WITHDRAWN
FOR SALE

3 8002 01461 1810

D0187969

# I Go to Extremes
## The Billy Joel Story

| COVENTRY CITY LIBRARIES | |
|---|---|
| 201461181 | |
| Bertrams | 26.03.07 |
| 784.0924 | £14.99 |
| CEN | |

# I Go to Extremes
## The Billy Joel Story

Bill Smith

**ROBSON
BOOKS**

First published in the United Kingdom in 2007 by
Robson Books
151 Freston Road
London
W10 6TH

An imprint of Anova Books Company Ltd

Copyright © Bill Smith, 2007

The moral right of the author has been asserted.

All rights reserved. No part of this publication may be reproduced, stored in a retrieval system, or transmitted in any form or by any means electronic, mechanical, photocopying, recording or otherwise, without the prior written permission of the copyright owner.

All photographs are from the author's collection.

ISBN 10: 1 86105 890 X
ISBN 13: 9781861058904

A CIP catalogue record for this book is available from the British Library.

10 9 8 7 6 5 4 3 2 1

Typeset by SX Composing DTP, Rayleigh, Essex
Printed and bound by Creative Print & Design, Wales

This book can be ordered direct from the publisher.
Contact the marketing department, but try your bookshop first.

www.anovabooks.com

*For Inezita*

## Acknowledgements

There were so many who helped make this book a reality. The following is a partial list, and I apologize for leaving anyone out. Each and every person I spoke to contributed an important piece of this very complex puzzle, and it never would have happened without the following:

Ralph Turchiano, Rachel O'Connor, Rocco Parella, Judy Joel, Tanaka Koji, Vinny and Pat Longo, Anton Mure, Rich Arfin, Wendy Greguski, Bob Cinque, Todd Kopetic, Richie Canatta, Sharon Czechowski, Howard Emerson, Artie Ripp, Jim Gorman, Bobby Jo Grazier, Mike D'Amico, Lee Eastman, Bobby Colisante, Susan Dippi-Keegan, John Dizek, Tony Izzo, Christina Webber, Russell Javors, Frank Molinari, Jeff Schock, Pat Salamone, Mary Barnett, Bobby Briell, Chuck Arnold, Mark Hyman, Rich Arfin, Jerry Fischer, Art Tallman, Rochelle Maucher, Michael Epstein, Patti Lee-Barrett, Jim Bosse, Denis Arfa, Greg Hicks, Barbara Hicks, Ray Nelson, Mike Pillot, Dolores Maceli, Bobby DiMarino, Jeff Littman, Paul Korman, Morton Estrin, Vicki Chicollo-Marino, Pam Raab, Gerald Barker, Cati Monck, Pam Rabb, Linda Mahanna, Billy Zampino, Bob Jarrey, Amy Bennett, Lisa Perez, Phil Ramone, Walter Yetnikoff, George "Shadow" Morton, Trish Bergin, Lew Forman, Jim Guercio, Denise Howe, Joyce Jurgensen, Gary McManus, Irwin Mazur, Steve Wick, Prof. Jeffery Gabb, Danny Kortchmar, Janet Luna-Marcus, Catherine Leonhardt, Mrs. Stegmeyer, Stephen Gaines, Mike Towle, Rosemarie Walker, Doug Geed, Jerry Schilling, Gene Siegel, Toni Schultz, Rich Rothenberg, Christina Schweitzer-Weber, Maureen Chatfield, Danny Ryan, Ed Sacco, Capt. Bert Waife, Richard and Linda Blauvelt, Bruce Mattei, Pat Manger, Richard McKenna, Ken, Donna, Tyler, Miles and "Bella" Clark, Desiree Day, Todd Bullivant, Bert Fields and Barbara Guggenheim, Jim and Nancy Bosse, Russell Wilkinson and Eileen Guggenheim, Diane Rogus, Bob Buchmann, Paula Christ, Ray Nelson, Leon Barnes, and Becky, Ben and Derrick Smith.

Dick Tarlow for his friendship, inspiration and support, and last but certainly not least, thanks to Billy Joel for his time, for opening doors which otherwise would have remained closed, and for his trust and his candidness.

# Introduction

I first met Billy Joel during the summer of 1971 in the park at Cold Spring Harbor, New York. He and his buddies would occasionally come there to hang out and do the things that many our age on Long Island were doing at the time: drinking beer, smoking grass, throwing Frisbees, and trying to pick up girls.

I didn't pay much attention to him that summer or subsequent other times I saw him there but I do remember vividly the time that a friend of mine showed up in the park a couple of years later with a record album under his arm.

"Remember this guy?" he asked a bunch of us standing around. "He's the guy that used to come here from Hicksville with his greaser buddies and hang out."

The album of course was *Cold Spring Harbor* and the cover picture was taken down at Eagle Dock, a local private beach where we all grew up swimming and later on picking up girls.

After that summer I didn't run into Billy for some time. Not that we were ever friends because we weren't. We were just a couple of guys who grew up at the same time on Long Island, and whose paths would cross occasionally over the years. I felt a kind of kinship with Billy, though, and still do, again I think a result of us growing up at the same time, listening to and being influenced by the same music, liking the same types of girls, and being raised in a home where our fathers had left when we were about 8 years of age, robbing us in many ways of our childhoods, and leaving us to grow up with troubled and alcoholic mothers further complicating our already great emotional pain.

Within years of the album's release Billy was enjoying a great level of success and he bought a house in neighboring Lloyd Neck, where I'd see him occasionally in town or at bars drinking. Again nothing special, most of the time just a nod or a hello.

Then I moved to Shelter Island full time and for a while forgot about Billy Joel until he too arrived on the East End, first to rent a house on the North Fork and then to set up stakes in toney East Hampton after his marriage to Christie Brinkley. Again because both of us were obsessed with boats and (in his case to a lesser degree) fishing, we'd run into each other and talk briefly about our obsessions. Then one day I got a call from Billy asking me if I wanted to go tuna fishing with him and some friends on his new boat, a beautiful 46-foot Jarvis Newman, that in my mind was the best boat he's ever owned. Being a fanatic tuna fisherman, I jumped at the chance first to go tuna fishing, second on this beautiful boat, and third with Billy. I brought another Cold Spring Harbor friend, Thorndike Williams, who had fished with me before, thinking from my talk with Billy that Thorndike and I would be running the fishing end of things while Billy captained his beautiful boat.

We met Billy in Montauk on the agreed day. There were four others on the boat in addition to Billy and us whose identities soon became apparent. We left Montauk that morning and headed for the tuna grounds which are 70 miles out into the ocean. Arriving at the fishing grounds Thorndike and I got the rods and tackle out and started to set out lures for trolling.

Then it happened, just as I was setting out a lure: a 50-plus pound tuna hit the lure causing the reel to free spool and wrapping the line around my left index finger. Instantly the fish, feeling that it was hooked, took off in another direction, pulling the Dacron line down tight around my finger as it cut through the flesh to the bone like soft butter. Panicking, my reaction was to pull my hand away which I did, freeing the finger, but mangling it even more in the process. Instantly the mood on the boat changed as it became obvious that this wasn't just a superficial wound. Frank Weber, Billy's soon to be fired manager, wanted to get a helicopter to medivac me off to the hospital, and others insisted we turn the boat around and head home. I insisted that we do no such thing, but instead Billy Zampino, Billy's best friend and a good guy, brought me a baggie with shaved ice that I stuck my mangled finger in until I got up the courage to stitch it back together as well as I could using some monofilament line and a needle. Weber, who was visibly nervous, followed me around the boat for over an hour repeatedly asking me if I was OK, and if I was sure I didn't want to go to a hospital until, really pissed off, I finally turned to him and said, "Listen Frank, drop it, I'm not going to sue Billy." That was the end of Weber, thank God, who spent the rest of the two-day trip pretty much inside the boat watching porno videos. Classy guy even then.

Luckily the fishing trip went on and we ended up catching fifteen tuna fish, the same blue shark twice, and a small swordfish which I released. It was a magnificent fishing trip, and particularly from Billy's perspective as he'd never caught a tuna before and never would have a trip like that again. Upon returning to Montauk we offloaded the tuna and guests while Billy and I ran the boat over to Shelter Island. He wanted to take a look at a marina there that at the time belonged to the father of a friend of mine. We never talked about the finger, instead bullshitting about boats, fish, and women. From then on when our paths crossed, and Billy introduced me to people, he often would add that, "This is the only guy who could have sued me and didn't."

With both of us living in the same area our paths continued to cross, usually related to some issue about commercial versus recreational fishing. I was involved deeply in environmental issues surrounding that and we would occasionally talk about specific problems. It was a weird world, though, that Billy had gotten himself into in East Hampton. Being who he is, Billy wanted to do the right thing, and I think he did, but some around him saw Billy as a key to bigger and better things for themselves, and often would feed Billy false information about my intentions, at times distancing us.

While I've never claimed to be a member of Billy's very tight inner circle, I do believe that we share a great mutual respect for each other that was consolidated when I didn't sue him after the fishing accident. I know this is true because he has repeatedly told me so and also related to me that it was the factor that caused him to decide to talk to me for this book, something he had never done before although he'd been asked many times, and I'm sure something that he will never now do again. He also trusted me enough to tell many people in his close-knit inner circle that it was OK to talk with me, something that because of the intense loyalty Billy's true friends have for him, they never would have done otherwise. It was a situation that many didn't understand. "Do you know how unusual this is?" I heard often, and from knowing Billy even to the degree that I did, I understood the magnitude of their statement. It made me that much more determined, many friends said obsessively so, to write an accurate and balanced book.

Billy Joel is a remarkable human being. There is no doubt that he is one of the few that are doing exactly what they were born to do with their lives. By all indications he and, to a somewhat smaller degree, his mother Rosalind have sensed this right from the start. In talking with the many people I did, particularly those who went to school with Billy, the music has poured out of him for as long as anyone can remember. Whether walking to school as a young kid playing air piano, or jumping up on a table to mimic Elvis, Billy Joel on some level has known his destiny his entire life and has had the tenacity and remarkable focus to achieve things in his life that he never could have imagined as a kid running around post-World War II Hicksville.

It's clear that many in the early years knew that somehow Billy Joel was going to make music his life—the teachers that saw the gift he was born with, and his friends who couldn't have fully understood it then, yet who knew that this likeable kid from the broken family down the block was going to someday make it as a musician.

It is quite a testament to the inner strength Billy inherited from his ancestors that he made it to where he is today. Many times the deck was stacked against him, and at some points in his life he faced seemingly insurmountable obstacles, yet he has always remained steadfast in his beliefs and was confident enough in himself to trust his instincts. But he's also been lucky to have had certain people in his life who also believed in him. His mother Rosalind who, despite her own considerable demons, supported her son at every opportunity. Then later his first wife Elizabeth, who in many ways took Rosalind's place, and who was intuitive enough right from the beginning to understand Billy's gift and potential. Like Billy she was also blessed with dogged determination and great focus. She achieved each goal she envisioned and, never one to be complacent, always set another goal after reaching one. Then, after Elizabeth and to a large degree which few give her credit for, there was his second wife Christie Brinkley. Theirs was for a time the perfect partnership, as each supported the other.

Throughout his times with these three women Billy pretty much remained on track. I say pretty much because the temptations of life on and off the road are great, particularly for a star of Billy's magnitude. Yet it was only after his break-up with Christie that he truly began to go astray, held together to a great degree because of his deep unconditional love for his remarkable daughter Alexa, a gifted young woman who, despite growing up in the world she did, today is remarkably grounded and who, like her father, has inherited not only a great love of music, but also a remarkable ability, as her performances with her new band confirm.

Billy, like all of us who suffer from addictions, had to hit his bottom, and in his case I believe it came later than it might have because of the people around him who enabled him, afraid to bring up the subject of his abuses, and also certainly because of the bubble that Billy to a degree lives in. Yet in true form once he was able to admit his problem he dove into the solution head first, determined to prevail, which also true to form, he seems to have done.

Now sober, making music again and with a stable life at home shared with a woman who sincerely loves him, his third wife Katie Lee, I think Billy Joel is going to be OK. He's not the type to continue to make the same mistake; he's far too smart for that. With love and another strong woman in his life, he has the support that he needs as long as those self-destructive demons can be held at bay. He may very well surpass his own achievements in the days ahead as he also continues to discover the inner peace that is also becoming more and more a part of his life. I for one hope so because this man, who has enriched so many millions with his music, who can be and often is incredibly kind and generous, deserves to spend his last days in peace. His gifts to many of us have been extraordinary, defining the timelines of many lives while also bringing great joy to countless millions through his music. I hope it's his turn.

Bill Smith
Paris
April 2006

# Chapter 1

Friday March 15, 2002 was one of those dreary, cold and damp days in New York City where nature stubbornly holds onto the last vestiges of winter before finally letting it go for spring. Nevertheless, Madison Square Garden had been sold out for months in anticipation of the joining of two of rock and roll's greatest icons on what was one of the biggest grossing tours of all time. Billy Joel and Elton John had joined forces four years earlier in what was a mutually beneficial partnership, both musically and financially. To have these two legends on stage at once was a no-brainer for promoters around the world as ticket sales and gross receipts confirmed repeatedly. For the two performers themselves, while it was certainly about the music as well, it was primarily about the payday.

Elton John, known for his extravagant tastes and seemingly limitless spending sprees, had been a successful rock musician since his first album was released in 1969. His lifestyle, however, had taken its toll on him both physically and financially. Known for spending upwards of three hundred thousand dollars annually just for flower arrangements, many in homes around the world that he owned but rarely visited, Elton was truly caught up in keeping the cash flowing in to support his flamboyant lifestyle. He toured constantly and released albums at a frantic pace that kept him on that money-generating gerbil wheel year after year.

Billy, on the other hand, was fresh off a series of financial disasters. His former brother-in-law and manager Frank Weber, along with his business manager Rick London, had misappropriated countless millions of dollars of his money in hare-brained schemes and business investments, in the end robbing Peter to pay Paul before finally being exposed in an audit suggested by record company head Walter Yetnikoff and Billy's then wife Christie Brinkley, who had no love for Weber whom she found "common" and "coarse." Yetnikoff had found it bizarre that Joel had to sell his New York City apartment to Sting in order to raise money for a oceanfront house in East Hampton, which Billy and Christie wanted to buy, and immediately knew that something wasn't right.

If that wasn't bad enough, Billy had just been through a long, drawn-out court battle with his former attorney Alan Grubman, a scrappy Jewish kid from Brooklyn, who was quickly rising to the top of entertainment law in New York City.

Billy was clearly in a highly precarious financial situation despite the tens of millions he'd already generated from his music, and he needed money. This tour with Elton was Billy's way of insuring what he'd vowed to himself so many times, that he "wouldn't ever worry about money again." Billy figured that investing the time and energy necessary in the "Face to Face" tour was worth the financial security that he'd leave it with. Moreover, fresh from his divorce from Christie, with his family life fragmented, the road offered Billy the world of camaraderie and privilege that he felt would at least temporarily fill the void inside him. As time would tell he couldn't have been more wrong.

Because of the lawsuits and divorce, Billy now found himself again in one of the deep depressions that have plagued him since a child. He began to self-medicate himself with his favorites: Scotch, wine and other substances, in addition to making the most of another advantage of being a world-famous rock star on the road: women. The tour turned into a whirlwind of travel and performances, creating a reality that in one sense sheltered Billy, but on the other hand only compounded his issues. The tour was planned so that Billy and Elton were given breaks of two or more days so that they could rest and attempt to have some semblance of a life outside the road. A reality that in Billy's case only made his loneliness that much more apparent, feeding his depression and self-indulgences, because sadly he didn't have the family life then that was so important to him to be able to return to on his days off.

This dream ticket landed in New York City just over six months after 9/11 for a series of sold-out concerts in the New York area, concerts that were so much in demand that some box-office tickets sold for over one hundred dollars each, at the time an exorbitant price. Nevertheless, with New York and its people still numb from the events of 9/11, this concert by two of rock and roll's biggest stars, one of them a hometown hero, was sure to boost people's spirits and be a welcome escape from those events still fresh in so many people's minds.

Billy got to the Garden that night about 6.30 and went directly to his dressing room, pretty much ignoring the usual insanity that was going on outside. He was not in great shape, his throat raw from singing and other more abusive activities. In addition he was totally exhausted and probably should have been in the care of a physician or at the very least recuperating and resting. Nevertheless, New York was Billy's hometown, his backyard. These were his people, the ones that so many of his lyrics depicted, and Billy felt a strong obligation to them, as he always did with his fans, to be there for them and to give them all he had.

Although drinking and at times drinking to excess were not unusual before one of Billy's shows, this time it was obvious to his inner circle and band members that Billy's drinking that day had exceeded what even they had come to see as "the norm." His behavior had been even more brooding than usual on this tour and especially tonight. Just watching him walking around backstage it was obvious something was wrong, which was confirmed by his blurred speech and excessive profanity. No one had ever seen him this bad before a show.

As showtime neared things seemed to get even worse, but nevertheless Billy made it onstage with Elton. As the sold-out crowd chanted over and over again for their hometown boy, the lights in the Garden finally dimmed and two pianos rose from the stage as American and British flags appeared behind them. Joel entered to a rousing chorus of "Yankee Doodle Dandy" and Elton followed in his iridescent green suit, a broad contrast to Billy in all black. Together they sang two songs to open the show, "Your Song" and "Just the Way You Are." Then Elton's band came on stage and they played "Don't Let the Sun Go Down On Me," with Billy announcing to the cheering audience that "This is our favorite venue in the world" before leaving the stage to return to his dressing room.

Alone now on the stage with his band, Elton played a rousing set of twelve songs for almost an hour, finishing with "Crocodile Rock," as Billy secluded himself in his dressing room. The hometown crowd was now completely pumped up for Billy's set and the stage darkened as Elton and his band left to go backstage for a break. The audience, however, didn't want anything to do with a break and began chanting "Bill-ee, Bill-ee" over and over, their cries filling the massive venue.

Within a few minutes, the lights again rose, Billy and his band entered the stage area to a deafening roar from the crowd, and Billy walked over to his piano and sat down. It soon became clear to the audience, who had been told earlier that Billy was suffering from a cold, that something was seriously wrong with him, something far worse then a cold. He opened his set with "Scenes from an Italian Restaurant": "Bottle of red . . . bottle of white . . ." He struggled with the lyrics and his voice, but everyone in the audience just thought it was his cold at that point, the one that had supposedly caused him to cancel a Tampa Florida show the previous week.

Billy finished "Allentown," his second song of the set, and then started playing a riff from the 1965 song "The Boy From New York City," by The Ad Libs, singing a line in falsetto. Then abruptly he stopped and turned towards the audience. "A lotta people are scared shitless these days," he said. "It's nice to be part of America again." The New York crowd, still clueless, roared their agreement.

Next Billy played some more riffs while he tested the range of his throat. Again turning to the audience, almost to apologize, he announced, "This is not Luciano Pavarotti time. This is rock and roll," before singing the opening of James Brown's "Papa's Got a Brand New Bag." "I'm just gonna blow it out," he added. "Whatever the fuck I got." But he still wasn't finished talking. "This is the most expensive room to rent in the world," he rambled angrily. "You paid a lot for your tickets and that sucks."

Billy then began playing "Movin' Out," followed by four other songs, before finishing with "River of Dreams," struggling the entire time to sing correctly as most of the audience now clearly understood what was unfolding in front of them. Finishing "River of Dreams," it was now time for more chat with the audience. "Some of you say he's not 100% tonight," he started, "but I'm trying. With the price you paid for a ticket, you can cash it in for another night. Go to the box office and let the SOBs at Madison Square Garden worry about it."

Then even more bizarrely he switched his thoughts again back to the "Concert for New York" that had been held on October 20, 2001 at the Garden. "We saw all these English guys like Paul and Mick," he said, "and I'm thinking, where the fuck are the New Yorkers?"

That seemed to pump him up even more, while bringing his anger about it all to a head. "I want to throw out a couple of things," he said and, his voice rising, "Bunker Hill! Antietam! That was a bad one!" Then rising to his feet, he turned to the audience and continued his ranting: "The Alamo! San Juan Hill! Argonne Forest! Corregidor! Midway! Guadalcanal! Normandy! Iwo Jima! Chosin Reservoir! Khe Sanh! Desert Fucking Storm!"

The sold-out crowd, not at all sure where this was coming from, or going for that matter, nevertheless tried nervously to go with it.

"Who the hell do they think they're fucking with?" Joel roared into the mike.

Then, due to the ingenuity of the light man, red, white and blue lights bathed the stage, successfully calming Billy down enough as he returned to his piano and played a riff from "Rhapsody in Blue," with saxophonist Mark Rivera finishing the whole thing off with a chorus of "New York State of Mind," the crowd now roaring in approval.

Billy reached down to pick up a New York City Fire Department hat off the stage floor, placed it on his head as the crowd continued roaring, and then, throwing fuel on the fire once again as his anger got the best of him, he leaned towards the mike and announced, "So I got a fucking cold, so what?" before starting again appropriately enough with "I Go To Extremes" and finishing his set with "Only the Good Die Young."

Within minutes Elton and his band made it back to the stage where the two bands and two stars played a five-song final set. Ironically Billy's condition at times made his songs more effective. As Elton and Billy lashed into "You May Be Right," Billy slumped forward on his bench and, sounding hopeless and in pain, garbled the line, "Don't, don't, don't try to save me," as he banged on the piano keys almost at random.

With just three songs to go, Elton, clearly focused on what was happening and determined to salvage what he could of the show, hammered out the chords to "Bennie and the Jets," while Billy, seemingly lost, instead produced a jarring soundscape from his keyboard, clearly making Elton and other band members uncomfortable. So much so, that when it was over Elton could be seen mouthing to no one in particular, "Thank God."

Finally the show finished with an unusual rendition of "Piano Man," with Billy sadly looking like he was about to nod off, but with Elton taking the lead and leading the audience with the haunting words, "Son can you sing me a memory? I'm not really sure how it goes . . ."

The concert itself confirmed Billy's inner circle's fears. Joel had forgotten lyrics he once knew by heart, he missed cues, and rambled on incoherently between songs. Elton John was visibly upset and ultimately had to lead Joel from the stage at the concert's end. The next day it was announced that the remainder of the tour would be cancelled temporarily due to a respiratory infection Billy was suffering. Everyone at the concert that night, and later those who read the stories splashed across newspapers around the world, wondered the same thing: how could this accomplished singer/songwriter, whose performances seemingly never missed a beat, have fallen so far?

The answer not surprisingly isn't a simple one, yet in many ways it can be defined by going back through the years and the events of Billy's life . . .

# Chapter 2

On June 12, 1923, the same day that Harry Houdini was freeing himself from a straitjacket forty feet above the pavement in New York City and that the New York Yankees lost eight to four to the Cleveland Indians at Yankee Stadium, a boy was born in a Nuremberg hospital to a prosperous German Jewish family, who in less then two decades would witness the beginnings of the Nazi horrors, yet be fortunate enough to escape, traveling through Europe and the Caribbean, before finally landing with his family in their new home in New York City. There in the Bronx, this now young man would go on to father one of the world's most prolific and successful entertainers. A son who would sell countless millions of albums, who would make and lose fortunes in the process, and like many of us, search insatiably for happiness, all while becoming a American cultural icon but at a huge personal cost.

Helmut Joel's roundabout postwar quest for peace and contentment in America was so immersed in difficulty and dismay that its failure was virtually predetermined. To this day, even his own son's knowledge of what happened to his father en route to the States has remained incomplete and flawed at best. Helmut Joel was the only child of wealthy merchant Karl Joel and his wife Meta Fleischmann. While the earliest Joel is assumed by Helmut to have been "the one in the Bible, the book of Joel; he was one of the minor prophets," the Joel family has traced its modern lineage as far back as 1806, when Faust Joel entered the world in Colmberg, a farming community near the Altmühl River in the Bavarian district of Mittelfranken. Faust's son Julius was a tailor whose expanding interest in textile production led to grandson Karl Joel's eventual success.

By 1927, at the age of 39, Karl and Meta had managed to save about 10,000 German marks, then worth about $45,000, with the dream of opening their own business. Karl had always wanted to work for himself, and now he was ready to start a business of his own and, after reading about a new business concept that was taking hold in the United States, Karl took his and Meta's life savings and started a mail-order firm for household linens and clothing. It bore the family name Waschemanufakturer Joel, and in its infancy Joel and his wife Meta turned their small apartment into their office, packaging all orders and carrying them from their small apartment in Nuremberg to the post office, en route to their growing customer list. In just one year business was good enough to warrant renting a small factory and to specialize in women's ready-made clothing that was now being manufactured entirely by Joel's rapidly growing company. Things happened quickly under Karl's leadership so, by the early 1930s, the Joel name was well known in Germany. Karl, Meta and their young son Helmut left the small apartment, and moved into a large villa in a well-to-do Nuremberg neighborhood. The future looked bright for the young family and by all indications the Joels were well liked and respected in pre-Nazi Germany.

Shortly after moving into their Nuremberg villa in 1933, ten-year-old young Helmut befriended a neighborhood boy named Arno Hamburger. The two were schoolmates and became fast friends. Arno came from yet another prominent Jewish family, and his father ran a prosperous wholesale meat business in the city. Arno also got to know Karl and Meta Joel fairly well as a frequent guest in their very comfortable home over the next year or so.

But after Hitler came to power in 1933 the new government turned its attention and force on the country's Jews. Within days laws were being decreed, aimed solely at Jews who amounted to only about one percent of the country's population, and numbered just 9,500 in Nuremberg. These laws constricted the rights of the Jewish citizens much like a series of ever tightening rings. The process began with regulations that forced the Jews away from certain livelihoods, while at the same time instituting other laws that required them to report to the new government how much money they had, and where it was kept. This momentum continued to build through 1935 with the passage of the Nuremberg Laws, which defined who, in the eyes of the government, was a Jew, and also escalated the process of stripping the Jews of their German citizenship.

Arno Hamburger's family became one of the first casualties of these laws, losing their meat business right away in 1933. On the night of April 14, the first Jewish victim, Arthur Kahn, aged 21, fell to a Nazi soldier's bullet on a dark street, all because "someone" had labeled Kahn as a communist. At nearly the same time, Arno's uncle was pulled from his home, and beaten nearly to death for no apparent reason other than that he was Jewish. Within days the senior Hamburger lost his meat business. It was a very straightforward transaction, and one that was to be repeated countless times in the days ahead. A Nazi Party member walked into his office one day, reminded Hamburger about his uncle's misfortune, and then alluded to the fact that next time it might be anyone from his family, warning him that next time the end results would be much worse. Hamburger folded, and the business was essentially stolen from him to be run by one of Hitler's new "Aryan Commissioners." This left the Hamburgers more or less in poverty.

The Joels, however, were still prosperous and made sure that young Arno was invited over often for meals. "They knew we didn't have much," Arno related, "but I always got cakes and candies from them. They lived very near the zoo, so Howard [Helmut] and I would go there each weekend to escape what was going on in the streets, and his family always paid my ticket."

At the same time, Nuremberg became the center of the Nazi party, and the oppression focussed on the Jewish population continued to grow rapidly in a sympathetic atmosphere fueled by Nazi propaganda. The Joels, sensing what lay ahead, continued to operate their company but in a much more subdued and cautious way, in an attempt not to call attention to themselves.

"Withdrawing was the only option," Howard Joel related years later. "You felt excluded from everything. Suddenly you were an outcast, and no longer accepted by your friends." To live as inconspicuously as possible became the Joels' primary objective. The Joels' mansion was located adjacent to a large field in Nuremberg, a field which the Nazis used each weekend to practice marches and drills. On these days Meta Joel closed her window shutters and stayed inside in fear for herself and her family, and of what might happen.

To make matters more personal for the Joels, *Der Strumer*, a weekly Nuremberg newspaper published by an anti-Semitic madman named Julius Streicher, started a campaign to discredit Joel and his company. Streicher was a borderline psychotic, who had befriended Hitler at the failed Munich Beer Hall Putsch in 1923. Their friendship would last until Hitler's suicide in 1945, and then a year later, Streicher was hanged after being tried and found guilty at the Nuremberg Trials for crimes against the German People. A crazy Nazi to the end, he was heard shouting Heil Hitler as the trap door opened under him, dropping him to what was for him a far too merciful a death.

A socially insecure mental case, Streicher was also a Hitler "groupie" prepared to do anything to gain his favor, and also with an insatiable need to be part of Hitler's inner circle. All this with a personal goal of getting some sort of high-level job in the Nazi propaganda ministry. Streicher's first attack on Karl Joel was in May 1933—just a month after the Hamburgers lost their business. Fortunately Hamburger has kept copies of the newspapers. The first article attacking the Jews reads, in part:

Karl Joel is a Yid. Lately strange things happened in his business. The female employees can tell quite a few things about the impertinent and dirty way that their boss approaches them. He pays starvation wages to people who work for him. Thus he is able to sell his linen rags at low costs and so ruins German businessmen . . . The Jew Joel pushes them against the wall.

Streicher's second article, under the headline "The Linen Yid of Nuremburg," in part reads:

> . . . This business is not as generally believed in German hands. It is definitely Jewish. The owner is a full-blooded Yid. Every week he dispatches thousands of parcels all over Germany . . . He uses his profits in a typical Jewish way. He organizes drinking bouts during which he is supplied with German girls and women.

The exposure in Streicher's paper frightened even the feisty and brave Joel, but he was determined to save his life's work and his family's reputation, so in vain he naively tried to counter the attacks through personal contacts, which only infuriated the Nazis even more. Then, in an effective campaign to discredit and embarrass Karl, the Nazis began to arrest him time and again in public places for minor offenses that he would soon be released from.

In an attempt to escape the growing oppression, Karl soon decided to move to Berlin, a city he had heard from friends would be more tolerant towards the Jews. Prior to moving he contacted an old acquaintance in Berlin, Fritz Tillman, now the city's Economic Town Counselor and, unbeknownst to Karl, himself a member of the Nazi Party. In ignorance, Karl trusted Tillman, a former cloth merchant and the man who in a short time would be put in charge of expelling Berlin's Jews to the Nazi death camps. Tillman, a man without any moral scruples, saw a future business opportunity and soon had his own designs on Joel's company. He set out to learn all he could about it from Joel before attempting to steal it from him. With this in mind Tillman secured the necessary permissions for Joel to move his company to Berlin and in 1934 Karl and his family left Nuremberg to begin again. Taking no chances, shortly after arriving in Berlin, Karl packed the twelve-year-old Helmut off to the exclusive St. Gall's boarding school in northeastern Switzerland and set out to rebuild his business. He rented four floors in a Berlin warehouse, and in a move he hoped would confirm his loyalty to his country, bought exclusively new German equipment to make his goods. He also purchased a new villa in a fashionable Berlin neighborhood, and cautiously and perhaps naively looked to the future. But by now even in Berlin things were turning worse rapidly for the Jewish residents.

At the time Berlin was perceived by Germans to be the epitome of freedom and opportunity, attracting thousands of Germans who hoped to begin anew by taking advantage of Aryanization. For Jewish residents, however, a different set of laws existed, and soon, as part of the growing Nazi oppression of Jews, Karl Joel was forced to put up a sign in the window of his business stating that it was Jewish-owned.

In June 1936, young Helmut returned to Berlin for his bar mitzvah, which was being held in a large Berlin synagogue. Helmut spoke at the bar mitzvah, and afterwards close friends and family were invited back to the spacious Joel home for a quiet gathering. Adults talked business and politics as they sipped wine and ate the large selection of food while children ran and played in the yard, forgetting for even just those few moments what they'd seen and heard on the streets, yet fearing what they felt lay ahead. But even on this joyous family day, the laws being decreed by the Nazi government were slowly but surely making the dream Joel had of keeping his business alive impossible.

By the next year Karl's business was grossing one million Reichmarks a month and he remained cautiously optimistic that as a loyal German he might be allowed to continue building his business as he strived to keep a low profile. Then suddenly his Aryan suppliers, under pressure from the Nazis, stopped delivering supplies to Joel on a regular basis, and he was forced to mark all his outgoing packages with a "J" identifying them as Jewish goods to his now 850,000 customers. Simultaneously, under new laws he was forced to hire a German plant manager who boycotted his business from within, and his sales dropped precipitously.

Avraham Barkai, a Holocaust scholar who today lives in Israel, defines it best: "As boycotts were organized, Jews were forced to lower their prices to try to stay in business. At the same time, the goal of the Aryanization program was to strip the Jews of all their wealth and property and to turn it over to non-Jews and the government." To show how effective this program was, Barkai relates that in 1933 "there were roughly 100,000 Jewish-owned companies in Germany. By the mid-thirties that number had dropped to about 20,000, and these Jews clearly understood that their time was limited."

Nevertheless, Karl Joel was a good and wise businessman and, despite the Nazi thugs now ruling the country, was very proud of his German heritage. He was also undoubtedly following the new laws to the letter in a futile attempt to survive. As he participated in the new registration process that forced him to give the Nazis a detailed inventory of his property and assets, he surely must have felt the noose tightening around his neck. However, with young Helmut still in school in Switzerland for safety's sake, Karl and Meta focussed on trying to hold on to their life's work.

Meanwhile, away at boarding school, Helmut continued to study classical piano in addition to other subjects, just as he had from early childhood in Nuremberg. Helmut's talent as a promising young classical pianist, with a sure musical career, was recognized by his teachers and briefly considered by the precocious young musician, but less so by his parents. "The possibility was there," said Helmut, "but my father wanted me to do something serious. I became an engineer instead, because that's what he wanted. In those days, you did what the old man told you to do." That unwritten law of the "old school" was fortunately never going to deter Helmut's own son.

Things were now changing fast in Germany for the Jews and not for the better. During the spring and summer of 1938 new laws were passed that completely stripped Jewish business and property owners of the right to participate in the economic life of Germany. The new decree stated in no uncertain terms that all Jewish property was to be turned over to the government's economic office, and to non-Jewish Germans. It was clear to Joel now which way the winds were blowing, and he quickly made plans to save what he could of his life's work.

Just weeks after the passage of the June 1938 law, Josef Neckermann paid a call on Karl Joel. By then the opportunist Neckermann was a one-year Nazi Party member, who already had "acquired" the prosperous Ruschkewitz department store in Wurzburg. It seems that in 1935, that at the young age of twenty-three Neckermann, who was second in charge at the store and a trusted employee, showed up at the store with a Nazi Party official. They walked into Sigmund Ruschkewitz's office and confronted the then elderly man who had founded the store at the turn of the century. This "meeting' went on while Nazi brown shirts stood outside the busy store warning shoppers not to go inside. Scared and alone in Germany, because his son Fritz had fled to Palestine in 1933, Ruschkewitz was forced to sell the store to Neckermann for what amounted to nothing. Shortly after the sale he lost his stately home and servants, and was forced to move into a pauper's hotel with his wife in Berlin before escaping toward Palestine to join his son, sadly dying of typhus on the trip.

Karl Joel's business was to suffer a similar fate in the days ahead. He tried to hold on, but it quickly became apparent that there was no choice. He reluctantly put his company up for sale, hoping to salvage what he could. News of his interest to sell quickly spread through Germany's banking community, and Neckermann surfaced as the favorite to "buy" the company. With the backing of his father-in-law, a deal was struck for one million Reichmarks or four and a half million dollars, for a company later estimated to be worth twelve million Reichmarks. Things moved very quickly as the right officials were paid off, and on July 11, 1938 the contract was to be signed. Neckermann and his father-in-law arrived at Joel's office with their attorney. Joel, however, was forbidden under the new laws to have a real attorney, and was forced to appoint an Aryan commissary to "represent" him. He once again naively put his trust in Fritz Tillman, who quickly set out to try to buy the company himself behind Joel's back. With their well-paid connections, the Neckermanns won out, and the meeting went as scheduled. Joel asked Neckermann for some sort of security to insure payment, and was told by Neckermann's father-in-law and financial backer that, "He'd better

worry about his safety rather then his security." Understanding the under-
lying message, Joel signed the company over to Neckermann, who then also
took possession of the Joels' mansion, furnishings, and even driver as part of
the deal.

Karl and Meta moved into a Berlin hotel room to await their money. For
two weeks, as the situation in Berlin grew more precarious for Jews, they
waited until finally a friend tipped them off that they were to be arrested "at
any time" by the Gestapo. Quickly Karl secured two false passports and he
and Meta boarded a morning train to Zurich, barely escaping a much worse
fate, as the Gestapo raided their hotel room that afternoon. They safely
arrived in Zurich where they rented a room in a boarding house and where
Meta phoned young Helmut to tell him of their arrival. "We are in Zurich,"
she said, "and are not going back to Germany." Unsure of what to say, young
Helmut answered simply "OK." Meta persisted, asking her son "Do you
understand? We can never go back." With no extra money for schooling,
Helmut was forced to leave boarding school and he joined his parents in their
one room in Zurich as they tried to plan their next step.

Karl was now becoming increasingly worried about his money and started
phoning Neckermann daily. Neckermann ducked his calls, and then one day
about two weeks later a letter arrived from Neckermann telling Joel he had
to return to Berlin to pick up his money. Joel immediately recognized the
letter for what it was, an ambiguous death threat. Crushed, he began to make
other plans for his family and himself.

Always the opportunist, Fritz Tillman knew of Joel's futile attempts to
get his money and planned another scheme of his own to try to rob Joel of
what he had been able to leave Germany with. He arrived in Zurich and
told Joel that as his old friend he would help him collect from Neckermann
for one hundred thousand Reichmarks. Karl, now desperate and still
trusting Tillman, wrote him the check. Tillman, shortly after receiving
the check, announced to Karl that all German Jews had been dispossessed
and, as much as he might regret it, there was in reality nothing he could
do for him. Finally seeing Tillman's true colors, Karl was again devastated
as he realized he'd run into a wall and had been used by Tillman all this
time. Then, to make matters even worse, upon returning to Berlin the
next day, Tillman cashed the check and pocketed the one hundred
thousand Reichmarks.

Not surprisingly Neckermann's account of the company's purchase from
Joel is vastly different. In his autobiography, *Memories*, written just prior to
his death in 1991, Josef Neckermann stated that he was "more or less doing
Karl Joel a 'favor' by purchasing his company." He claimed that he and Karl
met only once to discuss the sale, and then Karl vanished, implying that he
ended up with the company because Joel essentially had abandoned it—a

ridiculous idea. Nevertheless, the "sale" of Karl's life's work did go through, and the company was transferred to the Neckermann family.

According to Neckermann, he placed the one million Reichmarks in a government-controlled bank in Berlin, but that "it stands to reason that Mr. Joel saw little or none of his money" because he had fled to Switzerland by the end of July 1938. Neckermann also claims that instead of stealing the Joel home, he "rented" it from the Joel family, "partially furnished and with a children's bedroom set and other furnishings." Today, with ample time to rewrite the family history, a grandson of Neckermann states that, "Mr. Joel was not paid because the government controlled the payment, not my father."

According to Barkai, the Israeli scholar, "transactions like the Joels' had to be approved by party agencies. The payment into a government-controlled account was in most instances a bribe paid to the party by the German who wanted the business. In order to get one of the larger businesses, you had to have standing with the Nazi party. They took care of their people first. It was a sad story for the Joels, but a fine story for the Neckermanns."

Under the Neckermann family the company would go on to make clothing for the legions of forced laborers working as virtual slaves in factories, mines and other war effort situations, as well as making three million winter uniforms for Germany's soldiers fighting on the Russian front. During the war, with the Nazi Party's patronage, the company would prosper far beyond even the heights that Karl Joel had brought it to, and Neckermann would win a Distinguished Service Cross from Hitler himself. Of course, having slave laborers for "employees" also helped immeasurably.

Meanwhile, Karl Joel, knowing that he had to leave Europe, purchased three visas and boarded a ship to England. He hoped to migrate directly to the United States with Meta and young Helmut from Switzerland, but there was a quota on Jewish refugees arriving in the States, so they were forced instead in 1939 to travel to England for a very short time before boarding another ship for an unknown destination in the Caribbean. After three weeks at sea with their destination still a mystery, the ship pulled into Havana harbor and its passengers were finally allowed to depart. The Joels rented an apartment and made plans to enter the United States. They enrolled Helmut in the prestigious Belen Secondary School in Havana, where he studied electro-technology, while his schoolmate Fidel Castro was deeply immersed in the study of Cuban history. The Joels stayed in Havana for three years until immigration restrictions eased in the United States and they were able to enter the dramatically different post-Pearl Harbor America in 1942 with Visa Number 4219.

Unsure and rightly so, very cautious about what this new country held for

Jewish refugees from Europe, the Joels were determined to keep quiet about their Jewish roots. Arriving by boat in New York City, they took a handsome apartment in a fashionable section of upper Manhattan at 30 Bogardus Place, paid for with valuables and cash that Karl had smuggled out of Germany.

As a young boy Billy Joel visited the apartment only a few times before family issues came into play. "He obviously had someone furnish the apartment," Billy says today, "because I never saw an apartment that looked like that. It was very nice."

They also discovered that the rabbi who had bar mitzvahed young Helmut Joel was living nearby in Washington Heights, as were scores of other German Jews who were fortunate enough to escape with their lives.

Shortly after arriving, Karl started a modest hair-ribbon business at 395 Broadway in Manhattan to support his family. He and his wife worked together making hair bows that were sold to five and ten cent stores throughout the metropolitan area, and Helmut, now 19, made many of the deliveries for the new family business. Almost immediately upon arriving in America, the Joels had also changed Helmut's name to Howard in an attempt to better assimilate him into American culture, and with cautious optimism they looked toward the future as they quietly led their lives and kept informed about the progress of the war in Europe. Years later in an interview, Howard, speaking bluntly of these times, was to say: "I am alive today because my parents had some money left. Otherwise we'd all have died."

Then in 1942, Howard Joel met Rosalind Nyman, a native of Brooklyn's Coney Island, and a first generation American, whose parents had emigrated from England. Her father Phillip was a British native, and an amateur playwright and author who today would be labeled as "bohemian." Rosalind's mother Rebecca was a trained British nanny with an impressive lineage that can be traced back to the Russian Kravenskys of Czarist Minsk. Howard and Rosalind met while both were serving as non-matriculated members of the Gilbert & Sullivan Players at the City College of New York and their courtship began. Shortly after, they were both involved in a production of *The Pirates of Penzance*, Rosalind with a minor singing role, and Howard as an assistant to the conductor Julius Rudel. Coincidentally, Rosalind's own parents had also met at a Gilbert and Sullivan operetta presented at London's Royal Albert Hall over two decades earlier, which would later cause their grandson to comment that "I owe a great deal to Gilbert and Sullivan."

Despite the fact that Karl and Meta were not happy about it, as they felt that Rosalind was beneath their class, Howard and Rosalind's courtship went on for a few months, only to be interrupted by Howard being drafted into the U.S. Army in July 1943, just weeks after his twentieth birthday.

Coincidentally the rabbi's son also received his draft notice on the same day and both were chosen to go back to Europe because of his ability to speak fluent German. Howard was sent first to Italy, though, with the 45th Engineer Combat battalion and participated in the Allies' seizure of Anzio and the fierce battle of Monte Cassino. In one of life's true ironies he later found himself in Nuremberg in 1945 driving a Jeep for officers. While there he attempted to look up old friends, finding only a few left, including the old family driver. Then one day, as he was leaving Nuremberg and driving an army jeep towards the Dachau death camp as part of the 7th. Army liberation force, he passed the factory of his father, now partially ravaged by Allied bombing, but with one tall single smokestack still labeled "JOEL." Joel arrived the next day in Dachau and related the horror of what he witnessed and his sadness that "We were too late to help" to an interviewer in 1994.

Over the years there have been many misconceptions about Howard's background, including the mistaken belief that was never clarified until late in 1993 that the Nazis had imprisoned Howard Joel at Dachau. Sadly the truth as told by Howard is no less unsettling.

"It was true in a way, that I was in Dachau," Howard Joel related somberly, his heavily accented voice dropping to a murmur. "But I was not imprisoned there. I was with the army outfit that liberated Dachau, near Munich, on April 29, 1945.

"We went there," he continued, "looked around and took pictures of the heaps of the dead people. And then we moved on, because we were a combat troop, and never stayed anywhere. I had relatives that were in concentration camps, particularly Auschwitz, and some of them were put to death. But at Dachau it was terrible."

Howard completed his military service and returned to the Bronx in late 1945. Upon returning he was saddened to discover that the rabbi's son had been killed fighting in Europe. His parents were still running their growing hair-ribbon business but, with Germany liberated, they were making plans to return home as soon as possible to try and reclaim what once was theirs.

Meanwhile Howard continued to see Rosalind Nyman and asked her to marry him, which she did in 1946. The wedding was very small, just family, and afterwards they went to a Chinese restaurant to eat. Howard took a job as an engineer with General Electric, and the couple looked to the future. But, like many returning soldiers from World War II, Howard had changed. What his family and friends had once known as the lighthearted aspect of Howard's personality had largely vanished. "Tragically, he was never the same when he came back," Rosalind Joel told an interviewer. Her son concurs: "All his cynicism and sourness came from his experiences in the war."

It's clear that Howard Joel was never happy in America. He found the country lacking in culture and, like his parents, yearned to return to Europe to pursue his true love: music. He always found being an engineer totally lacking in self-satisfaction, and as a creative individual his job quickly became the primary disappointment in his life. In a telling statement made to his young son some years later, Howard complained, "This is how I make my living in America: I work for G.E., and everything is plastic, American plastic."

Adding to Howard's deep unhappiness was the fact that his family and Rosalind's never got along. Instead of the family get-togethers so much a part of American life in those post-war years, there was friction between the Joels and the Nymans. The Joels, clearly hard-working upper middle class with an even more prosperous history, continued to live in their comfortable Bronx apartment full of beautiful furniture and oriental rugs before returning to Germany to attempt to reclaim what they could of their past. The Nymans, on the other hand, lived in Flatbush in Brooklyn in a dark, narrow, typical tenement-type apartment and were looked down on by the Joels. Complicating this was the fact that Howard Joel's job at General Electric required that he travel often to Latin and South America, and his absences became increasingly frequent—something he at first resented and yet later looked forward to, as he and Rosalind grew more distant.

Karl Joel was always an emotionally distant man, but with an enviable work ethic, and in the old European sense he clearly did love his family very much. Yet after the war he was determined to correct the mistakes of the past and to return to reclaim his Berlin home, his company and, most important, his reputation. He made arrangements to meet Neckermann in Munich after the war at the Four Seasons Hotel to discuss this, but despite a series of meetings and communications made no progress in reclaiming his company. Determined, he filed a lawsuit against Neckermann on June 8, 1949 that would go on for eight years. Today even his son Howard does not know the exact details of the settlement, but it was established in court that the business was worth many more millions of Reichmarks more than the "sale" price of one million in 1938. Neckermann, in his autobiography *Memories*, contended that at the war's end the Joel business no longer existed, and that the new fabric business was built entirely by him. Despite this, documents produced by Joel's lawyers from Nazi archives easily proved that Neckermann had essentially stolen the company, and the German courts ruled in Karl's favor for two million marks in 1957. Neckermann agreed to pay, which also saved him from going to jail. Then, just days after the court's ruling, a letter from Hardy Bank surfaced which verified once more that Neckermann had never attempted to pay Joel any money at all for his company, and instead used the money deposited in an account set up for Joel in 1939 for himself, drawing from it as needed.

Even today, Johannes Neckermann, Josef's son, continues to try to rationalize the deeds of his father. He claims that Karl Joel got "more" than the one million Reichmarks promised in 1939, and that his father died "embittered" because of the efforts of Joel's lawyers, whom he referred to as "greedy." "It was not a good experience for my father," he was quoted as saying.

Sadly the Neckermanns were joined by countless others who took advantage of the Nazi laws to steal businesses from Jewish residents that they acquired under threat and with bribery. Even worse, many of the Nazi Party's well-connected "Aryan Commissaries" held onto their businesses even after the war ended due to political connections, and saw their wealth increase in the post-war boom, avoiding any scrutiny from German or Allied officials.

Karl, who always remained a European, never quite seeming to belong on American soil, took his settlement and with Meta traveled the world on an extended vacation before returning to New York and disbanding his hair-ribbon business in 1970. They then both returned to Germany where Meta died in Nuremberg on September 10, 1971. Karl lived another eleven years in a Berlin hotel room until, a deeply embittered man, he joined her on November 4, 1982, at 92 years of age. Today both are buried together in the old Jewish cemetery in Nuremberg.

Karl's struggle, determination, and willpower to obtain justice against insurmountable odds were not in vain. Not only did he right some of the injustices of the past, but he also passed on to his family the same characteristics that made giving up unthinkable for him, a trait which would be ingrained in a grandson who barely knew him but yet who inherited many of the same strengths. He too would go on to follow his dream despite a succession of failures and in the process help future generations of youth authenticate and define their lives through his music.

# Chapter 3

Karl's tenacity and sense of justice, as well as Howard's pain and darkness, are evident today in the next generation of Joels. "It's the loneliest job in the world," says one of the most successful musicians of our time. "Sure the rewards are great for what I do," Billy Joel continues, "but the moments of musical and lyrical inception come only when I'm by myself."

Telling comments from someone who has had to overcome more than his share of setbacks ever since he was born on May 9, 1949 in the Bronx, New York. Setbacks that in many cases would have easily defeated the average individual and erased their dreams a long time ago. But not in this case. Billy Joel is in many ways a remarkable composition of the traits that made his grandfather and father the survivors that they became. A fairly successful amateur boxer as a teenager, Billy doesn't seem to understand the meaning of defeat. Even when the odds are seemingly insurmountable, and the deck is clearly stacked against him, he still manages to emerge from the darkness and demonstrate a remarkable resiliency. This is due in part to his ability to put his trust in what he has always believed was his destiny: his music.

Music that by all indications has been part of him since before even he was aware of it. Music that flowed through him as a young child, and has never stopped. A gift that his parents first recognized when he was playing classical music on an old upright Lester piano as a young boy growing up in suburban Hicksville, Long Island, New York, and who, despite the limited financial resources in the Joel household, managed to come up with the money each week for piano lessons. Billy's mother found the teacher and at first would walk Billy down the road to Miss Francis's house for his lessons. "Her name was really Mrs. Neiman," Billy remembers, "but we all called her Miss Francis."

Francis Neiman was the neighborhood piano teacher who lived only about a five minute walk or two minute bike ride for Billy from the Joel home, a short trip he made weekly until he was fourteen. Her mother had been a concert pianist, and rumor had it that once she even played at Carnegie Hall. Miss Francis was very serious about her music, and very picky about whom she would and wouldn't give piano lessons to, although she gave everyone an initial opportunity. She also dedicated a portion of each Saturday to teaching ballet to neighborhood girls including Billy's sister Judy, some who were also her piano students. This she did in a portion of the attic that she and her draftsman husband Hank shared. Her "studio" was at the top of the stairs, and Hank's office through it and behind a door that was off bounds to everyone. She charged each student three dollars in the early 1950s for a one-hour piano lesson and the same for her ballet instruction.

Billy would make the trek to her house once a week after school and, because of the stern lecture he would get from her or his parents if he was late, was usually on time. He'd sit politely and wait in the small but brightly sunlit living room until the previous student was finished with their lesson, then take his turn at the always polished and in tune mahogany-stained Steinway baby grand piano which dominated the 240 square foot living room. It was placed so that the students sat on the bench with their back to the kitchen, with the sunlight pouring in the windowed south wall. Miss Francis would start Billy playing his scale exercises, while she stood behind him watching and coaching him or, as happened many times, correcting his posture, making him sit up straight. Often she would start her students and then go about the house doing her cooking and light cleaning, yet always listening, and if they hit a wrong key or slowed their tempo she would instantly appear beside the piano bench to correct them. By all indications she was a true musician herself and an excellent piano teacher who recognized talent in a student and then set out to nurture it. Billy's mother got along well with her because they shared a love of music and also because she was very effective in keeping an often fidgety young Billy focussed on his lessons.

Rosalind recalls:

By age three Billy was at the piano picking out Mozart. A year later on a cold fall day, I made him put on a coat, and took him down the block to Miss Francis's house for his first piano lesson. By six he was writing full songs with stories in them, just like the tales that he heard recited by my father.

Billy today has a slightly different perspective about taking piano lessons:

I never knew the piece I was supposed to learn, but I knew that my mother did. Take Mozart. He's a very refined composer, but how interested is a fourteen-year-old kid going to be in Mozart? I'd look at the dots on the page and think to myself "I'm sick of this shit." Then I'd start improvising, making stuff up as I went along and if my mother was there sometimes I'd get "Wow, you learned that very quickly, what is it?" "Oh, the second movement I'd tell her," and that might go on for a few days and then I realized finally that I was writing my own music. But Mrs. Neiman didn't care, she didn't want to hear what I wrote—she wanted to go by the book, which of course I didn't want to . . . But you know, it really isn't a bad idea to go by the book. Learn it and then throw it away.

Even during what later would be very trying times financially for the Joel family the music lessons would continue as would Billy's interest in the emerging different types of music, particularly rock and roll. He continued to practice his lessons as dutifully as he could, often even fooling his parents with their trained musical ears. Billy's father, a much more distant figure in Billy's life than his mother, also saw his musical talent, talent that undoubtedly had been passed to him through his parents. "There are some things that transmit genetically," Billy confirms. "Music transmits genetically, my daughter has it, my mother has it, I have it, and my half-brother who's a conductor has it."

Yet neither parent had any idea at the time that these lessons might nurture a rock and roll star, as evidenced by the one and only time his father struck him.

Howard had returned from work on the train from New York City that day. Billy, who was playing outside when he arrived home, knew it soon would be time to get serious and go inside to practice the piano lesson that Miss Francis had given him that week. He'd been playing with his friend in the backyard since walking home from second grade at Fork Lane Elementary School that late spring afternoon, and his dirty tight blue dungarees, plaid shirt and black high top sneakers with unmatching socks showed it. The Joels' large, triangular backyard backed up on Cherupski's farm one of the few remaining family farms in the area that often became a playground for Billy, his older sister Judy and friends, when they'd sneak in to take potatoes, tomatoes or corn. Unlike most other houses in the development which backed up on other yards, the farm gave the Joels' house an added sense of privacy which the Joels enjoyed. In addition to the farm, there was also a large reservoir which collected the rainwater from the neighborhood streets. Despite being forbidden by his parents to play there because of their fear that Billy or Judy might fall in and drown, it too became a favorite place to go and play.

For Howard, though, the home's backyard had been the deal sealer when he had first looked at homes in Hicksville. After all, the houses were all pretty much the same in design and appearance, but this one's backyard was bigger and more secluded then the others. After buying the house the backyard quickly became a place where Howard planted a huge flower and vegetable garden. This was his sanctuary from the growing turmoil in his marriage as well as his dissatisfaction with his job.

As Billy played that day he wondered what his parents might be talking about inside. He was beginning to sense an increasing distance between his parents, even though as a young child it was in the most abstract of terms. Yet somehow he knew things were beginning to change between his parents, and he sensed that it wasn't good. The fighting was now happening more often and coinciding with it was Rosalind's increased drinking.

As he played he knew that it was only a matter of time before he was called in to practice his piano lesson, so he continued to make the best of what time he had left playing in the dirt, yet kind of watching over his shoulder for one of his parents to appear to summon him inside. Billy's piano lessons were something his parents took very seriously. As music lovers, both of them were adamant that he take them, despite what later would become very limited family finances. He liked the lessons too, yet then as a recently turned seven-year-old kid there was a deepening conflict in him between practicing his piano lessons and playing outside with his buddies. He enjoyed both for the satisfaction he got from them. Playing with his friends was great because he looked forward to each day's seemingly endless adventures in suburban Hicksville, and he loved practicing his piano lessons because it satisfied the innate craving he had for music. As was common with some kids then who took piano lessons, his real friends never made fun of him or labeled him a "sissy," this because somehow even they knew that their friend's life was incomplete without his music.

Finally it came through the window of the master bedroom, in his father Howard's heavily German-accented voice: "Billy, time to come in and practice. Tell your friend you'll see him tomorrow."

Billy knew this was it and that it was futile to try and buy more play time, so he dusted himself off, said bye to his friend, and walked through the backyard and into the house. The old Lester upright piano sat in the small living room along what was the windowless east wall. His parents had put it there partly because they thought that putting it against a wall would help to keep Billy focussed on his playing and not allow him to daydream about playing outside. In the sparsely furnished house the old piano was a valued piece of furniture, and for Billy, it was also a revered place where his father would often sit and play after dinner, with Billy looking on in awe as this usually distant man played this beautiful music he had been introduced to over twenty years earlier in Germany. For the young Billy Joel these were pretty much the only times that he felt really close to his father, when they shared something very special—their love of music.

As Billy played that afternoon, the windows overlooking the backyard were to his right, and the tiny kitchen where his mother was preparing dinner was to his left and behind him. His father was still in the master bedroom changing out of his work clothes, and getting ready to shower as Billy was playing the Beethoven sonata lesson that Miss Francis had assigned him that week. Dutifully he started it for the third time in as many days, his tiny fingers moving remarkably easily over the keys of the piano, which was chronically a little out of tune. The old piano had three cracked ivory keys and one "clunker" key that was unfixable, and each time Billy's fingers landed on this key that emitted a hard-edged sound, Billy would instinctively cringe. For about fifteen minutes that day he followed the sheet music in front of him, dutifully practicing his lesson as he sat on the piano bench that doubled as a storage area for the sheet music. It was difficult for his short legs to touch the three pedals of the piano, which made him sit in a sort of slouched position with his legs and lower torso stretched out towards the piano, and his upper torso leaning backwards. As he played his body moved back and forth from left to right depending on which foot he needed to reach one of the pedals. By all indications it was a funny sight to see this little kid straining to coordinate his body's movements with his hands, but his innate ability to create this wonderful music, even as a young child, made it all work. As he played, from time to time he might hear his mother humming along, and also often felt her loving gaze as she quietly moved around the kitchen. This, too, added to the feelings of confidence and well-being that playing his music instilled in him.

As he played the Beethoven lesson his mind started to wander to the music that he'd heard Judy playing when she and her girlfriends would get together after school or on weekends. On these days when there were no parents around, Judy and her friends would often sit in her bedroom or in the living room, putting 45s on the little record player or blasting their transistor radios as they sang along or practiced dancing the newest dance steps while Billy, who was two years younger, looked on. After all, these were the older cooler kids, and two years made a vast difference at that age. They listened to songs by artists such as Fabian, Little Richard, Elvis, Buddy Holly, and others who then were driving the increasing popularity of rock and roll. Billy soaked the music up too—it took hold of him as it did to countless others and from then on there was no turning back.

As he continued to practice his Beethoven that day, his mind started wandering and flashing back more and more to the rock and roll music, and suddenly his lesson turned into an improvised version of a boogie-woogie theme that had popped into his head. Blind and deaf to anything else around him now, his fingers started banging out the rock and roll on the upright piano, and Billy immediately felt his spirits soaring as his fingers sailed over the keys.

Then just as suddenly as it began it ended as Howard, fresh from the shower and in his bathrobe, flew out of the bathroom and came up behind Billy, smacking him with an open hand across the back of the head. Stunned, Billy momentarily stopped playing, and then quickly realized what had happened. Knowing he'd screwed up, he still tried to fight his first instinct to see who the attacker was even though he knew. He didn't want to, but something inside made him look over his right shoulder to see his father standing there looking down at him with his dark piercing eyes, a look that indicated both total disapproval and disgust. Billy, who had an insatiable desire to please his father, hoping that if he did it might draw them closer, was now devastated for letting his father down. He knew what he had to do, though, and without saying a word, his fingers started again playing the Beethoven, shortly afterwards feeling his father return to his bedroom to dress and prepare for dinner. That night at least, he never wandered from his lesson again.

However, from now on it was not uncommon for Billy to be practicing a piece by Mozart or Beethoven, and then begin to improvise in the style of the composer, but only when he was alone or just his mother was in the house because if she were to ask he'd simply tell her that he was playing a little known second movement. This never would have worked with his father Howard, a much more serious classical pianist.

Howard in these days was clearly a man deeply possessed by and damaged by his past. He had little if any sense of humor and by all indications has remained that way throughout his entire life. A presence in Billy's life for the first seven years, he still remained a remote figure, who because of his own pain was unable to touch his son on the levels that fathers do or should do. Yet he also managed to instill in Billy a love of music as well as an awareness of the darker realities of life.

Billy remembers:

I recall my father being different than a lot of other people's fathers I knew. He was German and had a dark European sense of humor. He always talked to me like he was talking to someone his own age. He never spoke in that very condescending way that parents do with young children. I didn't always understand what he was talking about, but I always thought that compared to what I saw with other kids' fathers, I was being treated in a special way.

Perhaps one of the most telling things Howard ever said to his son, and something that would stay in the forefront of the few memories Billy has of his father in these early days, is the time Howard told him, "Life is a cesspool," which, as Billy points out, is "a heavy thing to say to a kid."

Howard was very much a perfectionist when it came to music, undoubtedly because of his great love of it, and also because he had been denied the musician's career that he wanted so badly as a child. This too is painfully apparent in his son, and also is at the core of what perhaps is Billy's biggest conflict, the fact that despite his huge successes, his father has never really acknowledged Billy's musical prowess. "What I do, to me, isn't as good as I wish it could be," Billy says. "My father believes that if I'd grown up in Europe, I would have been a better musician."

Yet would Billy's life have been different if Howard hadn't later left to return to Europe? As his father had done to him, would he have denied Billy a career in music and forced him into a more conventional occupation? Indeed, Howard later tried to steer his second son and Billy's half-brother Alexander, now a successful European conductor, away from music, and into law school. Alexander, devastated because he feared that he wouldn't be able to pursue his true passion, called upon Billy for advice. Billy wisely told him to pacify their father by going to law school for a year and then, once he had satisfied his father's concern, to go on a pursue his true passion: music. Today that advice is paying off as Alexander is one of Europe's most respected conductors.

We will never know how Billy's life may have been different had he been raised and schooled in Europe, but what is undeniable is Howard's influence on young Billy's love of and respect for music. "My father was my idol as a pianist when I was a kid," he says. "He was classically trained, self-disciplined, and could also read music. He'd come home from work at G.E. and play Chopin and Bartok pieces, working them through laboriously—this was his entertainment." Howard's "entertainment" and his mother's incredible support were to sow the seeds from which one of the great success stories of rock and roll would emerge.

But because Howard's taste in music favored the classics, he had little tolerance for anything else. "My father was completely disparaging of pop music," Billy confides. "He thought it was crap. Popular music for him stopped when he got to the big band era. He liked and respected musicians like Errol Garner, who he thought was incredible. He also loved Nat King Cole, but after that, nobody."

Just three years after beginning his own piano lessons, Howard's son would experience a series of events at home that would rob him in many ways of his childhood. The dark talks with his father, who essentially would remain a remote and unknown figure, unknowing or unable because of the great pain he suffered as a child to touch his son's soul, would soon end. Yet it was Howard who in all likelihood unknowingly helped to cultivate Billy's love of music. Unknowingly because, by all indications, Howard, in those days, found it impossible to easily express his feelings. His method, if there was one, tended to be more of the staunch old European way, identical to what he had experienced as a boy in Germany where music wasn't meant to be fun necessarily, but treated like most other aspects of life with complete seriousness.

Despite this, watching and listening to Howard playing the piano, often literally at his knee, was an important factor that allowed Billy's love for music to emerge for the first time, even then as a child, in its most abstract form. From his father's departure from the house on, it would be his mother Rosalind who would nurture Billy's love of music. She would remain steadfast in her support and insistence that Billy's piano lessons continue; even through what later would be her own very dark days. Yet somehow she knew even at that early age the talent that Billy had, and despite the precarious financial situation she and her two children often found themselves in, she made sure Billy had what was to be his life's greatest influence for the next ten years, his piano lessons. "I figured that if he was going to bang on the piano, he was going to bang on it right," she said.

Billy's memories of these days fit more realistically into those of a wise guy kid from Long Island than a musical prodigy: "As I got older I realized that if I was going to be a concert pianist, I'd have to practice six hours a day my whole life, and there was no way that was going to happen." Yet there was clearly enough of a passion to keep him at the lessons into his teenage years, even after once being pulled off the little league field in front of his friends by his mother to be marched down the street yet again to Miss Francis's house for a lesson. "I never wanted to be a Vladimir Horowitz. In fact then I never really enjoyed playing the classics, although I'm glad I did," Billy relates today. "Practicing every day like that makes you a high-strung maniac, it is so competitive. It got to the point where the lessons weren't fun, and I wanted to have fun." In that sense growing up in suburban Hicksville, New York, the young Billy Joel was no different from countless other children; it also changed the focus of his music from classical to rock and roll, yet who back then could ever imagine where that path would lead? Certainly not Billy.

# Chapter 4

Hicksville, NY is a former potato-farming community on Long Island named after the Hicks family who were once the area's largest landholders. It borders Levittown, the quintessential American suburb, and, along with Levittown, was developed into vast tracts of identical 750-square-foot two-bedroom houses with a living room and kitchen for the masses of GIs returning after World War II by William and Alfred Levitt, in what was to be the first "assembly line" housing development. For a very small down payment, a GI returning from the war could purchase one of two Levitt house models for under seven thousand dollars, and thus flee the urban life for what they all thought would surely be a more promising future for them and their young families. That is exactly what the newly married Joels did when they moved into their new home on 20 Meeting Lane on Saturday July 1, 1950.

Howard had been told about the Levitt houses by his good friend Morton Estrin, a classical pianist that he'd known since moving to Brooklyn, and then the best friend that Howard and Roz had. Morton would also go on to teach Howard's young son Billy, beginning at age seven in Hicksville, along with Francis Neiman.

"Since I was already well under way in the development of my career as a concert pianist and teacher, I immediately started to further my career so that I could afford my new house," Estrin relates. "One day, several years after both of us had moved to Hicksville, Roz Joel called me to arrange for me to teach her son Billy piano and so that relationship began. I taught him to respect and understand the materials and structures of music, little suspecting that he would evolve into one of the most prominent musical personalities of our time! I have taken pride in Billy's great success but I certainly don't take credit for it—that could only come from his particular genius."

Typical of the distant and cold relationship between Howard's family and Rosalind's, the day Howard was to travel by train to Hicksville to look at houses, he left Roz in the Bronx with Judy and Billy. He traveled alone by train out to Hicksville which then was still a rural area of sorts. Upon arriving he was shown some new homes just across the Levittown town line in the

West Village Green section of Hicksville, and picked the one with a large backyard that faced south and was bordered to the east by a reservoir that collected rainwater from the neighborhood streets. To the west was a farm that grew corn, tomatoes, potatoes, and other vegetables. The house was secondary to Howard—after all there were only two choices; it was the privacy that this particular location offered and his dream of a large garden that made the decision for him. After coming up with the sixty dollar down payment, and signing the contract that day, Howard returned to the city to tell Roz. Excited, she immediately began dreaming out loud about how she'd furnish the house in preparation for the big move. However, she was soon to find out that Howard and his mother Meta were to be the ones that ultimately furnished and decorated the house, with very little influence from Roz. This was typical of the callous disregard that the Joels had for the Nymans and even their own daughter-in-law who they looked down on as beneath them.

According to Billy's sister Judy, Howard's mother picked out all the furniture and even the fabric for the curtains. "My mother was not involved whatsoever in the decorating and my grandmother bought all this horrible fabric that my mother would never buy; it was all olive green. They never, never appreciated Roz at all. She really is a caring woman except for her flaws." Nevertheless, overshadowed by her mother-in-law, Roz swallowed her pride and quietly looked forward to hopefully distancing herself from her in-laws, once the family moved from the Bronx to Hicksville.

Hicksville was then, and today remains, an impersonal landscape of small homes, suburban families, and blue-collar working-class culture that Billy was determined to escape from even as a youngster. It is one of a number of planned communities that have become infamous and synonymous with America's soulless suburbs, places where block after block of houses sit on tiny plots of land, all without any real character, and virtually identical to each other. Billy always hated the feeling of being "trapped" in this suburban morass, and despite the relatively humble conditions that he himself grew up in, he always knew that a better life was possible, primarily because of the world his grandfather Philip Nyman opened up to him. "There's an identity crisis associated with living there," Billy says. "You're a nothing, you're zero in the suburbs. You're mundane, you're common. You have 2.4 children, a quarter acre plot of land, a station wagon, but who gives a damn about you?"

Yet despite his family's dreary economic situation, Billy would see at an early age the world that existed outside of this suburban abyss thanks to his grandfather. These experiences coupled with his music, music that by all indications permeates his being as much as the air he breathes, would be the primary factors that would form his dream and allow him to attain it.

From his bedroom Billy often woke to the sound of a tractor working the

Chrupskis' farm behind the house. Billy and his friends would often taunt farmer Chrupski by raiding his fields for corn, tomatoes, potatoes, and other vegetables that they'd then take to their very secret Fort X to cook on little fires made from leaves and sticks. Fort X was actually inside a giant culvert pipe that emptied into the neighborhood reservoir behind the Joels' house. Here the maze of neighborhood streets drained their rainwater, forming a large pond, and on days when it was dry, Billy and other neighborhood kids would sit inside the pipe that made up their secret meeting place, and dream and play as only kids can do. This was one of their favorite places to go and meet up. A place where they could sit and tell stories, smoke cigarettes that they'd smuggled out of their families' houses, and do things that all kids in suburbia do. Fort X was a wonderful and very welcome place for Billy to escape from the increasing tensions between his parents, prior to their separation, as well as later on after his father was gone when his mother Roz would be on one of her "tangents".

First, though, he had to grow up, and in 1956 Billy's life was to be suddenly shattered. His parents, who increasingly weren't getting along, separated and his father returned to New York City and eventually Europe to continue working for G.E. Suddenly the protective bubble Billy and his family existed in exploded. Money became much tighter and Rosalind Joel was thrust into the unenviable position of having to raise her family and to be the primary breadwinner, which in 1950s America was almost impossible for a woman, particularly a woman with children and no husband. The separation caused Billy to draw his feelings and emotions even more deeply inward and by all indications his father leaving the family when Billy was just seven, never to return, deeply scarred his psyche, as evidenced by his inability to really trust people even to this day. According to Billy, it also "forced me to stand on my own two feet."

But still, try as hard as you might to downplay the situation, in the late fifties the façade of the "nuclear family" was everything; "Father Knows Best' projected Hollywood's version of the perfect family to America and divorce was something that was spoken of in the darkest of terms. The Joels' marital situation immediately became the talk of the neighborhood. Additionally, a divorced or single woman at that time in a cultural situation not known for its progressive attitudes was always suspect, particularly a good-looking one like Rosalind. Because of their own insecurities, as well as the air of conservatism in mid-fifties America, other neighborhood wives looked upon her with fear and jealousy and, at the same time, in many cases as damaged goods, scared that perhaps one of their husbands might find her an attractive alternative to what he had at home.

"You know, not everybody in our neighborhood was all that overly nice to his family," Barbara Hicks, a childhood friend of Billy and Judy, says. "I believe it's partly because they were Jewish but also because they were the only family whose father wasn't around. My mother was very forward thinking so we never had a problem with that. That's why I think Billy spent a lot of time at our house."

Despite this and her own issues, Rosalind found the inner strength to carry on. "We were blue-collar poor people," Billy says about these times. "Not poor people. You don't stand on a welfare line when you're blue-collar poor, you somehow find work, and my mother did."

In fact, despite their precarious financial situation, Rosalind tried to instill in her family the dignity and pride that her mother and father had instilled in her. To her credit, Rosalind despite her own demons, managed to survive and hold her family together in what undoubtedly were more then trying times. "You never asked for a handout," Billy continues. "You would die first."

Rosalind had a reputation among many of Judy and Billy's friends as a kind and understanding woman, although the reality was that, at times, often for seemingly no reason at all, she would fly into rages, taking out her frustrations particularly on Judy. "Billy could do no wrong. And I'm an epileptic," Judy says. "I am a nice person, but I was never happy-go-lucky. I lived in terror of Roz." Add to that her occasional fondness for alcohol, which was like throwing gas on a smoldering fire. Roz didn't have an easy time of it, and these fits of rage and drinking were her only real outlet, which were usually directed at Judy. Billy could seemingly do no wrong after his father left in Roz's eyes. His gift for music, which she clearly recognized, also made her very protective and supportive of him, and through her trying times, both professionally and personally, Roz was always Billy's biggest champion. Yet to Billy, because of her tendency to drink too much at times, she was also somewhat of an embarrassment and he would rarely bring friends home except during the times she was at work, and these were often girlfriends and one or two very close male buddies.

Today Billy, always fiercely protective of his family, not surprisingly defends his father's decision to leave, although on a more personal and intimate level it remains one of his great and unresolved issues:

He never really abandoned us. He sent a check every week, but things changed after he left. Don't forget this was Hicksville, a typical suburban neighborhood, and overnight there was a family on the block with no father. My mother was a good-looking woman, and perceived by other wives in the neighborhood to be a threat. Also because of the stigma of divorce, we all carried the irrational image of "shame." Then if that wasn't bad enough, because of the times, the only work she could get was menial jobs, and our situation changed dramatically. We had less money, and for the longest time, no TV.

Rosalind worked as a book-keeper, a secretary and a receptionist, anything she could find that would keep a roof above their heads, food on the table, and allow Billy to continue his piano lessons. Billy's success is to a large degree a tribute to his mother who supported him in his music no matter how tight money got, and although she made sure there was always the extra money for his lessons, she never pushed him to make music his career. That decision she left up to Billy. Then when he finally was successful Rosalind still worried about her son's happiness. "She's not awed by stardom," Billy says.

From this bleak and often unspoken image of the dark side of America's fifties suburbia, few if any impressions left more of an indelible mark on young Billy's childhood psyche than the times when he would see his mother looking out the kitchen window onto Meeting Lane. "She knew that my dad wouldn't be coming home that day," he says, "but she was always hoping that maybe he would pull up front. I'd see her, and feel her pain, and once asked her what she was doing. She told me 'Just looking out the window. Maybe your father's coming home.'"

These times were to influence Billy and ultimately his music. Today in some of his work there is the unmistakable and often persistent color of wounded pride, struggle and loss, disappointment, as well as shattered faith and misplaced trust, and particularly a deep-rooted anger from those early experiences in Hicksville. Experiences that in many ways robbed him of his childhood, and thrust him at seven years of age into the position of man of the house, a responsibility he always took very seriously, and one that would set the pattern for future behavioral patterns in his life. Billy's grammar and high-school friends often speak of his loyalty to his family and his determination to "take charge," to look out for his family. His first wife Elizabeth perhaps says it best, "He enjoys being the Godfather," a role that grew out of these early days of struggle. He has always been determined to care for his family and to give them the lives he and his sister never had in Hicksville. He has been successful at it too, yet even today he holds his most private emotions and thoughts deeply inside the walls he put up around him as he first learned to as a child the day Howard left the house and never returned. These stay in a very private place inside Billy rarely to come out except in occasional situations with his most trusted friends such as Billy Zampino or his wife Katie.

It's also important to note that despite the lack of money in the Joel household during these times, the portrayal of Billy living in abject poverty, as a young hoodlum and druggie, as the press has often painted his youthful circumstances, could not be further from the true reality. The ability to pay for weekly piano lessons, even in the late fifties and through the sixties, is not indicative of gross poverty. Similarly, young drug addicts don't diligently study music for over a decade as Billy did, nor do they sing in the junior high school and high school chorus as Billy also did, and they aren't, as his two chorus teachers, Chuck Arnold and Gerald Barker, say "as gifted a student even then, as we've ever had."

The truth about Billy's childhood is that he was not any better or worse off than the vast majority of kids transplanted into Long Island's suburbs from places like Brooklyn, the Bronx, and Staten Island, who preferred leather jackets and engineer boots to school sweaters and penny loafers. According to many of his schoolmates, Billy may have been "no angel," but first and foremost always was Billy's dedication to his family, second his music.

After his father left, Billy's mother became aware that he needed a positive male influence in his life and reached out to her father, Philip Nyman, who lived in Brooklyn, to be a "father figure" in Billy's life, and also to help her raise what was increasingly a restless and very inquisitive child.

"He was the male figure in my life," Billy says today. "At the time I was getting into trouble and I didn't pay attention to my mother. I was a pain in the neck."

To say that Philip was a character is a gross understatement. A very proper and Edwardian English gentleman who spoke the King's English, he had first come to America through Ellis Island in 1912 at the age of twenty-two on the ship *Franconia*. Within a year he had returned to England to get his younger brother Harry and they both arrived in New York, again coming through Ellis Island after a voyage on the *Lusitania* in 1914 in what his grandson today feels was an attempt to evade the draft in England and to begin a new life in America. Philip and Harry left their sweethearts in England with the promise of sending for them as soon as they were settled. "I asked my mother once why grandpa and nanny had come over and she told me that she wasn't 'comfortable' talking about it," Billy said. "So I said, 'You mean Grandpa was a draft dodger?' Remember, at the time they were taking young kids off the streets in England and putting them in the Army to go and be slaughtered in the fields of Flanders for God, King and Country."

Within a year Philip sent for Rebecca Gershon and Harry for his girlfriend whose first name was Kate, known later to Billy and Judy as Auntie Kitty. Rebecca and Kate sailed from Liverpool on the ship *St. Paul*, and arrived on Ellis Island on August 7, 1915, Rebecca with her bed mattress carried all the way from England, and both couples were married the next day in New York City in simple civil ceremonies. Philip's wife Rebecca immediately set out to find work in their new home and shortly after began a career as a nanny for wealthy families throughout the New York Metropolitan area. She and Philip settled in Brooklyn as did Harry and Kate, and the young couples began their lives in their new country.

Philip was by all indications a great intellectual, a follower of Bertrand Russell, and, according to Billy, "completely self-taught." And it seems that Billy's grandmother Rebecca was a very down-to-earth, unpretentious woman who loved Philip very much, and unselfishly supported him and his bohemian lifestyle her entire life by working very hard.

Philip, on the other hand, was content spending days playing chess and checkers or arguing politics with people in Brooklyn's Prospect Park. This colorful and eccentric character would play an integral role in Billy's young life and to a smaller degree his sister Judy's too. He exposed them both to a very different world than they knew in Hicksville, certainly whetting Billy's appetite for learning, even if unconventionally. Philip's positive influence would open countless doors to the world outside of Meeting Lane and the West Village Green in Hicksville for Billy. According to Rosalind, he was Billy's real father figure, and Billy himself confirms this:

> He would sneak us into operas, ballets, and Gilbert & Sullivan by slipping the usher a pack of Lucky Strike cigarettes, and suddenly we'd be sitting in almost the front row. Even though I was a very rambunctious boy back then, and I'm sure a pain in the neck, my grandfather would always find time for me. We'd visit Central Park, the Museum of Natural History, the New York Public Library, the Metropolitan Museum and Opera, and the Bronx Zoo. We'd also go to the Brooklyn Academy of Music to see great classical performances or to see Nureyev dance. That was the discipline and education I got from my grandfather. He also had all these crazy friends. Some of them were wealthy people and some were hobos, and he'd bring them home to dinner all the time. That's the kind of guy he was.

Billy spent many nights sleeping at his grandparents' Brooklyn apartment as a young boy and remembers one night in particular when he was watching a late movie stretched out on the couch and his grandfather was sitting in a chair in the same room reading a book of logarithms, or mathematical equations: "He was quietly sitting there reading and all of a sudden he started laughing out loud. I looked at him and asked him what was so funny, and he pointed to one of these equations that to me looked like some sort of foreign language and said 'fantastic.' "

Philips generosity seemed to be limitless when it came to young Billy. Philip was a "staunch atheist" according to Billy, "and I was very close to him. He was the most inspiring presence in my life." These beliefs that were first introduced to Billy by Philip would go on to influence Billy's life and music in the days ahead.

Although Philip was a self-educated, very well-mannered and extremely well-read English gentleman, "none of this had brought him wealth or position." A jeweler by trade, but only briefly, he came from a family of English tinsmiths. "He never had a dime," according to Billy, "because all of his energies were funneled into the pursuit of knowledge. He would sit in bed at night and read books on a limitless range of subjects. He didn't respect anything but knowledge, and you'd better have known what you were talking about when debating him or he'd devastate you. He could be a pain in the neck, but he was a happy man, the only self-fulfilled soul I've ever known. He made a science out of doing what he wanted to do."

His influence rubbed off on Billy at any early age. Rosalind recalls:

By the time he was seven, Billy was a bookworm. If I went to the library, I had to bring home twenty books. History books, picture books, storybooks, anything. Billy was always very self-sufficient too. It didn't take much to make him happy as a child. Just give him a chair, and he'd spend an hour making believe it was a choo-choo train.

"Yes it's true," Billy confirms. "I think a lot of the romantic notions in my music come from reading Hemingway, Fitzgerald, and even Mark Twain. My grandfather was a brilliant man who inspired me to read, and who introduced me to a world outside of the confines of Hicksville that otherwise I might never have known." Philip would leave an indelible impression on him for the rest of his life. Billy relates:

He taught me so many things about the world, things that immediately somehow made sense. For instance, he was Jewish, but he thought it was the dumbest philosophy in the world. He told me once, "If you want to see philosophy read something by Nietzsche or one of the other great philosophers." He also felt that there were no such things as Jews or Christians, and that religion was the "last refuge of the terminally stupid." This was the type of stuff he'd dump on me at like nine years old, but you know what? It made sense, although today I respect the basic tenets of all religions, like do onto others.

Philip, like most people, also recognized Billy's musical ability right away and constantly supported him in it. While visiting in Hicksville, he would ask him to play pieces by greats such as Chopin and Beethoven, and "always encouraged me to keep playing the piano."

Billy's "Uncle" Harry, also a "very colorful character," according to Billy, would tag along at times on Philip and Billy's adventures. Harry was a former boxer who spoke with a heavy Cockney accent and who loved to have a pint of beer from time to time. The three of them would visit pubs with pianos in Brooklyn's Brighton Beach, Coney Island, and Sheepshead Bay neighborhoods together. "We'd be sitting there, me this little kid and two grown men, and Harry would turn to me and say in his heavy accent, 'Come on Billy give us a song, play us a song,' and we'd do these sing-alongs like they do in British pubs. Amazing stuff for a young kid to experience and even now look back on," Billy says. "And those were really my first gigs now that I think about it."

Although some would try to describe these young years of Billy's in less then positive terms they were indeed made up of the experiences that would later mold his personality and define his music. While things were not always easy for young Billy Joel, it is apparent that there were enough positive influences in his life from his mother, sister, grandfather, great-uncle, and even early on his father, as well as life in suburban Hicksville, New York, to inspire Billy to go on to achieve the great musical success he eventually did.

# Chapter 5

First, however, life and all its molding influences lay ahead for the kid from Hicksville. Howard Joel leaving the Hicksville house in 1957 never to return shattered Billy's already fragile world. Up until then Howard had been a distant figure at best to Billy and his sister Judy, often on extended business trips to Central and South America, and when home often preoccupied with his own demons, escaping into his backyard garden or to the piano as his relationship with his wife Rosalind deteriorated. He was a very unhappy man who disliked his job, would rather have been playing the music that his parents denied him for a living than working for General Electric, and as a European always felt out of place in post-war America. If that wasn't enough, his relationship with Rosalind, which started out as a great love affair, deteriorated rapidly primarily because of the vast differences between the Joel and Nyman families. Howard's parents, who were German Jews, looked down on the Nymans who were Russian Jews as "common," and always thought that Rosalind was beneath Howard, both socially and intellectually. "We were never close, they never got along with my mother," Billy says today. This friction created an immediate wall between the two families, with the dedicated son Howard siding more with his parents, driving the final fatal nail into the marriage's coffin.

As a result of Howard's growing distance from Rosalind and his children, Rosalind, already a bit of an eccentric with a taste for alcohol, began to increase her drinking, first in Howard's absences and then even when he was home. This escalated the bickering and then all-out fighting, which began to scar the children as it drove an increasingly big wedge between the parents while dramatically affecting the already dark mood that at times prevailed in the small Joel house from Howard's demons. "I remember him coming back from one of his trips and there were arguments and stuff," says Barbara Hicks. "It wasn't a real happy place to be when he was there." Finally, Howard, who had been looking for a way out, packed his belongings for a business trip and never returned. He moved into a small apartment in New York City, essentially cutting off any involvement with his family, except for sending a small support check each month or so.

Deeply hurt by his father's abandonment, the young Billy retreated into the innermost depths of himself, as the walls around him also began to go up. Although he had never had much of a conventional father/son relationship with Howard yet, as most young boys do with their fathers, he looked to Howard in awe, particularly during those rare times they spent in the Levitt house's small living room playing the old Lester upright piano together and sharing their mutual love of music. Now and for years to come there would be no contact. The young Billy now saw himself in a more vulnerable light. After all none of his other friends' fathers had left their families and few if any were Jewish.

Billy says:

There was no religion practiced in my family for at least three generations, and from what I understand back then that wasn't uncommon. We had Christmas and because all my friends were Italian, Polish or Irish, I went to mass on Sundays. I thought that's what you did as a kid. I had no Jewish upbringing. In fact, the first time I wore a yarmulke was at my grandfather's funeral. They buried him as a Jew, and he was an atheist; he would have hated that, despised it. I thought even then that it was hypocritical.

But the reality is that, after Howard left, things did deteriorate quickly inside the house at 20 Meeting Lane, as Billy recalls:

We were the gypsy family. The only family where there had been a divorce, the only one that wasn't Catholic and the only one without a driveway. There was no breadwinner so our situation went downhill pretty fast. For me, I was different from the other kids because they had dads. I remember, especially, a lot of guys my age had a dynamic going on with their fathers that I didn't have.

Always the one to hide his vulnerability and his personal pain, Billy quickly turns to the other perspective: "But there was an upside too. I was brought up by a loving woman and my sister."

Rosalind, also feeling the deep effects of being abandoned, began to spend an inordinate amount of time on the telephone with her sister Bert in Ohio looking for consolation, running up huge phone bills that taxed the already precarious finances in the Joel household. She also began to rely more and more on alcohol to numb her pain and anxieties, another drain on money. Embarrassed about her situation and her solution to her depression, she often would send Judy down to the local store with a note to buy some basics for the refrigerator as well as a quart of beer. Although Howard was sending a small check most months, money remained tight due to Rosalind's new priorities.

Despite her shortcomings Rosalind still managed, despite what must have been insurmountable odds, to hold her family together, but at a great personal cost too. She would often disappear into her bedroom for a few days, deep in a depression that she would attempt to escape with a quart of beer or some wine. These were the times that Billy and Judy had to "tip toe" around the house. Friends knew better then to stop over, which was fine, because bringing friends home was not a common event for Billy and Judy anyway.

"I went to his house a couple of times," says friend Bobby Colisante. "But it was not a place where he wanted to be. He didn't have a television, but it was the place where the piano was."

They both seemed to be embarrassed by the rudimentary nature of the tiny house compared with others in the neighborhood, but now Rosalind's increased drinking and erratic behavior was becoming the talk of the neighborhood. This, in addition to their Jewish roots, Howard leaving, and their precarious financial condition made them stick out like a sore thumb in the neighborhood, which also only made them that much more of a target for those with their own skeletons in the closet who needed a place to point the finger.

"I remember feeling bad for them as a family," Barbara Hicks says. "Because besides being ostracized in the neighborhood, it always seemed like things never worked out for them. My mother knew Roz pretty well, and I remember that she tried very hard to hold it together, then she'd just be kind of absent." She continues: "I think that was always one of Judy's big problems because she was always responsible for a lot of things in the house that most young people were not responsible for."

Indeed, when Roz would descend into these dark moods, things in the tiny Levitt house had to be absolutely quiet, because to wake or disturb her was to incur her wrath. The music from Judy or Roz's records that usually filled the house was silenced, as were Billy and his sister, who knew the drill all to well. More then once friends of Judy's who had stopped by to visit and listen to records or play dolls witnessed Roz come flying out of her bedroom, dressed in her pajamas or disheveled clothing, screaming like a madwoman as she drove everyone outside. But then on other days when things weren't so dark and Roz was not as burdened by her situation, she could be like one of the neighborhood kids, listening to records with them or even playing some of her own and singing and dancing with them as they looked on in awe at her talent and beautiful singing voice. You never knew what to expect when you visited the Joel house, and Billy and Judy were often away at a friend's house anyway, trying to escape the behavior at home, which they didn't fully understand. Then, like it had never happened, Roz would pull herself together and go find a job until the next episode.

So to say that things inside the Joel house were anything like the stereotypical suburban lifestyle then being perpetuated by Madison Avenue and television would be far from truthful, but then again where other then television and Madison Avenue did the perfect suburban dream exist?

Billy today agrees: "Here we are living in the Betty Furness of lifestyles, and Roz was a single and attractive woman. She found it difficult. She could not find a good job, although she was very intelligent and often over-qualified; all she could get was book-keeping or secretarial work."

Despite her demons Roz had an inner strength that often prevailed. Because of the suicide of her own sister in 1947 due to post-partum depression, she was determined to hold her family together and when she wasn't battling her demons would take what amounted at the time to menial jobs in the Hicksville area to support her family. She worked as a receptionist, book-keeper, and secretary at just about every business or office within a five-mile radius of her house at one time or another, and by all accounts was thought of as a competent employee, although a bit eccentric. At a time when divorced women were looked upon as some sort of damaged goods, Roz's inner strength and dignity prevailed until things got to be just too much and the demons would win out again. Then she would return to the drinking, lose her job, and descend into the depths of her depression until she was able to pull herself out again.

Although Roz had a reputation with Billy and Judy's friends for being less then predictable at home when her demons got the best of her, she was also fondly thought of by them because of her ability to relate to them on their level, often acting like more of a friend then a parent. On her good days, and there were many, she could often be found baking cookies or snacks for the neighborhood kids, and when they'd stop over she'd often listen to records and sing and dance with them or play her own records, which often were Gilbert and Sullivan or Richard Rodgers scores, and again singing and dancing as she acted out the roles to the delight of the neighborhood children. Appearances were also very important to Roz, who was a good-looking woman. She one day told Judy and one of Judy's girlfriends who was at the house helping Judy iron bras that "looking and dressing well was the most important asset a woman had," and again by all indications many of the husbands of the neighborhood thought of Roz as an attractive woman, much to the dismay of their own wives.

With the hand she had been dealt, Roz did an amazing job raising her family in the fifties and sixties. Any spare money that was around was often used to put gas in one of the clunker cars that the Joels had, if it was running, and to head up to Long Island's North Shore to Cold Spring Harbor or the

Oyster Bay area with Billy and Judy and their friends, who were always invited. Whitey, the Joels' mixed breed dog and Billy's close friend, would sometimes go with them too on these trips. They'd BBQ and picnic, always near the water in a park or beach, and then swim and play while Roz read or napped nearby. In fact one of these excursions was where Billy, whose deep love of the water is well known today, had his first experience as a boat captain. At about the age of twelve, he and a friend swam out to a small rental row boat with a motor in Cold Spring Harbor and, starting up the outboard, slipped the mooring line and puttered around the harbor for an hour or so, until scared they'd be caught, they returned the boat to the mooring and swam back to shore, with the boat's owner never finding out.

At the end of the day on one of these picnics on Long Island's Gold Coast the Joels would head off in the car to drive the country roads that were so vastly different then Hicksville's suburban morass, and look at the big and beautiful houses in these communities before returning to Hicksville. Here is where Billy would often dream out loud to those in the car about which one of the mansions he was going to buy when he became rich, something he's ended up doing many times since then.

Cooking was a pastime Rosalind enjoyed during those times when things were running right in the house. Her favorites were pasta dishes, shepherd's pie, and the cookies, but it was deli food and deli buffets that Billy and Judy and their friends loved the most. These were special occasions and real treats that only occurred when things were going smoothly in the tiny Joel house. Judy would usually be the one sent, along with one of her friends and a wish list they'd all made up, to pick up a bunch of cold cuts, chips, sodas, and salads at the local deli. They'd then be set out in the tiny kitchen on top of the linoleum table where everyone would help themselves, usually while Roz played records and sang, or at times while Billy would play the piano for everyone, always amazing them with his ability to play classical, show tunes, and rock and roll with equal ease. It seemed that music always filled the Joel home during these good times, often led by Roz and her albums of show tunes, but also by records that Judy and Billy played on the portable record player. So although things inside 20 Meeting Lane were often precarious in many ways, and bore no resemblance to the "perfect" image of families perpetuated by television, the one stabilizing force for the family was the music that filled the house and the soul of a young Billy Joel.

# Chapter 6

Fork Lane Elementary School rose out of the vast post-World War II Hicksville potato fields just as the thousands of Levitt homes had. It was just down the block from the Joels' house on Meeting Lane, and a quick walk or even quicker bike ride for young Billy and his sister. Brand new when the Joels moved to Hicksville, it was where Judy and, then two years later in 1954, Billy first started school, and where they met many of their friends, some of whom would later turn up in Billy's songs as colorful characters. Typical of the schools built in suburban areas during that time period it was and today still remains a sprawling, ranch-type building surrounded with playfields, a tennis court and Levitt houses.

Many of Billy's friends from those days speak of the little kid with the white socks, black high top sneakers, dungarees, and flannel shirts walking around the neighbor streets often only with his beloved dog Whitey, yet clearly in a world of his own. In fact one old schoolmate related how she once saw Billy on his way to school one morning, with his arms outstretched and fingers moving "furiously." Totally unaware of what he was up to then, she know realizes that as he walked to school that morning with his dog Whitey he was off in his own world playing the "air piano" to some piece of music that was running through his head.

Fork Lane was also the school where Billy was to meet the first school music teacher who would leave a deep and indelible impression on him: Mary Milidantry. She, like so many others yet to come, would recognize the talent of this funny-looking little kid. Fresh out of teachers' college she approached her job with the enthusiasm of someone who for as long as she could remember wanted to teach music to young children. In addition to teaching music and playing the piano, Ms. Milidantry was also the chorus teacher, a common package in small suburban schools back then. It was her responsibility not only to teach the children music, but also to direct and produce the school's musical presentations for the students' families. By all indications she had a large and positive impact on her students and on Billy. According to Linda Mahanna, a schoolmate of Billy's, she was "demanding, but nurturing at the same time," and "would make her chorus practice by standing in the back of the gym, while she stood opposite them at the entrance as they sang," and if she couldn't understand every word of their song she was known to throw tantrums, and "bang on the piano's keyboard" until her kids, now totally intimidated, "got it right."

Always the born entertainer, Billy loved chorus, and his little voice could often be heard above all the rest at practices and school plays. Additionally, even then Billy was a showman, and not at all intimidated by doing solos, which is interesting given that he has never been comfortable with the way his voice sounded. In fact in second grade Ms. Milidantry had the school put on a presentation of George M. Cohen songs with Billy doing a memorable and very animated version of "Give My Regards to Broadway" complete with a little straw hat and a cane that, by all indications, drew the crowd in the gym that night to their feet for the first of many times yet to come. Billy Zampino, who today remains Billy's best friend, joined Billy in this. "I remember that we went to the local Army Navy store to get our costumes," Zampino says. "We were dressed out in full military regalia that night."

How the two Billys met isn't real clear to either today. Billy likes to tell the story that his mother gave him a quarter and told him to "go find a friend," and he brought Zampino home. Zampino remembers it a bit differently though. "We both took piano lessons from Miss Francis, so I'm pretty sure it happened there," he says. "I remember being amazed at Billy's prowess on the piano even then, and I think that's where our friendship began." Regardless, the friendship has endured. "One day we were climbing the willow tree in his backyard and both tumbled out when a limb cracked or something," Zampino relates. "We were both scratched and slightly bloodied. To Billy it seemed an ideal time to become blood brothers. We have been ever since." Zampino may very well be Billy's closest confidant, able to ground him better than most and get Billy to that place inside himself that is most important to him, a place which if he strays from he often finds himself in trouble. It's the classic conflict that lies at the heart of Billy Joel the Hicksville kid versus Billy Joel the world famous rock and roll star. He wrestles with it constantly, and it is the source of his greatest demons because he loves both worlds, but when push comes to shove, it's the Hicksville kid that Billy wisely realizes is the most important because it's who he is at his most inner core.

Second grade was also when Billy would start for the first time really beginning to write down the music that was in his head. Up until now creating his music had always been something he'd done while sitting at the piano practicing his lessons, or improvising, but now he actually began to write down notes and even names for his compositions.

When not in school, Billy's life on Meeting Lane usually revolved around hanging out at other kids' houses and doing the things that kids in elementary school did back then. In addition to their Fort X, Billy and his friends would play stickball, climb the monkey bars at the school playground, ride their bikes, raid the fields at Cherupski's farm or hang out in the big barn that was one of their play spots.

By all indications Billy was a pretty good stickball player although he was shorter then most of his friends, with little legs and hands. Nevertheless, because of his speed and his ability to hit the ball he was always in demand when it came time to pick teams. According to Christina Webber, a friend of Judy's at Fork Lane School:

> Billy was quick, oh yeah, he was speedy, for such a little guy, with such little legs he was very fast, we used to fight over him to see who would get him to play stickball on the street. We used to play stickball on Meeting Lane and sometimes we would go over to the schoolyard over on Fork Lane and play there, and we would fight over him.

Back then Billy had a reputation for being "distant" and somewhat of a loner, no doubt partially because of his preoccupation with his music, but also because kids (as they can be) were often very mean to Billy and Judy. Again because of their situation at home, and the talk about it in the neighborhood, they were easy targets. That, coupled with the innate insecurity that a young boy of Billy's age lived with due to his father's abandonment, were the seeds that were planted very early on, and which were to follow him throughout his life. From there first the anger and then the rebellion against any authority figures, which were primarily men, sprouted and remain today in Billy. He is someone who doesn't make close relationships easily, although a few meaningful relationships with male friends have endured from that time.

Others like Jim Bosse, also a Hicksville kid and early bandmate, and who many think is "James" in the song, enjoy a friendship and mutual respect with Billy for what he has done with his life and his music. Yet in general, because of that day when his father left the house and never returned, Billy remains someone who is not easy to get close to, but also someone who if you do, can be one of the most generous and loyal, yet demanding, friends ever.

Being the loner wasn't always necessarily always a negative thing for Billy though. Often those times when he'd be playing stickball, riding his bike with friends, or just hanging out and he'd disappear, he could be found back at his house alone, because his mom was usually at work, sitting at the piano practicing. These were the times, and they were often by all accounts, when the music would overwhelm him and he'd have to stop what he was doing to go and give in to it.

Playing at friends' houses, or acting out little skits, was also a common event for young Billy Joel. "My grandfather was from Texas and was very involved in Native Americans' rights, even back then," says Barbara Hicks. "Because of it he had all these Indian costumes. So one day I remember Billy, Judy, and I dressed up in some, and we were over at their house acting out like little Indians, when all of a sudden Billy sat down at the piano and started playing Indian-type music, you know what I mean with the boom, boom, boom, boom beat. Anyway Judy and I were dancing around the living room with this little kid playing the music on the piano, and I remember thinking that this little kid was different, that he had real talent."

Barbara continues:

My mother also loved music and used to hang out with Roz sometimes. Unlike other women in the neighborhood, she wasn't threatened by Roz because she was pretty. Actually I'm sure she actually felt a lot of empathy for her and her kids because they were always ostracized in the neighborhood, and also because things just never seemed to go right for them if you know what I mean. Things like her old Renault car not starting in the morning so she could get to work, so she'd have to call a garage to get it started, or take a cab and waste what little money they had. Anyway, there'd be these times when Roz would be around, when you'd see her, or she'd even be at my house visiting my mother, and I know my dad thought she was good looking because he's told me so. Then there'd be those times when Roz wouldn't be around, but then again, neither would Judy, and then you knew things weren't good at their place.

Both Billy and Judy were smart kids and good kids. But boy did they run into problems in that neighborhood at times. Even in school they ran into trouble at times. I remember that we had this one teacher at Fork Lane, and she could be unbelievable to them both. Very cruel, and I'm sure it was just because of their predicament.

As well as the tough side of life there were plenty of good times too. Art Tallman, a classmate of Billy's, remembers an event that left a deep impression on young Billy Joel:

In third grade Billy and a friend Bobby Breeden had put together a little skit for one of Miss Milidantry's talent shows. Billy was to be Elvis, and Bobby was a member of his band. They practiced it at Billy's house, and then one day during lunch in the school cafeteria that also doubled as the auditorium Billy jumped up on the stage and, banging on the piano, started playing and singing Elvis's "Hound Dog," swinging his little hips and everything. Well, some teacher flipped out and grabbed Billy and pulled him off the stage, but not before a group of fourth-grade female spectators began to form. It was the most amazing thing I'd seen until then, this little kid singing his heart out and mimicking Elvis.

Billy also recalls the story: "I remember thinking, 'Hey, the girls in fourth grade are digging me. Digging *me!*' They'd never even known I was alive until then, but that day, up on that stage, they sure did." Needless to say, that was something that was to leave an indelible impression on him.

After school there was always plenty to do for young Billy. On those days when he didn't have piano lessons he could be found riding his bike with friends, playing baseball or stickball, or playing at someone's house or Fort X. Hicksville still retained its "small town" atmosphere until the early sixties, when the big Mid-Island Plaza mall opened. Like all small towns, there was a sweet shop on Main Street where the kids would congregate after school. It was across from St. Ignatius church whose presence dominated Hicksville's Main Street, and it had the old-fashioned soda fountain and a case full of penny candies. Billy and his friends would hang out here drinking vanilla crèmes and buying penny candies, and also listening to the rock and roll music that was being played inside on the bigger kids' transistor radios.

Even though Hicksville was primarily a blue-collar working-class community the parents and teachers were determined to try and bring their children up correctly, in the manner which would make them gentlemen and ladies. But the sixties were right on the horizon, a period which would change this, although as in other suburban towns it all started quietly.

Ballroom dance lessons were part of the curriculum at Fork Lane for the older grades and dances were an annual event at Fork Lane School for the 6th. graders before they graduated and went off to Junior High School. Mary Barnett was a classmate of Billy's who had a crush on him. "He wasn't interested in anyone except himself," she said. "It seemed he was always off in his own world. But I liked him, and besides, he was short and so was I, so I asked him to the dance. Billy showed up in a black suit, with a white shirt and tie, very proper, and I wore a blue dress and black shiny shoes. First we all sat down in the gym which was all decorated and had dinner, very proper, and then afterwards they played the music and we all danced with the teachers looking on to make sure everyone behaved. Back then we did." That wouldn't last much longer.

Many kids announce the onset of adolescence with a dramatic change in behavior to their parents. They begin to separate from their parents and strive to become more independent. At the same time, children this age are increasingly aware of how others, especially their peers, see them as they desperately try to fit in to that world. They'll often start "trying on" different looks and identities, and they become acutely aware of just how much they differ from their peers, which results in episodes of distress and conflict with parents.

One of the common stereotypes of adolescence is the rebellious, wild teen continually at odds with his parents and authority figures. As teenagers start to pull away from their parents—usually the parent that they're the closest to—a multitude of conflicts can arise. Furthermore as teens mature, they start to think more abstractly and rationally. They're forming their own moral code. And parents of teens may find that kids who previously had been willing to conform to please them will suddenly begin asserting themselves and their opinions strongly and rebelling against parental control—and Billy Joel was certainly not an exception. With Howard leaving and Roz in such an unstable state so much of the time, Billy was forced into a position where he grew up much faster then those around him. As a result he experienced much of what life throws at you before his friends and peers did, which in many ways robbed him of his childhood. For instance, Roz was famous for making up excuses about where her husband was, something that Billy also picked up on. When Roz would show up at parent teacher meetings, which wasn't often, she would tell the teachers that Billy's father was "in the merchant marine, and unable to make the meeting." Understandably embarrassed by the situation at home, Billy was known to tell his friends the same story in his younger years; this "white lie" and others that he was fond of telling his friends was to earn Billy the nickname "BB" for "Bullshit Billy" later on. School plays and presentations were a little different for Roz though. These she could show up with a sister, Phillip or her mother and avoid the stigma of being a divorced woman. After all, Billy was usually the center of attention at these with his great talent, and Roz could bask in the satisfaction of knowing that, removing her from her all to often-dismal situation, if even for just that one night.

Junior high school was for many reasons going to be a great turning point in Billy's life, even if he didn't see it until much later. Music would take on a new seriousness and importance in his life as he also began to take his first steps out into the world on his own, asserting himself as an individual, and continuing his evolution, again with the help of some people and teachers who were to play important roles in his life. "There were only a few ways you could go in school then," Billy says. "This was before The Beatles even, so it was pretty much the collegiants or the preppy who were usually into sports, or the greasers who were into other things like drinking, girls and experimenting with glue and pot. I wasn't a preppy." Others also saw the change beginning in Billy. He was going from being that cute little kid, with the big dark eyes and smile, to a more serious and even sullen adolescent hanging out with a "faster" crowd. But according to Jim Bosse, a member of

Billy's first band The Echoes, Billy always had "a maturity and intellectual level that was definitely higher then most kids we hung out with." And when people who initially were turned off by Billy's tough guy persona got to know him they were surprised at just what a nice person he was under that hardening shell.

One thing that stayed constant with Billy throughout it all was his inherent love of music. Continuing his run of luck with good music teachers, Billy was introduced to Mr. Barker, who now was the boys' chorus teacher for Division Avenue Junior High School. He had taken the job because the previous teacher, a good-looking woman, couldn't handle the rowdy group of 40 or so boys that signed up each year. In the 7th grade taking a music class was mandatory in Billy's school, so if you didn't want to take general music and learn an instrument, you had to take chorus. Since Billy was still taking piano lessons, even though their days were numbered, with his new tough guy image, he chose chorus and ended up with Mr. Barker, a teacher known for his "no nonsense" approach to teaching. One he had to maintain since usually those in his class, particularly the boys, were there to try and skate through what was a full year commitment. Barker ran his classes like drill camps, penalizing students even when they were minutes late and taking no crap from the adolescent "wise guys" who ended up there.

Gerald Barker recalls:

I remember it was the first or second day of school and Billy came up to me and said, "Mr. Barker, I like songs. Do you think I could sing for the chorus?" I looked down at this little kid who couldn't have been older then twelve thinking that the older and rowdier kids were sure to laugh or boo him down. But there was something about him, his sincerity, so I said "OK, come tomorrow." Then he tells me that he's got a friend that plays the guitar, and that he'll bring him, and sure enough they both showed up the next day for practice and played me two songs. They did it beautifully. Right then I knew that Billy would make music his life's work. After all, he was talented and there was something about him that made him stand out from all the rest, even then.

This also was just about the time that Billy's voice was beginning to change and Billy was worried about it. He trusted Mr. Barker and discussed it with him, so they both worked on it, and on perfecting a new sound successfully. Mr. Barker continues:

He'd come in and sing these songs that he'd written with a friend, the same kid that played guitar with him. It took a huge amount of nerve to sit there in front of this bunch of rowdy kids and sing, but he did it, and the kids really responded to him, this little kid having the nerve to sing the songs he'd written, amazing. So when I had a solo that had to be done, I'd usually give it to Billy. He had the presence to pull it off, and that is something that is natural to one, something that they're born with.

Unlike some other teachers whose paths crossed with Billy back then, Barker is able to remain objective and honest about the influence he may have had on Billy's future life: "Mary Milidantry is the one responsible for his musical career. She was the one and everyone who taught him knows that." It seems that Billy would agree. At a hometown concert at Long Island's Nassau Coliseum in the late seventies, Billy announced from the stage: "Tonight there are two women here that are the most important women in my life, my mother and my music teacher Miss Milidantry."

However, Billy himself has acknowledged Gerald Barker's influence on his singing voice. On a concert stop in Reno, Nevada, where Barker lives today, they ran into each other backstage before a show. Mr. Barker had brought a photo he had of a young Billy Joel dressed in a dinner jacket and singing in the choir for Billy to sign, which he did. He also brought a copy as a gift for Billy, and they had a great reunion.

Barker remembers:

I got backstage simply because I was the only person at the concert dressed in a suit and I guess they thought I was somebody. Anyway I'm walking down the hall and I run into this guy, and in my New York accent I tell him, "My name is Barker and I'd like to see Billy Joel." No sooner had I said it then Billy comes running down the hall and grabs me and gives me big bear hug. We talked for a little while and I gave him a copy of the picture which I could tell he was delighted to have, and he autographed my copy too. Then if that wasn't enough, at the show he announced that I was there and dedicated the concert to me. It was a wonderful evening.

By all indications Billy was now firmly immersed in a world of music that continued to nurture him. If it weren't at school where he continued to impress both his teachers and his peers with his talent, it was home on the old Lester piano practicing, or listening to music with Judy and her friends. Regardless, music was at the innermost core of Billy's world, and by all indications his great talent was beginning to emerge not just as a piano player, but also as a singer and overall performer. Fortunately for Billy he had this sanctuary in which to take refuge and escape the often precarious and stressful situation at home.

# Chapter 7

On October 24, 1962 a thirteen-year-old Billy Joel and two friends hopped a train in Hicksville on their way to their first rock concert. Arriving in New York City, they got on a subway and headed uptown to Harlem's Apollo Theater to see James Brown and the Fabulous Flames play. The three of them purchased their tickets at the box office and, excitedly, and very naively, walked inside to find their seats. Soon after entering the lobby it quickly became apparent to them that they were the only white people inside and the adrenaline each was feeling in anticipation of the concert quickly turned to an unfounded fear. The three white kids from Hicksville, who at the Village Green or in the halls of Hicksville High School were considered pretty cool, were clearly out of their element now and in a light state of panic as they moved to their seats, trying to play the role of hardasses, masking their trepidation. They took their seats, and forced a conversation among themselves, hoping the show would soon begin. Still unnerved, they were just about to leave when the theater lights went down and Brown came onstage. Suddenly their fears fell by the wayside and they became transfixed by this mythical figure onstage that until then they'd only heard on New York's AM radio, usually at night as they lay in bed listening to their transistor radios.

Billy said:

It was incredible. He moved across the stage on one foot and came back the other way on the other foot, with the greatest footwork and singing I'd ever seen. He tore the place apart for over two hours, until finally exhausted and soaking wet from perspiring, he'd put on his cape and try to leave the stage. Then the people backstage would drag him back out again for one more song, which worked the crowd into an even greater frenzy. This went on for another five or so songs until he finally disappeared. It wasn't the most sophisticated show, and the compositions were fairly primitive, but the performance knocked the hell out of me.

Only later would Billy and his friends realize the significance of this night. Brown had wanted to record a live album, but his record company at the time refused to bankroll it. Brown put the five thousand dollars up which resulted in *James Brown Live at the Apollo*, an album which included such powerful classics as "Please, Please Me" and "Night Train." It soon jumped to number two on the Billboard charts and introduced Brown to countless millions of new, mostly white fans.

The concert also galvanized Billy's future: "Pop music hadn't really hit me till then, but after that—James Brown, Sam and Dave, Wilson Pickett, Otis Redding and the Phil Spector records did it for me. That was the first music I really felt."

At home he started tuning his transistor radio into New York City's R&B stations, and practicing interpretations of what he'd heard on the piano. Hooked, he kept going to concerts, like The Temptations at Palisades Park in New Jersey, a top venue back in the sixties. Long Island was also a hotbed of garage rock and roll at the time, and Billy was immersed in it. Billy says: "We had so much reaction and rock and roll attitude, we'd listen to soul music a lot and we used to go to this black record store near the Hempstead bus station and buy records; it was great record shop. We'd get a hit 45 and look at the other side, the B side, because these songs we usually just as good and not well known. In fact one of our first recordings with The Hassles was 'You Got Me Hummin,' a Sam and Dave B side. Everything before that we did was English, The Beatles, Gerry and the Pacemakers . . . so this was soul. We also did Traffic. The first guy in our first band, Jimmy Bosse, he lives in Colorado Springs, he has most of our early recordings, and so does one of The Echoes' early drummers Billy Zampino."

At Division Avenue Junior High School Billy's evolving musical ability was continuing to be noticed both by students and teachers. Mr. Barker, the Junior High School chorus teacher, was always punctual. He also had a reputation to his students as a strict teacher yet he commanded their respect and today most have fond memories of him.

As Barbara Hicks recalls:

Gilbert and Sullivan stuff, a couple of solo opportunities, "Three Little Maids," and modern major-general from *Pirates of Penzance*, he would always volunteer for solos, and what he brought to the table was improvisation. In other words, he wouldn't follow the script. What he would do, and I always thought this was kind of brilliant, would be to take the song. Take the song improvise it so that the audience would be cracking up . . . a true showman, a ham. Added an extra dimension to our performances

One day he was late for some reason and we were all sitting around, you know fidgeting, etc. Well, Billy walked up to the piano and started playing rock tunes mostly. Had the whole group spellbound—very few of us realized he could play the piano to that point. And listening to him made me think this guy was like a virtuoso sitting there pounding out stuff off the top of his head as we all stayed there silent for about 10 minutes.

At about the same time Billy Joel was turning onto this new music, his teenage adolescence was kicking in full power. He started hanging more and more with the Parkway Green Gang, a bunch of "hitters" or "greasers" from the neighborhood made up of self-proclaimed "tough guys" who usually were anything but, but who were more in love with the image then the lifestyle.

"When they built Hicksville and Levittown, they also built nine "Village Greens," says Vinnie Longo, a childhood friend of Billy's. "Each green had a swimming pool, and a bunch of places to play and hang out, and then near each one there was also a drugstore and a diner, where you could hang out too. Billy and I hung at the West Village Green on Newbury Road," Vinnie continues. "We'd do all the stuff that everyone else was doing, like sniffing glue, drinking cheap wine and beer, and hanging out."

But luckily for Billy there was also an alternative to this "tough guy' behavior, that some of his friends and acquaintances weren't fortunate enough to have.

"As teenagers, we went together to see *My Fair Lady* on Broadway, and sat through the film version of *West Side Story* at least 12 times," Billy Zampino says today.

Here again Billy's mother Roz, despite her precarious financial and personal conditions, was determined that Billy and Judy were both going to see the world that existed beyond theirs. These trips and events, coupled with the world that Billy's grandfather Phillip had already opened for Billy through his stories and voracious reading habits, were to be the things that kept the flame of hope burning red hot in a young Billy Joel.

But meanwhile you had to find an identity and fit in to survive and Billy did. While not exactly Bernardo and his buddies from *West Side Story*, Billy and his friends at the Village Green nevertheless emulated them as much as a bunch of kids from suburbia could. "We wore the black leather jackets, purple shirts, tight black pants, black socks, and Astro boots with that stupid little rocket logo on the sides. If you were cool, and we all thought we were, you'd rip the rockets off," Billy remembers. "Also engineer boots and tight blue jeans," he adds with a smile. The girls teased their hair, used lots of make-up including white lipstick and white nail polish, and dressed in tight black pants and skirts, tight blouses and sweaters, and smoked cigarettes constantly. They'd all travel the streets of Hicksville in little groups, and hang at the Parkway Green pool during hot summer days and nights. "We weren't nearly as tough as we thought we were, but belonging got us all through somehow," Billy says.

There was a sense of security associated with being part of a group like this, and Billy, still unsure of himself and his masculinity, due primarily to being raised in a home where his father abandoned him and where he was always surrounded by women, welcomed the camaraderie. It was at this point that Billy and his friends also started experimenting with drinking cheap Tango wine, fighting with other local gangs, and sniffing glue. Seeing this change unfolding in Billy his mother Roz decided that Billy needed more of a "masculine" influence in his life. Sure he had his grandfather Phillip who Billy adored, but Roz had in mind an environment with a lot more macho attitude for the young Billy. She'd heard about a police boys' club down the road from the Joels' house in the Mid-Island Shopping Plaza that had a model building room where kids could come and build model airplanes and cars with grown-ups, and shortly afterwards, she was dragging Billy inside to meet the adults that ran it.

Billy remembers:

My mom used to bring me there a lot. She thought I needed to do stuff with guys. Originally it was the model airplanes, they built some beautiful World War I era planes, wooden ones, and I started to really get into it too. It didn't take me long to realize that a lot of the guys that were there were not there to just build models. They were there to sniff glue, and there was plenty of it around, so naturally I fell into that scene too for a while.

Billy was also taught boxing at the Mid-Island Plaza Shopping Center just downstairs from the model-building room where they had a makeshift gym set up with a boxing ring. A cop named Terry Burns was in charge of the program and he and Billy hit it off pretty well right from the start.
Billy recalls:

I stumbled on the place right away. They were teaching boys how to box. I was small and slight back then so they classified me as a welterweight. I discovered that I was a great counter-puncher, a good defensive-style boxer. I had what they called a European style, I had good footwork and good rhythm. In America it's all knock the guy out, but I had good timing, which may have come from being good at music.

I learned boxing because I got tired of getting beaten up when I was going to piano lessons. On the way to Miss Francis, there'd be a couple of guys waiting for me outside her house. "Hey, Billy where's your tutu," they'd say, as she used to teach ballet too. I'd drop the books out of my hand and get my ass kicked, I got tired of it . . . I got really tired, I never liked bullies.

I saw my mother get bullied, when she first got divorced. She could never get a decent job. She was a young good-looking woman but in the late fifties and early sixties no one got divorced back then, and every job she got she was bullied in. I watched her get beaten up by the system, and ground down by the system, and it was awful. I watched this happening to her and it created all this rage and hostility in me, I was so angry . . .

Anyway I fought a total of twenty-two fights and I lost a couple I think, and then I got my nose broken, which put an end to my boxing career. I didn't mind so much that it got broken, hey it was macho shit, but I was afraid boxing might damage my singing voice, so I quit.

Ralph Turchiano met Billy in the early sixties one day when he and some of his friends ran into Billy doing impersonations on a street corner for some other kids.

"He could do imitations of people so good, that if you closed your eyes, you'd think it was them," Ralph says today. "Then later on I know he did them as part of his concert act until he realized that his music was enough."

Ralph became one of Billy's close friends back then and has stayed in touch with Billy all these years. He remembers when Billy had his brief but successful boxing career:

He was boxing at the Police Boys' Club. He had this long torso and short legs and when he walked he waddled. A friend told me he'd seen Billy one day walking down the road with a girl, when five or six guys pulled up alongside of him and started mouthing off. You know shit like, "Hey, you long-haired faggot, who is that you're with?" Billy, who was clearly outnumbered, told them, "Pull the car over, I'll show all of you, each at a time" And you know what? They drove off. I'm sure 'cause they were caught off guard by Billy's ballsiness, but maybe also because deep down they liked him, we all did.

Billy enjoyed the brief boxing career he had, and like everything else in his life that he became involved in, was always looking for ways to make himself better. Conscious about his small hands, and worried that they weren't "tough enough" because of his piano playing, Billy took to dipping them in a bowl of vinegar at home, because he had heard somewhere that this would make them toughen up. One day Roz discovered this, and flipped out on Billy because she was afraid that it might interfere with his ability to play the piano.

Shortly after ending his boxing career, Billy joined his first band The Echoes on February 21, 1964 after being asked by Howie Blauvelt. Howie along with other Hicksville kids Jim Bosse and Kenny Retcher had formed the band and were practicing whenever and wherever they could. Blauvelt decided that their band needed a keyboard player to better play the British standards that were becoming so popular, so they asked Billy who was well known as a good piano player to audition.

"We invited him to one of our rehearsals," said Jim Bosse, "and of course he was way ahead of us, so we invited him right away to join. He soon became our front man due to his talent."

Before he prematurely passed away from a heart attack, Howie Blauvelt told the story of his first garage band:

I was in the fifth grade. We had a talent show and this kid played the guitar. All the girls went wild for him and I said, "I gotta do this!" So I got a guitar and learned how to play, I practiced hard for about two years. Later on, after I knew enough chords, I played with some other kids and we formed a band, The Echoes. We had two guitars so I switched to bass and hey—it was fun! There was a space for it, you know, it was great. We had fun when we played. This was just before the English Invasion so we played dance music: "Twist and Shout", "La Bamba," "Perfido," "Wipe Out," and lots of instrumentals . . . too many instrumentals! We eventually needed a singer bad so I said I knew this guy that sings and he plays piano. I asked my friend Billy Joel if he wanted to join our band.

Billy himself says:

I couldn't believe it: I actually got *paid* for this stuff! That locked the back door. There was no way out for me. I was hooked. At the time I couldn't understand why they asked me to join. Everybody was playing guitars and I couldn't imagine where my piano would fit in. At first we used to stick an old Kent microphone into the back of the piano—and we were all plugged into one amplifier, an old Magnitone amp that had this little reverb chamber that we'd turn all the way up, thinking we were the Righteous Brothers or something. We were pretty lousy in the beginning I guess, but shit I didn't care; I was playing in a rock band.

At first The Echoes copied California standards like The Safaris' "Wipe

Out" and The Ventures' "Walk Don't Run," but they also did top 40 hits such as "Wolly Bully." They landed their first paying gig at one of Hicksville's Holy Family Church teen dances in 1964, when Billy was fifteen, with each member getting about five dollars for their efforts. "I think it was Dave Bagoli's father that got us our first job there," says Jim Bosse. "He was an usher or something so he had the connection." Regardless of who it was, this was to be yet another turning point in Billy Joel's evolution as a musician, as well as yet another source of material for songs he'd write in the years ahead, as that night, a preppy, good-looking, red-haired Catholic cheerleader, who never before had paid him any attention, stood in the front row, eyes fixed on Billy as he played. It was Virginia Callahan, who he would later immortalize in "Only the Good Die Young."

From now on, with Billy playing the organ, The Echoes specialized in playing the British Invasion songs of the time by groups like The Rolling Stones, Dave Clark Five, and The Zombies. Billy's favorite band at the time was The Zombies, whose keyboard player Rod Argent he particularly liked. The Echoes, dressed in their blue jackets with black velvet collars, cut a quite different image then the other "surf" bands at the local dances. They played anywhere they could: school and church dances, the Teen Canteen at Hicksville High School and private parties. The band became their social life and they all hung out together after school under the leadership of Billy who was by far the most serious musician of the group and who quickly became its leader.

"One day we decided that we should be doing more vocals," Jim Bosse says, "and so we all decided to give it a try. The mike never got to me. Once Billy tried singing it was obvious that he was the one. He could mimic any record we put on to sound exactly like the singer."

They practiced in Bosse's cellar or at Billy's house because that was where the piano was, and besides Billy's mother was usually working after school which gave them the place to themselves. They eventually wore their welcome out at all the places and started looking for something more permanent. They had already gone through a bunch of drummers including Billy Zampino, and now had Dave Bagoli playing for them. His parents were unusual in the sense that they were very supportive of their sons' music, so the Bagliolis' house with the large insulated cellar became their practice center. Billy, with a little financial help from his mother, bought a fold-up Vox Continental organ with an orange top just like the Dave Clark Five's, which allowed him to bring it wherever he was playing, and The Echoes got really serious about practicing every day after school, often till late at night in the Bagolis' basement.

There was even a brief and relatively unknown trip to the recording studio for the keyboard player of The Echoes in the fall of 1964. Billy remembers:

"These two brothers had a tiny recording studio in their cellar and asked me to come play piano for them on some session they were recording. No one knew what the hell it was all about."

The session turned out to be arranged by an eccentric Long Island musician named George "Shadow" Morton. "Shadow" got his nickname from songwriters Jeff Barry and Ellie Greenwich because he was famous for never being around when he was needed. Shadow had hired Joe Monaco's studio that day and had asked a friend of his, George Stermer, to find him some cheap musicians to help with his recording. Shadow had never written or produced anything before this, but had talked his way into this recording studio promising a hit song. A little nervous now that he had the studio rented and musicians waiting to record but no song, Shadow was on his way to the studio, still unsure of how he was going to pull this off, when it came to him as he crossed the railroad tracks. Pulling his car over he jotted down some lyrics to a melody that was in his head, and continued on to the studio. Once there this genius of improvising took the two pairs of sisters, Mary and Betty Weiss and Marge and Mary Ann Ganser, aside and taught them the lyrics, while he instructed the young piano player what to play. Within two hours of walking through the door the song "Remember (Walking in the Sand)" by the now-named Shangri-Las was recorded and would go on not only to be a hit but a pop classic. Ironically, when it was released, a production credit was given to one Artie Ripp who would later emerge as one of Billy's producers, and for a while one of his biggest nemeses.

But even today no one involved is sure if the piano piece was the one recorded by the fifteen-year-old Billy Joel, who never got paid for it anyway. Billy relates:

> It was something working with Shadow. He came sailing into the studio that day with dark sunglasses and a cape on, announcing to no one in particular, "Hey man, I'm Shadow Morton. How ya doin'? What's happenin' here? OK, we're gonna lay down some heavy stuff today," and he'd put the mike near the musicians, and we'd sit around and play while he instructed us what to do. It was really primitive shit, but somehow Shadow managed to get some incredible sounds out of it all. Then he'd bring in the singers and lay down their tracks, so no one ever really knew what you were playing on or weren't. To this day when I hear that song I think to myself, "Hey is that me?"

Billy also believes that on another session with Shadow he played some piano chords that ended up on the Shangri-Las' hit "Leader of the Pack," but he's not totally sure about that and neither is Shadow.

What Billy is sure of though is that in 1967 he was hired to play the organ for a new Bachman Pretzel television ad that Chubby Checker was doing. The vocal line "There's a new twist in Bachman . . ." was part of the lyrics, and Chubby Checker was the man with the song "The Twist" that had reached number 1 on the charts on two separate occasions. Billy was paid two hundred dollars for his services and also got to meet Chubby Checker at his house, where he saw the "weird-looking" double gold record hanging on the wall.

Meanwhile gigs started to roll in for private parties, fraternity parties, school dances, bars, and an event Long Island was famous for, "The Battle of the Bands." The Echoes were usually the winners of these events, and never finished in lower than third place, including a contest at the 1965 World's Fair in Queens, NY.

Billy's playing schedule wasn't without its downside though. Playing gigs till late and then breaking down before getting home in the early morning hours for some sleep began to take its toll on Billy's school time. Cutting classes or school altogether became more and more a common event. Many times Billy dragged himself out of bed, to get himself breakfast, then pretended to go off to school, but instead hid in the brush behind his house or down the street at someone else's place until he saw his mother leave for work. Then it was back home to catch up on his sleep and after waking to do his own reading. Many times his sister Judy would return from school to find Billy upstairs in his room, covered in a blanket, with books around him. "He used to read encyclopedias you know," she says. "Then we'd play these question and answer games to test each other's knowledge, and he never lost."

Within months after beginning to play the Long Island circuit the band discovered that there was another group called "The Echoes" so they briefly changed theirs to "Billy Joe and the Hydros," a testament to just how quickly Billy's leadership had been recognized. The name never stuck though and they tried "The Emerald Lords" for a while, eventually choosing "The Lost Souls" by November 1965.

As The Lost Souls, their local success and reputation continued to grow and they were able to capitalize on an offer from Mercury Records to record an album. At the time they had two managers, one named Bob Parish and another Richard Ryan. Things never clicked with Parish so he was canned in favor of Ryan who finalized the deal with Mercury records.

"He is the one that had some kind of connection and got us signed," said Jim Bosse. "I'm not sure what happened to it. We recorded about half an album and then it stopped."

On those tapes was the first song ever written by Billy called "Journey's End" that Howie Blauvelt helped out with. "It was a great song too," according to Howie, "and Billy and I wrote another song together called "Time and Time Again." But the album was doomed. Mercury shelved the project mid-way through and forced the band to change their name to The Commandos, which in the midst of the growing anti-war sentiment in the United States was fatal for them. The album was never finished, yet today some of the recordings are with Billy's best friend Billy Zampino and Jim Bosse, now a respected classical guitarist living in Colorado.

For the next year or so the band, now again called The Lost Souls, played the Long Island club circuit and practiced religiously. They found themselves playing more and more bars despite being under age and the late hours began to take its toll on school for all of them. Missing school became the norm and soon Howie and drummer Dave Bagoli dropped out of Hicksville High School in favor of playing music. Billy wasn't having an easy time of it either in school. By now his "tough guy" persona was getting him into trouble with teachers and the administration. Not that he wasn't getting decent grades, because he was. Billy always had the ability in school to do well, not great, but well enough, because of his voracious reading habits, his ability to retain all of what he reads and his incredible memory which he still has today.

Nevertheless he became a target at Hicksville High School because of his rebel attitude and looks. In one memorable instance Ray Nelson, a then friend and classmate of Billy's, remembers when a history teacher, who was constantly up the asses of guys like Billy in the high school, was in a tirade one day in class. Billy, Kenny, and Ray were sitting in the back of the classroom, and paying attention to some girl who was there instead of the teacher, when the teacher went off on them.

"He started yelling at Billy and us," says Nelson. "He's screaming that we weren't going to amount to anything in life, and that we would come home from work after working hard at a menial job most likely as laborers, and just sit on the couch and drink beer. Well, Billy stood up, I'll never forget this and getting right in his face tells him, 'Someday I'll be able to buy and sell you a hundred times over.'"

Another memorable Billy/teacher incident occurred in Billy's senior year at Hicksville High School with Chuck Arnold the music teacher. Chuck taught Billy for three years and not surprisingly found his talent then to be great. "We were not close," Arnold relates, "but we shared a mutual respect. I liked him; he was a wonderful kid who wrote beautiful melodies."

Arnold had a classical piano too and had also "crossed the tracks" to play in some "grungy cocktail" lounges which Billy knew, so Billy was aware that he wasn't just another piano-playing snob, and they shared a mutual respect that continues today.

"Billy was bright enough to know that there was more to life then the West Village Green," Arnold continues. "I know he was influenced to a large degree by all the music that was around him in the sixties—who wasn't? The music just seemed to pour out of his veins."

Arnold and Billy were also competitors of a sort in high school as witnessed by an event that many of Billy's classmates back then remember. It seems that Billy was chronically late for classes in high school, all classes except music that is. One day in Billy's senior year, he and the rest of the class were waiting in their music theory class for Mr. Arnold to arrive. Billy was seated at one of the two pianos in the room, and the rest of the class was milling about when, according to Mary Barnett, Mr. Arnold walked in uncharacteristically late. Barnett relates:

> Mr. Arnold saw Billy sitting there at the piano, and he walked over and sat at the other one. The room got quite because it was obvious something was going to happen, and then all of a sudden Mr. Arnold played a short jazz riff on his piano and turned to Billy. Not one to turn down a challenge, especially regarding music, Billy played the same riff, but with more ease. Then Mr. Arnold played a classical piece, and sure enough Billy followed with the same. This piano dueling went on for a few minutes as we sat in the bleachers dumbfounded. They went back and forth and then finally Mr. Arnold played a jazz piece again, and Billy, putting one hand behind his back, played the same damn piece and just as well if not better. Then Billy got up from his piano and walked out of the class, never returning that day, but Mr. Arnold, now completely blown away, just let him go. It was the most amazing piano dueling I'd ever seen, and today to think about it and Billy's career gives me goosebumps.

Despite not being into it at all, Billy stayed in school but his excessive absences resulted in a call to the guidance office in April 1967, his senior year, to tell him that he wouldn't be graduating. He couldn't understand it, after all his grades were still pretty good, certainly good enough to graduate, but it seemed that some at the school had it in for him and refused him his diploma. The truth is that the state mandates just how many days a student must be in school annually and Billy didn't make it. He would have had to go to summer school to graduate, which was an unacceptable thought to him after suffering through 12 years already. Fed up, Billy just quit going to school, telling his mother, "I may not be able to go to Columbia University, but I will go to Columbia records." If only he knew at the time how prophetic these words were.

# Chapter 8

For Billy there was no turning back now. It wasn't just the money he could make from playing his music or the fringe benefits, such as the girls, or even the attention in the school hallways or around town. It was all of that, of course, but it was also creating the music as well as the lifestyle that struck a nerve at the innermost core of the young Billy Joel. He was one of the fortunate few who early on knew his destiny.

"I never even thought of how much," Billy says with regard to money. "All I ever wanted to do was to make a living as a musician." Make a living he would and then some, but first life and its lessons awaited.

Long Island back then was a hotbed of music. The Beatles' music was leading the way in changing the way we looked at ourselves and our world, and other bands like The Rolling Stones, Dave Clark Five, and The Who were doing the same if only to a slightly smaller degree. Music, especially rock music, was everywhere and influencing everything in our lives it seemed.

It was in a sense a true revolution unfolding through the music. Every teen wanted to be a part of it in some way, and as a result an explosion of garage bands sprang up on Long Island. Countless suburban kids were buying guitars, drums, and other instruments and forming groups of their own practicing in basements or garages and expressing themselves musically. For them it became a welcome alternative to the life they had come to know, as well as the dismal future that they saw ahead for them—as represented in the lives that they saw their parents living in their identical houses, with their often unfulfilling jobs. Kids sensed, and rightly so, that there was more to life than what they grew up in and read about in magazines or saw on television. Most refused, even as teenagers, to accept the expectation that their lives would be a perpetuation of their parents' sameness and superficiality. Many of them began to rebel against this dreary reality that they saw their parents imprisoned in, using the best methods they could find. As a result, on Long Island the many teenagers getting involved in music created a sound that later became known around the world as "The Long Island Sound" thanks to successful bands like Vanilla Fudge, The Lovin' Spoonful, The Vagrants, and

The Young Rascals. Not surprisingly, Billy Joel was to be in the midst of it all.

"The Rascals were *it* then," says Arma Andon, a friend of Billy's from this era and later an executive at Columbia Records. "Everyone came to see The Rascals and their jaws would drop. We also had The Vagrants who were the unwholesome version of The Rascals, and I think The Hassles tried to fit in somewhere between the two."

The Hicksville band that started as The Echoes and through a series of personnel and name changes had evolved into The Lost Souls was enjoying a level of success of its own that allowed Billy to keep his head above water, and to even help out at home a little, which made him feel good about himself. They were making upwards of one hundred dollars per show, which was not bad money in the mid-1960s for four high-school age musicians. More importantly, though, it gave him countless opportunities to fine tune their art collectively and individually as they practiced constantly and played for audiences often. Billy and the other band members of The Lost Souls began to get really good and as a result they worked, and pretty consistently. School dances, private parties, fraternity and sorority parties, and then later in 1965 or so they began to work the bar scene on Long Island even though some of them weren't yet eighteen.

They ended up at the Long Island Fair on August 30, 1965 after competing against and beating over 100 other Long Island bands in competitions that were then sponsored by the department store Macy's. After winning they went on to play against another large group of bands, this time from the entire New York metropolitan area, at The World's Fair in Queens, New York, coming in second.

A few miles away from Billy's house on Meeting Lane was a small strip mall in Plainview, New York where there was a rock and roll club called the Cat and Fiddle. It was a fairly large club for its time with a bar and a large dance floor, and was housed in an old Jack Lalane exercise gym and run by a guy named Danny Mazur.

"Danny was a Long Island club owner with a pinky ring," Billy said. "I think he had some mob connections there. I don't think you could run a club in Plainview and not have connections."

The Cat and Fiddle took on the more serious name My House under Danny's management as the Long Island rock and roll scene exploded. He was soon booking some of Long Island's biggest bands including The Four Tops, The Ronettes, The Young Rascals, The Lost Souls, and The Hassles, and his club became known as one of the places to hang out in for great music.

Billy's band started playing at My House in 1966, usually as an opening band. They quickly began to build a following of fans from around Long

Island, and Irwin Mazur, Danny's son and then a dental student in Philadelphia, who later became Billy's manager for seven years, quickly took notice of Billy's immense talent and stage presence. They played there until mid-1967 when just before graduation in June they split up when Jim Bosse decided to go to college.

"I decided to go to college," said Jim Bosse. "I remember telling Billy's mother Roz that I was going, and she said to me, 'You know, you are going to have a nice professional office someday and that's a good thing, and Billy will have that too but with music.' She was sure that he would have it, either from classical or rock and roll. It didn't matter—she was always very supportive of Billy. A lot of parents that had invested in a classical music background would have been upset by rock and roll, but despite the fact that she had very little she managed to get Billy lessons and music classes."

Also playing at Mazur's My House was a band called The Hassles, who were from Long Island too. They'd started in 1964 as The Road Runners when schoolmates Richie McKenna, the son of a New York City cop from Syosset, who was a guitar player, and Jon Small, whose family owned a wallpaper store in Jericho and who was a drummer, decided they wanted to form a rock and roll band. Soon lead singer John Dizek and an organ player named Harry Weber who were in another band that was self-destructing were onboard, and they were playing the club circuit. They drove their equipment around from club to club in a van that was painted in psychedelic colors and flowers which at the time was pretty ballsy because vehicles like that were real police magnets. They also decided that "The Road Runners" wasn't projecting the image they wanted and after some thought decided on the name "The Hassles" because of the bad luck they seemed to have everywhere they traveled with equipment and vehicles breaking down.

"We had this roadie named John," Richie McKenna says, "and it seemed like whenever we played a gig someplace either our van or a piece of equipment would break, so that's how the name The Hassles happened."

Jon Small was perhaps at the time the most accomplished musician between himself and McKenna. At eight years of age in 1955, he became a professional drummer with a band called The Starfires.

"The Starfires played mostly after school parties and sweet sixteens. By the time I was twelve, in '59, we really started to make money," Jon said. "The work was steady and we stayed busy. By '63, we were playing covers at The Runway on Hempstead Turnpike. I was making $150 to $200 a week and I was only in tenth grade. I had more money in my pocket than any of my friends. But there was a drawback. I was able to pick up plenty of girls, but when it came time to leave with them and I had no car, well . . . I couldn't go anywhere, I was too young to get a driver's license."

John Dizek reminisced:

Jon Small knew Harry Weber, Harry knew me from a group I was in called The Takers (with Larry Zampino, Bill Tracy, Allen Kahn and Bob Snoody) and I knew Richie McKenna. I met Harry in school. I was sixteen, he was twenty-one and had just come back to high school to get his diploma. He was a real character. Harry had an old car that used to break down all the time. We used to travel from parking spot to parking spot. Wherever it broke down, we'd stay in the car and harmonize. Harry taught me harmony. He had a guitar and I had a harmonica. We'd sit in that car, stoned, and sing and harmonize for days. Literally. We'd get cars to push start us—we'd tell them that we just need a push when, of course, we needed far more than that. After a while, they would give up and drive off . . . and we'd sit in the car and harmonize. Once, when we broke down on the Long Island Expressway, we heard about ourselves on the radio—"an obstruction on the L.I.E. is backing up traffic two miles"—and it was us, sitting in the car singing!

In 1966, the Finals of the Battle of the Bands Competition were held before a James Brown concert at Forest Hills Tennis Stadium. The Hassles took home the first place trophy with their cover of Freddie Scott's hit "Are You Lonely for Me, Baby?" As their popularity rose, they found steady work. They entertained political royalty at a birthday party for then Senator Robert Kennedy in the Hamptons, and they almost played for the most enthusiastic audience ever, according to John Dizek:

Sid Bernstein, the guy that brought The Beatles to America, wanted to sign us and almost had us. He and our manager, Danny Mazur cooked this scheme up: when The Beatles played Shea Stadium, we tried to crash the show. We came to the show in a big limo, our roadies got there earlier with the van. So, we're sitting in the dressing room with Bobby Hebb and "Cousin" Bruce Morrow being cool. We saw The Beatles come in . . . Now, here's the plan: we were going to run on stage and start to play and not get off the stage. Let them drag us off! The kids would have gone berserk but The Hassles would have been known internationally! What a publicity coup! Well, anyway, it never happened. We got nabbed at the last moment and never got to the stage. We ended up in the dugout and watched the show with The Lovin' Spoonful.

John Sebastian said: "I don't remember that. I remember being in the dugout but I don't remember The Hassles being there. But, you know, there was a lot going on and, of course, memories are hazy . . . then again, we weren't in real good shape, if you know what I mean." Irwin Mazur, however, for seven years Billy's manager, does remember that day:

At this point I was managing The Hassles. We were playing this club called The Phone Booth in Queens, and right near it was Shea Stadium where The Beatles were going to play the next night. Someone in the band said something like "Wouldn't it be great to get onstage and play there?' I said, I'll tell you what, come to my house tomorrow with the roadies, who at the time were Brian Ruggles and a guy named John Abrant. So they show up at my place just as planned. I grabbed this captain's hat that was lying around in some closet and give it to either Brian or John and tell them, you be the chauffer. He puts it on and we all pile into my father's big brown Cadillac, while the van with our equipment follows. We get to Shea Stadium early and the place is pretty empty although kids are lined up everywhere to get in. At this point I've got no plan at all, but a bunch of kids see the long-haired kids in the Cadillac and they start surrounding us. Next thing I know the cops are showing up and they wave us through this entrance in to the stadium! Now we're inside and I see this big blond guy Malcolm who was the original roadie for The Beatles. I go up to him and say "We're the opening act. Where is our dressing room and when is the sound check?" Well, he looks at me dumbfounded and says that no one told him about this, but he'll see what he can do. Just about then Sid Bernstein shows up and blows our cover, but he loved the fact that we'd pulled this off, so much that he told us, "If Brian Epstein says it's OK, you guys can play". Well, it turned out that because we weren't members of the union we couldn't go onstage, but Brian, who was very gracious anyway, let us sit in the dugout and watch the concert and then we all got to meet The Beatles anyway.

The Hassles were soon working regularly and became the house band at Mazur's My House, attracting more and more fans as their talent evolved. "Those were great days for music on Long Island," Mazur reminisces today. "We had The Rascals, The Vagrants and a band that started as The Pigeons but became Vanilla Fudge. They were a phenomenal band with a big following, but The Hassles had a large following too. On some nights we'd have over one thousand people packed into "My House" which for the time was big time." Big time indeed. Mazur wisely knew that he had something with The Hassles, and many say today that he kept The Hassles at My House too much. They were the house band after all, and a big gate and bar draw for Mazur. Speculation is that if as their manager he'd booked them into more clubs in New York City, for instance, many today feel that there is a good chance that they would have been discovered and gone even further then they ended up doing. But by keeping them securely booked into his club, he was guaranteed a large gate and bar business. John Dizek today agrees: "Our management was bad. They used us to support themselves. They kept The Hassles at My House during the most crucial time. We should have been touring to support our album which was starting to happen. We never really had the chance to make it." Soon after the first album was released Johnny Dizek could take no more long nights. At year's end, he quit the band and rock music forever. With Dizek's departure, a powerful visual aspect of the group was lost and the role of lead singer would soon settle on Billy Joel. Although a novice when it came to managing bands (The Hassles were his first), Irwin Mazur nevertheless was a quick learner, and watched the music scene beyond his father's club in Plainview for trends in not only music, but the make-up of bands themselves. This was the era when bands like The Buffalo Springfield, The Byrds, The Yardbirds, Cream, Spencer Davis Group, and others were breaking up and then re-forming into newer "supergroups" as the top talent of each band left to join up with others. Mazur saw this and looking right in his own backyard realized that if he took the best from The Hassles and combined it with the best from The Lost Souls, he might have a group that would easily attract a major record contract.

He was acutely aware of the huge talent that the organ player Billy Joel of The Lost Souls had, and that also turned out to be the only weak spot that The Hassles had in their organ player, Harry Weber. Weber was a good musician, but he suffered from debilitating depressions that at the time were for all intents and purposes untreatable. In the mid-1960s there was no such thing as Prozac or Wellbutrin, so Harry self-medicated constantly in a futile attempt to alleviate his pain. As a result he developed a serious drug problem and couldn't be relied on to always show up. His behavior on and off the stage was erratic at best and usually worse. Harry was a deeply troubled and free spirited soul, some would say a Brian Jones type character, but without the considerable talent that Jones had. Nevertheless, he did have talent, and he could play the Hammond organ fairly well. Sadly, though, he shared the self-destructive aspect of Brian Jones' personality and like Brian pushed it constantly to the edge. Harry loved to party, and to party harder then anyone else. Whereas smoking marijuana seemed de rigueur, Harry's choice was sniffing glue. Onstage, Harry's peculiarities set him apart. He sat low behind the organ with his hands creeping up over the keyboard. The instrument hid him. On occasion, he'd let out an odd scream. Kenny Holly, lead guitarist of The Gents, another Long Island band, once described Weber's wail as "the greatest scream, really blood curdling . . . really weird." To complicate matters, drugs were everywhere now on Long Island and particularly in the music scene, and many musicians as well as non-musicians were tempted by them. Somehow Jon Small never succumbed to them, though Jon, who was now seeing Harry's sister, Elizabeth, saw the results firsthand and up-close: "When the band started, it was the four of us together, although Harry and I fought over a lot of things. I became the leader of the band because I had some idea of what to do. Also, they were heavily into partying and I was not into drugs at all. I wanted more than they did." As The Hassles improved, Harry had gotten worse, marked by extreme periods of violence. The Hassles were just beginning to get steady work when, on a tour of Florida, Harry went over the edge. Johnny Dizek remembers that night well:

Harry got kicked out of the group on that tour. He was sniffing a lot. One time, on stage, I was singing my part and waiting for Harry to come in. I looked back to see where his harmony was . . . Harry was playing the organ with one hand and had his head in a bag sniffing! Harry was crazy, the more glue he did the uglier the scenes got. It finally got to the point where he could sniff glue and play at the same time! That set was a joke. After the show, in the dressing room, for absolutely no reason whatsoever, he jumped Jon Small. We had to fire him.

Jon Small, now his brother-in-law evidently agreed: "Harry was crazy . . . he was always crazy. There were times when he was bearable, but those times were short lived as he became more into the glue and the scenes got uglier and uglier." Upon returning to Long Island, Mazur set out to replace him with Billy. Since Billy was playing his club on alternate weekends he knew of him, and of his talent. Besides, firing Harry now gave Mazur the opportunity to merge The Lost Souls and The Hassles resulting in what he thought would be a Long Island supergroup that he could then turn into a lucrative record contract. With that in mind he set out with the group's leader Jon Small and Jon's wife and Harry's sister Elizabeth to audition new organists.

"I remember that Billy came in to the club to audition with The Hassles," Mazur said. "He had a little Farfisa organ that he played with The Lost Souls and even with just that he sounded great. I told him how much The Hassles were working and that he would have Harry's Hammond B-3 to play and he said, 'I'm in.'"

Mazur thought that if he could get Billy to leave The Lost Souls and join The Hassles he would have a great sound. Luck was with Irwin as just about that time, in June 1967, The Lost Souls were breaking up. Mazur realized that Billy Joel was not only a great musician, but also took his music career very seriously, and besides since he hadn't graduated with his class, he wasn't going anywhere. Billy didn't want to do anything but play music, so when Mazur asked him if he wanted to join The Hassles Billy agreed with one condition, that Howie Blauvelt come with him. Howie was known as a great bass player, and as the guy who had invited Billy into The Echoes four years earlier he was also a friend of Billy's. Because The Hassles had a B-3 Hammond organ, they really didn't need a bass player, but they wanted Billy, so the deal was made.

Harry Weber had been thrown out of the band before, but always let back in. This time he was devastated, and with his primary identity in life now gone, he began to sink into his world of drugs and self-destruction at an even faster pace. He played in and tried to put other bands together but ultimately he started using heroin, and as it became his primary focus, drifted further and further away from the music world.

Billy and Howie joined Small, McKenna, and Dizek in The Hassles and the future looked bright for the eighteen-year-old Billy Joel. That first summer together The Hassles started playing in a small oceanfront bar called The Eye in Westhampton, New York, which was owned by Joe Steinfeld. The Hamptons then bore no resemblance to what they are today. In 1967 it was a well-balanced mix of local farmers, fisherman, and merchants who were joined in the summer by "summer people," most of whose families had owned second homes there for generations. Everyone got along well, but it was also 1967 and the "Summer of Love," so sex, drugs, and rock and roll were everywhere.

"The Eye was not for the faint of heart," Arma Andon, a bartender there then, says today. "Not only was there plenty of booze and other recreational substances, but there seemed always to be fights out in the parking lot too. It was the Wild West psychedelic style."

Indeed it was: acid, pills, booze, and girls were everywhere, and The Hassles with their large following from up the island only added to that when they played there and their fans would make the drive out east to party and listen to the music, then sleep it off in their cars in the parking lot of the nearby beach.

Billy, because of his seriousness about his music, somehow never really seemed to fall into the craziness quite the same way the others did, although that doesn't mean he acted like a choirboy either. "He was always a bit aloof from the rest of the band," Arma Andon continues. "I always got the impression that he was serious about what he was doing. We'd talk in between sets and became friendly." Even then Andon and others could see Billy Joel's emerging talent and the way he stood out from the rest of the band.

Finally it all came to a head, and in 1975 Harry was dead. Some said it was suicide brought on by his drug addiction and dead-end lifestyle. That he walked in front of a train one night in Syosset, New York after a night of partying very hard and was killed instantly. Others say that the real cause of death was a lot more sinister and dark, that in fact it wasn't suicide at all, but that he had been killed by drug dealers that he crossed and that he owed money to and that he was badly beaten up and placed on the train tracks that night. Richie McKenna, who was close with Harry, subscribes to that theory.

"Harry was basically assassinated," he says. "He was living in Syosset, when one guy overdosed in the basement of the house and basically Harry covered it up and hid the body, for a day or two. The family of the guy caught up with Harry in a bar in Syosset a year or two later and beat him up and put him on the railroad tracks."

Either way, there is no denying that Harry's premature death was a result of his own actions, and directly or indirectly Harry lived life on the edge, and eventually it all caught up with him. Meanwhile, though, The Hassles continued to fine-tune their music as their audiences grew.

# Chapter 9

Through their almost three years together The Hassles played bars and clubs on Long Island and in New York City, building a large and dedicated group of fans, many of whom would follow them from venue to venue. During their time together in the band Billy and Jon Small developed a deep friendship based primarily on their mutual love of music that today remains intact. They were the two serious musicians of the group, and the ones that had their eyes focussed on the future. But unfortunately it wasn't enough to hold the band together as during the recording of their second album titled *The Hour of the Wolf* the band found itself passing into rock and roll history.

There had been a lot of stress building among the band's members for some time, but the growing success of the band had been enough to hold it together until finally the various problems and conflicts, jealousies and resentments became too much. Chief among the internal conflicts was the direction the music of The Hassles was taking. Billy and Jon felt that their inability to reach success beyond the shores of Long Island and New York City was due to their music which now was more slanted towards AM radio top forty. They wanted the music to go in a different direction; one that they felt was more serious and indicative of their talents as true musicians. FM radio was emerging now as a force to be reckoned with and the music that prevailed there was slanted more towards the psychedelic sound coming primarily from the West Coast. This was the music that they wanted to focus on and which the two of them were now writing more and more much to the dismay of the other band members. Finally when sales of their second album stalled Billy and Jon pulled the plug to set out on their own.

"After three confusing years of screaming teenyboppers and bad music, I quit to look for something heavy," Billy said.

Jon Small recalls the end of The Hassles in less then positive terms:

Billy and I hated the band. We didn't like them or their playing so we terminated The Hassles. We wanted to continue to play together so we formed a two-man army called Attila the Hun. We spent most of our time practicing in the basement of my parents' wallpaper store in

Jericho. We played a bunch of clubs on Long Island—our best night was at The Daisy on Merrick Road and Route 110.

Attila the Hun was one of the first truly heavy metal bands, inspired in some ways by Billy's love of Led Zeppelin.

Billy agrees:

Jon Small and I decided we were going to make a heavy metal album and I wired up a Hammond B-3 organ through ten custom amplifiers, these big, loud guitar amps, and it was totally distorted. I played a keyboard base which was well made. And Jon played the drums and we played a lot of minor thirds, the essence of heavy metal in those days, and we were the loudest band. It was just two guys and we made so much noise and we knew we were loud because good friends would come to see us in these small clubs and they would run away. By the end of the night there would be nobody left in the club except really angry bartenders and we made one album, *Attila*, made for Epic Records. There was a picture of us in a meat locker with carcasses of beef, dressed like barbarians with chains. I didn't want to do this but the art director of Epic talked me into it and that was the last time that happened.

Attila the Hun was also inspired by the success at the time of an album by Lee Michaels. Michaels was a Hammond B-3 organ-playing rock musician from San Francisco who rose to one-shot stardom after recording his third album with just himself and a drummer nicknamed "Frosty." Frosty, who weighed three hundred pounds plus, and looked more like one of Attila's Huns than Billy or Jon ever would, was known for his John Bonham-type drum solos played with his bare hands, while Michaels, originally a southern California hippie who would have looked at home either on a surfboard or stage, usually played shows barefoot and shirtless to the delight of his female fans. Michaels had recorded two albums prior to 1969 that went nowhere, but then hooked up with "Frosty" and they recorded their first album together in just six hours in a San Francisco studio. Then from 1969 to 1970, thanks to the song "Do You Know What I Mean?," they enjoyed the successes and excesses of one hit wonders. Billy and Jon knew about their bluesy, rock and roll type music and came up with the brilliant idea of taking their sound one step further to emulate and even surpass the heavy metal sound of Led Zeppelin who at the time were exploding onto the rock and roll scene.

Irwin Mazur stayed on as their manager after The Hassles broke up because he believed in Billy's talent, but he was less than enthusiastic about this new idea. Nevertheless he supported Jon and Billy in their new experiment. "I thought it was a ridiculous concept from the beginning," Mazur says today, "but I supported them anyway. I had to go into debt to get them a set of huge Marshall amplifiers and then I called on Larry Cohen who at the time was head of Epic Records. He agreed to listen to the tape and signed them to a one record deal."

*Attila* was released in July 1970. The album was a musical disaster. Produced by Billy, Jon, and Irwin Mazur, and containing such forgettable original songs as "Brain Invasion," "Godzilla," and "March of the Huns," all written by Billy and Jon. Years later Billy would describe the album as "psychedelic bullshit" and although he remains a fan of bands like Led Zeppelin, Billy is not a fan of the *Attila* album that was influenced by them.

Fortunately during this musical quagmire, life was going on for the young Billy Joel. He was now living in the Fairhaven apartment complex, about two miles north of Meeting Lane, in an apartment across the hall from Jon and his wife Elizabeth, who now had a young son Sean.

Billy says:

I just had to get out of my mother's house and Elizabeth helped me get an apartment. Those were the days when I didn't have any money. I mean I had zip. So I would hang out in front of their place looking very hungry. She was always a good cook and those great smells would be coming from their door. I had a lot of dinners at their place. We were great friends before we were anything more.

Great friends indeed. Those who knew Billy and Jon back then confirm the deep friendship that they shared as well as Jon's incredible loyalty to Billy. They seemed to many like inseparable brothers, brought together by their mutual love of and seriousness about music.

As usual Billy during these days remained more focussed on his music than anything else that was going on around him. The world seemed to be on a destructive course as the United States invaded Cambodia and escalated the Vietnam War, four students were killed at Kent State, and The Beatles broke up, but somehow only The Beatles' breakup mattered to Billy though. "I idolized The Beatles, especially Paul—nobody could come up with the melodies he could."

Elizabeth in addition to being a wife and mother at this time was going to college part time and also when her schedule permitted was immersed in doing anything that she could to help make The Hassles a success. The demands on her time were great and she hired a nearby neighbor as her mother's helper to watch Sean when she was away or studying.

Bobby Jo Grazier was then a fourteen-year-old girl who lived three doors down in the garden apartment complex. She became Sean's babysitter in 1969, and got to see the dynamic first hand between Jon, Elizabeth, and Billy very well. "I met them all just after The Hassles broke up," she says. "I'd go shopping with Liz, watch Sean and I spent a lot of time around them all. I also had a huge crush then on Billy."

At the time the six years' difference in their ages was too much, even if Billy had wanted something to happen, which of course he didn't. At the time Billy was seeing a beautiful red-headed shampoo model named Patti Lee from nearby Bethpage, New York, who he had met one night at My House when from the stage he saw her standing on the dance floor with her back to him and mistakenly took her head of red hair for that of old girlfriend Vicki Chicollo. Billy and Patti had been hanging out for about a year now and Billy had already proposed to her at least once, being turned down because she knew they were too young and she wanted to go through chiropractic school anyway. So any childhood crush that Bobby Jo had at the time would remain just that. Nevertheless, Billy Joel left an indelible impression on her.

"He seemed so skinny then and he never had a dime, so I used to raid my parents' piggy bank and leave money anonymously for Billy in his apartment," she says today. "I also took a roast beef from our freezer and one day went in and cleaned his apartment and cooked the roast for him. I remember thinking as I cleaned the place that everything in it was centered around his music."

She remembers Elizabeth even then as, "not very warm . . . If she liked you, you were OK, if she didn't like you, you certainly got the impression that she did not like you. She was manipulative . . . without a doubt . . . it was all about prestige with Liz."

Many from these days and the days ahead would echo similar sentiments about Elizabeth's personality although usually all agree too that she played an integral role in helping Billy Joel become who he is today.

Elizabeth Weber has by all indications always had her eye on the gold ring. A kid from Syosset, NY, a middle- to upper-middle-class town just north of Hicksville, somewhere between blue-collar Hicksville and the then Waspy and old money Cold Spring Harbor. Elizabeth has always been a very smart, savvy, focussed, and tenacious woman. Unlike most teenagers then whose focus if there was one at all was a lot shallower, Elizabeth knew what she wanted (money and power) from life, and was going to do anything she had to in order to get it. She was going to high school in Syosset, and hanging with musicians when she met Jon Small at one of the local clubs, through her brother Harry Webber, the troubled organ player in The Hassles.

Jon was no slouch either. In a time when being a long-haired, good-looking musician translated into being a magnet for endless streams of groupies, Jon knew how to work it. He was a great-looking guy, with a reputation then as a class "A" ladies' man who took full advantage of his looks, his position as a musician in a rock and roll band, and the lax sexual attitudes that prevailed at the time. Elizabeth fell hard for Jon. After all he was a "prize" who everyone thought would never settle down, yet Elizabeth set out to get him and in typical Elizabeth style did just that. By the time she was eighteen she was pregnant which sealed the deal for her. She felt that Jon was going places with his good looks and music, and that with her help she thought that he'd eventually make the kind of money that she wanted, which in reality turned out to be true, but not before she'd changed her priorities.

Elizabeth at the time like many Long Island teenagers fell head first into the rock and roll world. She loved the music and the excitement that it generated, but also was keenly aware that there was money, and lots of it, to be made in the business. What better way to end up rich and live an exciting life than to hook up with a rock and roll musician. So she set out to learn all she could about the business. Those who knew Elizabeth then all agree that she maintained an incredible determination and focus to "better herself." There was no way that she was going to end up as a housewife in a suburban tract home.

Living in the Fairhaven apartments, Jon, Elizabeth, and Billy often got complaints about loud music and people coming and going from other, often older, tenants. Most important for Jon and Billy, there was no place to practice their music. The three of them thought that if they could get a big enough place together, that they could move all their instruments and equipment from Jon's parents' store and have a place to practice, and also to write their music. They started looking for a secluded house and found an old stone house set off the road in a wooded setting about twenty miles east of Hicksville in Dix Hills, New York. They scraped together the rent and deposit money, and with the help of friends moved their belongings and instruments to their new home. By this time the relationship between Billy and Elizabeth was also evolving from one of friends to something more intense. Bobby Jo remembers first seeing the "flirting" between Elizabeth and Billy, usually initiated by Elizabeth and at times in front of Jon. "I never saw anything real obvious, but I was only fourteen years old too and had my own crush on the guy. Liz was a lot smarter than to be obvious about it," she says today.

During the summer of 1970 and into the fall Billy and Jon waited for the *Attila* album to take off, but according to Irwin Mazur, "The *Attila* album was released, and nothing happened." "*Attila* received rave reviews from two people," Billy reflected later on after his next album was released. "Both of them our road managers."

Despite this Billy and Jon pressed on that summer playing clubs in the

New York area and even opening for Grand Funk Railroad, then a rock and roll supergroup. Even with all their hard work and dedication Epic dropped Attila the Hun in late 1970, so once again Billy Joel and Jon had to formulate a new plan.

Billy contacted his old partner Howie Blauvelt and offered him a role in a new group he was assembling. This collection of local rock and rollers going under the name of El Primo was Billy's attempt to form a Long Island supergroup, which was put together from the ranks of four bands: The Hassles (Billy and Howie), The Phaetons (Gerard Kenny), The Rich Kids (Denny Belline), and Man (Jeff Schwartz).

With this wealth of talent, El Primo composed and performed many original songs in addition to doing covers of other bands' music. None of their music ever found its way onto an album or even some obscure and lost tape. Regardless, El Primo played some great music during their short tenure.

Bruce Gentile, a drummer and acquaintance of Billy's, remembers seeing Howie and Billy playing together again with El Primo at a Long Island club: "They had two keyboard players, Gerard Kenny and Billy, with Howie on bass. It was the first time I'd seen Billy sing lead with only a mike stand in front of him. Howie evidently had talked him into being the front man."

Howie Blauvelt, who later at the early age of forty-four suffered a fatal heart attack brought about by the excesses of the day, reflected on El Primo:

We were booked to play Chesney Wolds, a club in Island Park right across the street from The Action House, a hotbed of music in those days. I showed up to the gig late and they threw me out of the band. Of course, I was pissed but my dismissal only lasted one week. One week later, they played the club again with a new bass player. After the first set, the owner told them, "Get Howie or get out!" and I was back in El Primo.

In the end it didn't matter: El Primo broke up before the end of 1970 anyway. Howie went on to play in a number of bands including one called Ram Jam who recored the hit song "Black Betty" in 1977. It is an aggressive version of the Huddie Ledbutter's song, and became a bar band staple and a heavy-metal response to what was then the dark musical days of disco fever. It also enraged such groups as the Congress for Racial Equality and the NAACP, both of whom accused it of being "insulting to black women." Howie toured with Ram Jam, trying to push the band to the next level, when personnel changes and the lack of a follow-up hit forced them into the annals of "one-hit wonders."

However, Howie Blauvelt's bass playing affected an entirely new generation of hard and heavy rockers. After Ram Jam, Blauvelt worked in several bands and then finally during the early 1990s, found himself a member of a Long Island blues band named Spitball that was just starting to come to fame when he suffered his heart attack and died.

Meanwhile, big changes were on the horizon for Billy Joel.

# Chapter 10

Billy had known Elizabeth and Jon Small for three years and through many incarnations, and now things between the three were really coming to a head. Billy was desperately in love with her, yet deeply remorseful over what he was doing to Jon, his best friend and Elizabeth's husband. Always a deeply sensitive person and a loyal friend, Billy never wanted their relationship to cause Jon any pain, but he'd allowed himself to get caught up in a situation which he hadn't intended. Elizabeth was an attractive and very ballsy woman even then, who knew what she wanted from life and was determined to get it. At first she'd thought Jon was the seemingly perfect package of looks and talent, but the more she got to know Billy during his three-year tenure in The Hassles, the more she recognized his incredible talent as well as his tenderness and sensitivity, a perfect combination she surely thought.

Billy was in an especially vulnerable place in his life. After being in bands for seven years, cutting three albums and some fragments of others, he was now without a band and any income. He was living away from home for the first time and found himself with no real place to live and no means of income. Without a trade and a high school diploma the future looked more than bleak to Billy, who now was more preoccupied with just trying to survive than he had been just months ago with writing and playing his music. Billy was truly at a loose end now, just trying to keep his head above water by taking odd jobs and sleeping wherever he could, which included all-night laundromats when necessary because they were warm. Since his father's leaving, things had never looked worse in Billy's world.

Elizabeth and Jon were having their problems too. The relationship with Billy was common knowledge now and Jon, a dedicated friend of Billy's, was torn. He loved Elizabeth, who was now working in a doctor's office to help pay the bills, and he wanted to keep his young family together, but he also felt a deep kinship and respect for Billy which tore at him even though Billy had been sleeping with his wife.

Bobby Colasanti, who was a friend and confidant of Billy's back then, remembers the events that summer of 1970 that led to Billy's suicide attempt:

I ran into him that night, at The Fantastic a bar in Hicksville. I was going into the bar and Billy was sitting out front and he said. "Hey I need to speak to an old friend, have you got a few minutes, can I talk to you?" "Sure," I said to him, "let's go walk" . . . so off we go and he starts pouring his heart out to me.

We kept walking and he's telling me all about his relationship with Elizabeth, and how much he loves her, but that he loves Jon too and doesn't want to jeopardize that friendship. He was really undone by Elizabeth, he was really crazy over her, but she was married. They couldn't do it because of John and because of her marriage, he was his friend, so everything was terrible, going wrong. He was feeling really bad, you know, he was living there, if he did not live there he would have been homeless basically . . . Things were not going well for him musically at the time, he had a young man's falling out with his mother, so that was not even available to him to go back to her at the time . . . everything was bothering him.

I dragged him into the bar and we drank what we could with our little amount, and I said have another one, Billy, you'll get over it, you will be fine have another drink . . . he says no, no, I'm leaving and he did, he walked out of the bar . . . I walked home later that night, and heard he had checked himself into the hospital.

Irwin Mazur, now an executive with Oppenheimer and Company in Los Angeles, was still managing Billy, and also got dragged into the drama that night:

I'm managing Billy and also working for Morris "Moshe" Levy. He was famous in the music business then as a manager, promoter, you name it. He also had a reputation, that if you were smart, you knew not to fuck with Morris Levy because he was a very well-connected guy. In fact one guy that tried to screw him ended up being found dead near an upstate New York farm that Moshe owned.

Anyway, I'm still managing Billy, and I'm totally convinced that he can make it, that he has an incredible talent, and all that stuff, but that he needs to make some changes.

So I get a call from Billy late that night, "I gotta see you," he says . . . It's about 10 or 11 at night, and I tell him, "OK, meet me at the Syosset diner."

I tell my wife I'm going, and get out of bed to go meet Billy, and he looks like shit, he divulges his situation to me, about him and Elizabeth, behind Jon's back. He is being tortured, he was sleeping at the laundromat, and his life is shattered, maybe not as extensive as he has made out, but things are definitely shitty. So I say to him come over and sleep at our place, which he does. We set him up in the living room, on the couch and I go back to bed. Next morning is a Sunday and I get up to go see how he's doing in the living room, and he's not there. He's gone. But on the dining room table, I see the lyrics to a song scribbled on a piece of paper, called "Tomorrow is Today" . . . it was on the *Cold Spring Harbor* album. The words are "what's the use of living, if tomorrow is today" a real funeral song. Later that morning I get a call that Billy is in a coma, he tried to commit suicide.

Billy himself recalls: "I was 21 and I had no prospects. No high-school diploma, my band had broken up, the girl I was with had split up with me. It was a period of intense self-pity . . . Fortunately things did not go as planned." Billy was caught up in this triangle that he felt at the time would never work out.

Billy's sister Judy remembers that day clearly too. She and her then husband Frank, her junior high school sweetheart, were living in Hempstead, NY, just west of Hicksville. Just days before, Billy had asked Judy for the name of her doctor. Judy says:

He told me that he couldn't sleep, and that he was going crazy. I gave it to him and he goes for an appointment and comes out with a prescription for fifty Nembutals! Fifty! He should have given him maybe five. Anyway that night he ended up taking a handful of them at my mother's house, and then because he didn't want me to get in trouble, he goes and buries them in the backyard, before he called his friend Jon Small to apologize, and collapsed.

Jon Small immediately drove over to Billy's mother's place on Meeting Lane in a blind panic and found Billy passed out. Judy continues:

He woke up Roz, and one of them called an ambulance to take Billy to Good Samaritan Hospital. Anyway Roz called me to give me the news, and I'm thinking to myself, "God, I killed my brother!" . . . there were no words. They get Billy to the hospital, admit him, and pump his stomach, and we're all standing there around him in his room freaking out as he's in this coma for a couple of days. I felt so helpless, but then one day some nurse asked me to keep his lips wet with this lemon stick, so I did, when all of a sudden he inhales the thing, getting it stuck in his throat and gasping for air. I went running out of the room screaming and got the nurse, who came in and flipped him over in his bed and started pounding on his back until he spit the lemon stick up.

Now he's coming to and he looks around and sees all these crosses everywhere, and he starts to cry, because at first I think he might have thought he was dead. Then when he realized he was in a hospital, he starts repeating over and over again, "I shouldn't be alive, I shouldn't be alive" . . . he was not happy that he was alive I think.

Billy stayed in the hospital a day or so more with Jon Small coming to visit, but not Elizabeth. Then, after checking out, he went home to Roz's house where he stayed in a deep depression, with his best and most loyal friend Billy Zampino looking out for him.

In a bizarre twist of fate, Jon Small, knowing now of Billy's suicide attempt and more concerned that he was going to lose his best friend at the time than his wife Elizabeth, also attempted suicide, and fortunately survived. According to Dennis Arfa, Billy's long-time booking agent and close friend: "This woman was like Helen of Troy, as she had these two men dying over her."

Billy stayed at the Meeting Lane house for about a week before his demons won out once again. "I guess it got to be too much again," Judy continues. "Because he tried to kill himself again, this time by drinking some lemon oil furniture polish that was under the kitchen sink."

This time it was Judy's husband Frank Molanari who took him to Meadowbrook Hospital, which unlike Good Samaritan has a psychiatric ward. This is the part of the story that Billy often makes light of when quizzed on his suicide attempt, never mentioning the first and more serious attempt with pills. Admittedly he checked himself in for the standard three weeks of observation, soon realizing that the majority of his roommates suffered from problems much more serious than his, problems that many of them would never emerge from.

Judy recalls:

I'd go to visit him, and my grandmother would give me five or ten dollars to give to him. We'd sit and talk and I gotta tell you there were some really crazy people in there. One guy I remember thought he was the King of England, but all in all, the place was full of crazy people, a lot like the book *One Flew Over the Cuckoo's Nest*. Billy would ask me to help get him out, but because he'd signed himself in, there was nothing anyone could do.

That was until Irwin Mazur and Billy put together a plan to spring him. Mazur went to visit Billy one day and found him pretty out of it from the drugs the doctors had given him. Nevertheless he was coherent enough to realize he was in a shitty situation and asked Irwin to help him get out of there. Together they hatched a pretty ingenious plan to get Billy released before his twenty-one days were up. Mazur relates:

Up until about eighteen months or so before I was a dental student, and had learned my way around the bureaucracies of the medical world and hospitals which were much more simple then than they are today. I went home that day and a few days later showed up at Meadowbrook in a suit complete with attaché case and a white lab smock on. I never said I was a doctor, but I never said I wasn't either. But I got Billy's records, and signed his release, and that's how he escaped from that place.

Billy was now out of the "snake pit" after about two weeks and determined never to look back. He had seen where his self-pity could get him, and he also had seen what it was like to be truly crazy and to have problems that you might not ever be able to emerge from. The unfortunate experience had put his life into a clear perspective and he vowed to himself after getting out that he would never allow himself to be that self-indulgent again. This was a promise that he has kept to himself and to those that he cares about to this day, even though over 30 years later he would commit himself twice again to facilities to treat his recurring depression and excessive drinking. "I got out and the door closed behind me and I walked down the street and said, 'Oh, I'll never get that low again.' It was one of the best things I ever did, because I've never gotten to feel sorry for myself, no matter what's happened," Joel said. Later on he briefly talked about his experience and wrote the song "Only Human," which would focus on the problem of teen suicide.

Now out of the hospital and determined to turn his life around, Billy went again to see Mazur to tell him that he was quitting the music business. "Irwin, you don't understand. Elizabeth and Jon have broken up because of me, and now she's pretty much left me too. I'm done. I'm going out to the Midwest and be a bartender. At least there no one will know me and I can get a clean start." Mazur begged him to change his mind: "Billy, you can't quit, you've written some great music lately, and to quit now would be stupid. I'll tell you what," he continued. "Give me thirty days to get you a record deal, and if I don't do it in that time, you can split." Billy agreed.

It seemed certain that Billy had truly hit the first of what were to be a series of "bottoms" in his life, but due to his amazing tenacity and resiliency changes were on the horizon.

# Chapter 11

Billy Joel has always been surprisingly modest about his talents:

> I knew all along I wanted to be a musician, but basically my goal when
> I set out was just to be a really good musician and to make a living, not
> to be rock star, and then when I was in my late teens, I was in rock
> bands and I thought the whole thing is over for me, I just want to
> write—I'm not a matinee idol, and I don't think I have a great voice.

Just a couple of months prior to the meltdown in Billy's life, Irwin Mazur,
who right from the beginning recognized Billy Joel's great talent, made Billy
promise that he was going to start writing songs of his own, and that, at the
very least, Billy was to write one song each week that he was satisfied with.
Irwin then watched the record business closely and knew by the trends that
were now emerging that the sensitive James Taylor type of songwriter which
was so popular in the late sixties and early seventies would be a perfect "fit"
for his artist Billy Joel. All he had to do was get him a record deal.

Billy comments: "I don't sing like Rod Stewart, like Joe Cocker, Ray
Charles, Nat King Cole, Frank Sinatra, I don't have a sense of vocal style . . .
so I said I'll write songs for other people, so I wrote these songs during the
early seventies when there were singer-songwriters like Carole King, Cat
Stevens, and Elton John, and all of a sudden things were changing."

At the time Mazur's brother Ruby, today a well-known artist, who
designed the Rolling Stones' famous tongue logo, worked at Gulf and
Western's Paramount Records as an art director. Irwin asked Ruby to help
get a connection inside. Ruby made the connection for his brother with the
head of their Artist and Repertoire department and also got a demo budget
for a new Billy Joel album. "Now we had some money to get Billy into a
studio and record a demo tape," Mazur said. As a result a five-song demo tape
with such songs as the now infamous "Tomorrow is Today," She's Got a
Way," and "Everybody Loves You Now" was made.

The demo tape was recorded at Ultrasonic Studio in Hempstead, New
York, just down the road from Hicksville. When it was finished Paramount,

who had what essentially amounted to a "first-look" option, listened to the tape and passed on Billy. At the time, they had a young British singer/ songwriter/piano player named Elton John who with his writing partner Bernie Taupin had just written a bunch of songs for one of those sappy teen-era movies that Paramount was soon to release titled *Friends*. The hard-working Elton John already had released four albums since 1969 and was just beginning to emerge as the great artist that he is in the United States. Knowing this, Paramount who at the time was never known as a far-sighted or innovative force in the music industry, in fact quite the contrary, decided to put all their eggs in Elton's basket and pass on Billy. They got half of it right.

Now Mazur, not one to admit defeat, and still believing deeply in young Billy Joel, set out to shop the tape around New York City to other record companies. At the time the music industry in New York was centered around the area between 42nd and 57th Street and Sixth Avenue, and Irwin knocked on every record company door, being rejected at each one as he heard such responses as "No thanks, he sounds like Paul McCartney" or "He sounds like Elton John." Frustrated, Irwin found himself walking around the streets of New York thinking, "Man, you fucking guys don't get it! You just don't get it!"

Time was running out for Mazur on his 30-day deal with Billy, and he had exhausted all his options in New York City except one in trying to find a record label for Billy.

He was still working for Morris Levy at the time marketing records, which amounted to essentially doing what had to be done to get DJs to play the records of performers that Morris had in his stable.

He decided to stop by and to play the tape for Morris and see what he would have to say about it. There was no way he was going to let Morris sign Billy, but he knew that Levy had great instincts when it came to music, even if his tactics were usually less then honest.

At the time, Morris Levy was a notorious music business mogul who was involved in many facets of the industry. So much so that early in his career *Variety* magazine dubbed Levy the "Octopus" of the music industry because he had an outstretched hand in nearly every area of the growing business. Later in his career he would be nicknamed "The Godfather," which reflected both his power in the industry and his reputed mob ties.

Levy had little formal education. He quit school at the age of 13, after assaulting his 75-year-old homeroom teacher, and grew up on the streets of New York. This was the education that would later make Morris famous for being a kind of tough, cutthroat character in the music industry. For a while in his teens he ran away to Florida where he eventually landed a job as a darkroom boy developing pictures of the customers who frequented the underground clubs he worked in. After being discharged from the Navy, he got involved in the nightclub business again, persuading his old mob bosses to purchase a place in the Latin Quarter of New York called Topsy's Chicken Roost and allowing him to run it. Soon Levy had clawed his way to the forefront of the bop movement, booking jazz musicians such as Dexter Gordon and Charlie Parker into the Cock Lounge, an adjoining nightclub he also now owned. Then when an opportunity arose for Levy to go out on his own, he did so by opening Birdland, one of the most legendary clubs of the jazz era.

By 1957 he was the founder of Roulette Records a company that signed many of the early fifties and sixties acts including The Heartbeats, The Edsels, The Five Satins and later the one-of-a-kind Tiny Tim. He now enjoyed the reputation as a disreputable character who was famous for swindling his artists out of their owed royalties. In short, for the time Levy represented everything adventurous and underhanded about the infancy of rock and roll.

It was through Birdland that Levy began his phenomenal rise to the top of the music industry. The start came innocently enough, as Levy was approached by a representative for ASCAP and told he must pay the publishing company a monthly stipend for the privilege of booking live music. Thinking that a rival mob was moving in on his operation, Levy consulted his lawyer who confirmed that the ASCAP representative was legitimate in collecting money on behalf of songwriters and their publishers under an act of Congress. Realizing an unbelievable business opportunity, Levy formed a publishing company, Patricia Music, and acquired the rights to songs first performed in his clubs, like the jazz standard "Lullaby of Birdland."

Now with both Birdland and his publishing company doing well, Levy formed Roulette Records, originally intended to be only a rock and roll label, but Roulette also recorded Birdland acts such as Count Basie and Joe Williams. Through Levy's contacts Roulette absorbed other independents, such as the Gone and End labels. Then at one point after befriending disc jockey Alan Freed, Levy actually owned the phrase "rock & roll" for a while, collecting money from the use of the term that Freed had coined. It was around this time that Levy also began the sleazy practice of forcing his name onto the songwriting credits of his acts' releases, which allowed him to collect even more money when they were published.

By the sixties and seventies, Levy's vast publishing empire was such that it even affected The Beatles. When their *Abbey Road* album contained a composition, "Come Together," that sounded remarkably similar to a Chuck Berry song ("You Can't Catch Me") whose rights Levy owned, the publishing mogul sued Lennon for infringement. In exchange for dropping the charges, Lennon agreed to include three of Levy's copyrights on his *Rock 'n' Roll* album. When Lennon stalled, Levy, never one to lose out on a dollar, stole the unfinished tapes and released them as a TV mail-order album entitled *Roots*.

At his peak, Levy owned several record labels, a vast publishing empire, and a chain of record stores worth $30 million alone. But when the music industry went corporate in the seventies and eighties, Morris Levy found himself the last of a dying breed. The hustlers and hoodlums that he had done business with were being replaced with young, legitimate executives such as David Geffen. Giving up many of the small independent labels he controlled, Levy eventually sold his largest label, Roulette, as well as his publishing rights for more than $55 million. In 1988, Levy's mob ties eventually caught up to him as he was exposed on national TV as a conspirator in the extortion of a small-time music wholesaler named John Lamonte. Sentenced to ten years in jail, Levy died while awaiting an appeal. Many say that his death marked the official end to the swashbuckling days of the music industry.

Mazur nevertheless trusted Levy's instincts and believed in the artist whose tape he was carrying around. He was also running out of time and was open to any suggestions. He went to see Levy and played the tape for him.

"I want you to hear something," he told Levy as he walked into his office.

"What is it?" Levy replied.

"It's a kid I've been working with, just listen to it."

Mazur put the tape in the machine and turning it on sat down at Levy's desk to watch for his reaction. He watched as Levy sat at his desk, head down and listening, but not giving up the slightest sign of how he felt about the music. After almost three songs had played, Levy got up and turned the tape off. He stood over Mazur, who was now looking up in anticipation of what he thought.

"You're fired," Levy told him. "Get out of here."

Totally caught off guard, Mazur could only come up with, "What? Why are you firing me?"

"Because it's obvious that you don't want to be a sales and promotion man anymore," Levy answered. "You want to be an A&R guy."

Now it was beginning to sink in to the shell-shocked Mazur. A flurry of thoughts ran through his mind all of them bad. "I'm fired, no job, no more one hundred fifty dollars each week coming in," he thought to himself. "I'm ruined, my wife is going to have a baby anytime now, and I'm broke!"

He rose from the chair and walked across the room to the door to leave. As he grabbed the doorknob he heard Levy ask from across the room, "How much do you want for the kid?"

There was no way that Mazur was going to get himself involved with Levy. After all he'd worked for the guy now for years, and had seen some of his moves first hand. He knew that the only one who'd see any royalties would be Levy, and broke, ruined or not, he wasn't handing Billy over to this guy. "More than you'll pay," he said over his shoulder as the door closed behind him.

Levy's interest had now convinced Mazur that Billy had great potential. After all if Levy wanted him, he had to be good. With all his avenues exhausted and about fifty dollars to his name, Mazur walked over to the Gulf and Western building to see his brother Ruby again. He had to regroup, he wasn't giving up, he believed in the artist whose tape he was now putting in the machine for Ruby to hear, and he was going to get him a contract. He had to; he didn't have a job now!

Mazur put the tape in the machine in Ruby's office to play for the umpteenth time while he and Ruby sat and tried to brainstorm the next move. As they were sitting there talking and listening to the tape, a head full of long curls stuck itself in the door and half in, half out of the room, Michael Lang had heard it and was asking no one in particular, "Who is that?"

Mazur turned to see who was standing in the doorway. "It's a kid I'm managing," he answered.

"Really? What's his name?"

"Billy Joel," was the reply.

"Could I borrow it?" Lang asked.

Lang now had Mazur's attention. He had actually asked for the tape, and besides Mazur knew who Lang was and that he had a record label. "Sure," he said, and handed Michael the tape.

Michael Lang's name is recognizable to anyone who grew up in the sixties. He was the front man for the original Woodstock concert in August 1969, the best party that's ever been thrown. He put the Woodstock concert together with three primary partners after opening one of South Florida's earliest and most successful head shops in Coral Cables, then a hippy stronghold in the southeast. He made a bunch of money selling hippie paraphernalia and some say other organics popular at the time, then, getting bored, sold the shop.

After leaving the head shop, Lang moved to New York and with his partners threw the Woodstock party. Now a little more then a year later he was running a record label that he called Just Sunshine. Its name, many say, was influenced by the orange barrels of LSD that at the time were everywhere and shared the same name.

Lang took the tape home that night and listened to it. It turned out not to be his thing, but he did know someone on the West Coast that might be interested in it he told Mazur—the famous record companyy mogul Artie Ripp. "Can I send it to him?' he asked Mazur in what would be another turning point in Billy Joel's life.

At the time Gulf and Western Industries was one of the first large corporations to begin to diversify its interests. Then the music business was just beginning to evolve from a multitude of very small and independent labels to what it is today, an industry dominated by large and powerful corporations. Executives at companies like Gulf and Western saw the potential for large money that the emerging music industry was capable of generating and speculated that with their resources both financial and otherwise, they could dominate a large section of the music industry. In a sense they were right, but in doing so also seemingly helped to drain away the incredible creativity that was then occurring, ultimately resulting in what we find today, a music industry whose success is measured in its ability to market to the public, more than in the creativity of its artists.

Lang's record label was one of the many that fell under the umbrella of Paramount records, which was acquired by Gulf and Western Industries in 1970; another was Family Productions.

There was one problem. Gulf and Western knew little if anything about running a record company so they hired Tony Martell away from the CBS record group and set out to develop partnerships with the smaller, independent labels. The theory was that with their resources and influence, G&W could take these artists nationally and even internationally, making themselves lots of money in the process. The future looked positive for Paramount until Martell's son T.J. developed leukemia, and rightly so Tony's priorities changed. He couldn't focus on his job, even during those times when he was there in his spacious twenty fourth-floor office. It was to be the beginning of the end for what G&W executives had held so much promise for, but it wasn't to be.

Fortunately Tony Martell was able to turn what resulted in a losing battle with his son's leukemia into something very positive. As his son lay on his deathbed, he made his father promise that through his contacts and influence he'd raise millions of dollars for leukemia research so that others "wouldn't have to go through what he did." In an incredible testament to a father's love for his son, the T.J. Martell Foundation had raised over two hundred million dollars to date to help find a cure for leukemia, cancer, and AIDS.

On a trip to California soon after, Lang took the tape to his friend Artie Ripp, who loved it. Ripp was a streetwise kid from Queens, New York who never finished high school but who had a lifelong love of music and the music business. As a teenager in 1958 he sang in a band called the Four Temptations who had a Top 20 hit with the song "Barbara" that Ripp co-wrote. This experience made Artie realize that number one he "sucked" as a singer, and two he really wasn't a writer. He did love the music business though and the excitement it generated, and during this time went to work for the legendary George Goldner, a record producer and founder of the independent label Gone/End Records. It was here that Ripp began to learn the music business inside out. As an emerging A&R record production person, Ripp contributed to the success of many of the late fifties' biggest R&B groups including The Chantels, Little Anthony and the Imperials, and The Flamingos.

From there he went on to work for the legendary Don Kirshner who at the time owned Aldon Music, the leading independent record company. Here he established relationships with people like Carole King, Neil Sedaka, and Barry Mann among others, who were then writers.

In 1963 Ripp founded Kama Sutra Productions at 1650 Broadway in New York City, with two partners and the understanding that he and he alone would be responsible for making any decisions that had to do with the growth and operation of the company, as long as he could fund them. This was a pretty bold act as there was only $1400 in the bank at the time.

Shortly after founding the company Ripp put together a $12,000 deal that allowed him to produce the single "Remember (Walking in the Sand)" by the Shangri Las from a song demo that he found in the Kama Sutra files. Since at the time he didn't have a record label he contacted his old friend Goldner to license the record to his Red Bird Records and subsequent to its release the record became a number one hit.

Based on this success Ripp was asked to produce a record for a band named Jay and the Americans and took them into the studio to record "Come a Little Bit Closer." At the same time his Kama Sutra Productions was also releasing Shadow Morton's "Leader of the Pack" with a young Billy Joel playing the piano, but receiving no credit. Subsequently both records were in the Top 10 for many weeks, with "Leader of the Pack" going to number one and "Come a Little Bit Closer," at the time an innovative mix of rock and roll, pop, and Latin music, reaching number three.

In a little over a year he had formed working relationships with not only Shadow Morton, but also such well-known producers and songwriters as Richie Cordell, Gary Katz, Bo Gentry, and Richard Perry to mention a few. With these alliances he set out to dominate the independent record production and music publishing worlds and formed Kama Sutra Records, making a USA distribution deal with MGM records. Almost immediately he signed The Lovin' Spoonful and helped master their first hit "Do You Believe in Magic" for their introductory album with the same name released in 1965.

Within 18 months Ripp's Kama Sutra Records was responsible for more than 25 percent of MGM's record sales thanks in large part to Ripp's Lovin' Spoonful and Sopwith Camel as well as two top forty hits titled "A Younger Girl" and "Mr. Dyingly Sad."

Not one to rest on past success, Ripp formed the record company Buddah Records in 1967 with an executive team that included well-respected names such as Neil Bogart, Cecil Holmes, and Bob Krasnow. He was now in complete control and decided that Buddah would become the first independent record company to distribute outside third party–owned labels. He sold Buddah in 1968 after succeeding at this to Viewlex. Now with a majority equity position in Viewlex, an AMEX company, which at the time was in the record duplication and educational products business, Ripp purchased the record, film, and merchandising rights to the Woodstock Festival from its producer/creators Michael Lang and Artie Kornfeld by writing them a check for $425,000 at the end of the festival. Money that surely they welcomed after that initial financial disaster. When Ripp told his partners at Viewlex about the deal they squashed it out of fear that it was useless and that any association with Woodstock would hurt their image and stock. This made Ripp furious and he quit as chairman and sold his stock in August 1970.

In 1970 Ripp formed Family Productions Records and began a relationship with Jim Judelson's Gulf and Western Industries. Little did Ripp know that this would end up as perhaps his best-known career milestone. Shortly after arriving in Los Angeles, Michael Lang was sitting in Artie Ripp's house in the early morning hours, talking about the record business and making plans, when Lang remembered that he had this tape. He retrieved it from his jacket pocket and handed it to Ripp. "I think you might find this interesting," he said. "It's not my thing, but it may strike a chord with you. See what you think."

Ripp put the tape in the machine and started playing it. Lang could see that he liked it right away by the expressions on Ripp's face and his focus on the music coming from the speakers.

Turning the tape off, Ripp turned to Lang and asked him, "Is the singer the piano player?"

"Yes," Lang answered.

"Did he write the lyrics?"

"Yes," Lang answered again.

"Great. Where did you get the tape?" Ripp asked.

"From Irwin Mazur in New York," Lang answered. "The guy evidently has been turned down by every record company in New York City. No one wants to sign the guy. They aren't interested in a singer/songwriter/piano-playing musician."

Ripp was interested though. He got Billy's music. Without even knowing Mazur at the time, he understood what Mazur had in a young Billy Joel and why it was driving Mazur almost nuts in New York City trying to hawk this singer/songwriter to record companies who clearly didn't recognize the unique talent of young Billy Joel. Artie Ripp, like Irwin Mazur, understood that Joel's music and lyrics were different from most of what was out there.

Ripp could see that Billy's music wasn't just a bunch of superficial words accompanied by a similar type of music. This guy got it. He got life and could see and feel it on a level that few others did. He was a storyteller. Perhaps more important, Ripp could see that Billy Joel had an extraordinary gift for projecting this through his lyrics and his music, both of which touched Ripp in a place deep inside him.

Ripp says today: "It was clear that this was somebody that was not a tin pan alley song writer. This is somebody who was really writing biography. I was really taken with what it is he had to say and how I felt that he represented things that people felt and that people could easily relate to and that he was presenting it in such an engaging, musical and emotional context."

Ripp was so impressed that he said to Lang: "This guy can write and sing his ass off. This guy is going to be huge someday. He's got an extraordinary talent. I want to sign him to my label, and I'll give you a piece of it for bringing him to me. Who is his manager?'

"Irwin Mazur," Ripp told him. "He lives on Long Island."

"What's his number?" Ripp asked him, reaching for the phone. "I'm calling him right now."

"You can't call him now," Lang answered. "It's after four in the morning there."

"What do you mean I can't call him?" Ripp answered. "Didn't you just tell me that the guy has been turned down by every record company in New York City? This guy is waiting for my phone call. This guy is waiting for his phone to ring and for someone at the other end to say 'I love Billy Joel, and I want him on my record label.'"

Lang gave him the number and Ripp called Mazur at four in the morning. "How much do you want for the kid?" Mazur heard as he picked up the phone. "My name is Artie Ripp. I'm standing here with Michael Lang who just played me the tape. I think your kid is great and I want to sign him to a record deal."

Mazur, breaking out of a deep sleep, couldn't believe what he was hearing.

"I'll guarantee you an album and a single. I'll put him in the studio with some great musicians, and I'll give you enough money every month so that your kid can focussed on just writing his music and songs, and to get an act together."

Mazur couldn't believe it. Despite how much he believed in Billy Joel, he was beginning to think that the thirty days would run out and Billy would leave, go off to some job in the Midwest and possibly obscurity.

"I want it all in writing," Mazur told him.

"You've got it," Rip answered. "Meet me Tuesday at one o'clock in front of the Gulf and Western building, and don't play that tape or talk to anyone else. Understand?"

The conversation went on for about another thirty minutes as Mazur and Ripp worked out the primary details, and Mazur made sure that Ripp wasn't just some nut. "I'll see you Tuesday," Ripp said as he hung up.

There was no way Mazur could sleep now, but it was also way too early to call Billy, so he went out and hung in the living room, until finally he couldn't take it, and had to make the call. "You wanted a record deal in thirty days Billy? Well, I got you one," he announced.

Billy says today:

One of Lang's artists was making an album which was being produced by a guy named Artie Ripp. Don't ask me how it happened. It just happened. I was sent to L.A. and Artie was there, and he was going to produce my album, I didn't know who he was, and I believe he was a record producer, and then suddenly during this time there was a switch over with the record companies, and I got flipped over to Artie Ripp's record company which was called Family Records, and Michael Lang got one of Artie Ripp's acts, a Hendrix-type band called Velvet Turner.

In a little over one month Billy had gone from losing his girlfriend, to attempting suicide twice, signing himself into a nuthouse and breaking out, to getting a record contract. To say it all had been surreal would be a gross understatement.

However, Billy recalls:

I ended up on Artie Ripp's record label and production company which is based in L.A. and did not have an attorney representing me at the time. I was 21, I was old enough to sign, I signed away my publishing, my record rights, my copyrights, my record mechanicals, my touring monies, I just signed away everything, I was like "Hey, I got a record deal!" Its an old story in the music business, no one is clean.

Unfortunately in this case Billy was right. Because of his eagerness and naiveté, as well as Mazur's desperation because of his own precarious financial state, they signed away the copyrights, royalties, and the publishing rights of Billy's music to Ripp, a reality that would come back to haunt Billy for years to come and which would inspire a new word in the record industry—"Ripp-Off."

"I didn't know what I was signing," Billy said after the fact. "But I probably would have signed anything to get that deal. I was only twenty . . . I didn't know anything about publishing or monies that were owed to me."

It's sadly a familiar story in the music business and one that hasn't changed ever, and in all likelihood won't in the near future. Most musicians after all are not business people, and all too often are more focussed on getting that contract they've been thinking about than reading the fine print. So when someone comes along, especially someone with a recognizable name like Artie Ripp who had over fifteen years already in the record business, and flatters you about your music, while promising you fame and fortune, you sign. Billy agrees. "It's so easy to take advantage of a musician."

As happy as Billy was to finally have a record contract he also was burned out on the whole rock and roll singer thing. Having put in his time with bands since his early teens, he was sick of touring and he didn't want to ever go back on the road. His "vision" of a successful Billy Joel was to be happily sitting at home and writing songs that other musicians would record and pay him royalties for. In fact, that was his whole plan, but as plans do at times his would take on a somewhat different reality.

Artie Ripp also wanted Billy to continue writing as Mazur had challenged him to do earlier, but his vision for Billy was somewhat different and in the end closer to what the reality would be. He knew since hearing Michael Lang's tape that Billy was an extraordinary songwriter, and thought that if he could get Billy to write enough songs that they could then record an album. That became Ripp's and Mazur's goal, and to some degree Billy's too, but without having to go back on the road and promote them. Meanwhile Billy was trying to come to terms with the radical changes in his life professionally.

"As you sign a record contract, you go through this change," he says. "Because as soon as you put your name on the paper, you're an artist. The record contract says 'Billy Joel herein referred to as the artist,' and automatically you're an artist just by signing."

As part of Billy's deal with Ripp, he was given a monthly allowance and a piano to move into his place. Things were looking good for Billy, although he was still unaware that anything he did write essentially wasn't going to be his.

It appeared, at least on the surface, that his personal life was changing for the better too. With a record contract, and a monthly allowance coming in, Billy now had some semblance of security for the first time in his professional career. Elizabeth took notice and Billy's relationship with her also reached a new level until one day when Jon Small walked in on Billy and Elizabeth in an embarrassing situation. Shortly after Jon and Elizabeth called it quits and she took young Sean and left the house in Dix Hills to move in with Billy in a house out on Long Island's east end.

"She was manipulating to her advantage and she was playing the cards and the clowns that she was dealing with. She was making the most of it," Artie Ripp says today.

Many others who witnessed the events then agree with Ripp's perception, although most are somewhat less diplomatic about expressing them. "Yeah,

Liz was very cold and very calculating," Bobby Jo Grazier, the mother's helper, says today. "I don't know when it actually crossed over between Liz and John and Liz and Billy, you could almost see it but not see it that summer," she continues. "Looking back I could see it happening, but when we were young it seemed like we were all just hanging out together . . . for whatever reason it was that Liz was pulling Billy's strings."

Billy, Elizabeth, and Sean set up house in Hampton Bay's, New York, and the future, at least for the moment, looked bright for them all. Billy was writing songs and getting ready to record an album, and Elizabeth was attending college nearby on Long Island.

Billy soon had a number of songs that he was happy with and the time came to record an album. Ripp knew the right studio people and musicians and Mazur didn't care, it was an exciting development to move with Billy to California and record the album, and besides as Mazur put it, "We were so broke at the time and did not want the checks to get lost in the mail, so we all moved to LA." So in the early summer of 1971 Billy Joel moved to Los Angeles.

Upon arriving, Ripp and Mazur immediately drew up a list of musicians for Billy to interview in the studio, many of whom were were not lightweights.

"I knew that Billy had to have guys that would hear his music the way he did," Ripp said. "They had to be able to communicate musically."

Ripp booked studio time at the Record Plant and started setting up auditions with the likes of "Sneaky Pete" Kleinow, Rhys Clark, Sal De Troia, and Larry Knechtel to name just a few. As the artist, Billy wisely had the final say on which musicians would be used. Ripp used the money that he'd raised from record companies as well as whatever money he could scrape together to put together this album for a then essentially unknown Billy Joel, so it had to be done on a pretty slim budget. "Whether they were ultimately the best guys to be with, who knows?" Ripp says today. "Those were the guys that we could afford, that we could put behind this Billy, who wasn't earning a penny. Don't forget at the time no one was standing in line to see him play or buy his records." Despite whatever financial constraints they had to deal with, they still managed to put together a winning list of musicians. "At the end of the day I'm confident that we put together a list of musicians that he felt comfortable with and not challenged, and that was important at that stage in Billy's career," Ripp says.

This studio experience had to be vastly different for Billy than any others he'd been involved in. This time he was the main character, not a member of a band who all supported each other musically. There was a lot of responsibility and pressure on Billy Joel this time, more then he'd ever experienced career-wise before, and he quickly realized that there was an extraordinary amount of responsibility on his shoulders to pull this thing together. It wasn't going to be a walk in the park for Billy this time, and for a guy who had more then his share of rejections and failures already at just twenty-two years old, Billy deep inside himself must have been full of doubt that he could make it happen. He was fortunate though to have some of the top musicians of the time to work with, and even if they hadn't played a hundred or so gigs together like he had with The Hassles or even The Commandos, these guys, like Billy, were professionals. Nevertheless, Ripp did have concerns initially, although ultimately he did believe in his artist. "He had no confidence," Ripp says. "But I knew that he was an extraordinary, unique, and extremely creative individual. Like certain great creative individuals he has his share of idiosyncrasies and devils that run around inside him."

Ripp and Mazur knew that they had to do everything they could to insure that Billy remained as creative and happy as possible, and Billy, now living away from Elizabeth and Sean, missed them in those times when he wasn't in the studio. Jon and Elizabeth's divorce had just become final and Billy wanted them with him in Los Angeles. Ripp knew that he had to help so he flew both of them to Los Angeles. "I knew I'd better make sure that Billy was able to concentrate on his creativity rather than to concentrate on the dramas in his life, so I said, 'OK, your girlfriend and her kid are important to you? Great, we'll move them out here, and you'll have your own place' and that's what I did."

The title of the album came from the name of the affluent waterfront town north of Hicksville, where a young Billy Joel would go for picnics with his mother and sister as a child, and later drive around the narrow streets looking at the big homes on the water that Billy would dream about living in one day. It was the same town that Billy referred to in the beautiful song "Everybody Love You Now," and the one that within ten years he in fact would move to. The *Cold Spring Harbor* album was recorded with a minimum of overdubbing because Ripp wanted to capture the essence of a live performance as closely as he could in a studio, and overdubbing lead vocals would never work. Billy evidently agrees. "I think of myself as a piano player and a songwriter," he says. "My singing is all tied to my piano playing. There's never the total separation you get with a first-rate mix . . . but that's become an aspect of my sound, a distinctive trait. If I must overdub, I'll literally sit at the closed piano and pound my fingers on the lid."

The album was finished and Billy, Elizabeth, Sean, and Irwin Mazur returned home to Long Island while Artie Ripp was left with the responsibility of mixing the album. Meanwhile things at Gulf and Western's music division were melting down. With no leadership due to Tony Martell's preoccupation with his son's illness, Paramount Records was essentially free-spooling. That is, running itself. There was no effective leadership and employees had little if any idea what they were supposed to be doing each day. Even though at this point there were fourteen different independent record labels under contract to Paramount, no one seemed to know who they were, or for that matter where.

Family Productions was one of the fourteen and with the *Cold Spring Harbor* album tracks recorded all that remained was to mix them and release the album. First, however, Ripp was dealing with his own demons. In addition to having Billy Joel signed, Ripp also represented a young country and western artist known as Kyle. He had recorded an album prior to Billy's that was now released and seemingly being promoted by the team of Sandy and John Gibson. Sandy was in charge of publicity, while John, currently a Fox News broadcaster, then was in charge of promoting Family Productions records to radio stations. This they had done successfully, and the Kyle album was getting airplay. The problem was that because of the rudderless ship Paramount, there were no records being pressed and shipped to stores. As a result there was no money coming into Family Productions and Ripp was in a financial mess.

Ripp started to unravel and those around him saw the changes in his attitude and moods. He knew that if he was going to keep any money coming in at all that he had to get Billy Joel's album mixed and mastered and get it into stores. The result was the now famous "chipmunk" sound of the *Cold Spring Harbor* album. Some say that he rushed the album through because he needed to keep a stream of cash flowing; Ripp's version of what happened is understandably different:

> This was the ultimate Murphy's Law situation. If anything could go wrong it would and in this case everything ended up going wrong. The two-track stereo tape machine that I mixed the master to was running slow which I didn't discover it until it was too late and the 50,000 records were manufactured and out the door. It seems that the second studio engineer never ran a speed test each time we had a mixing session to make sure that each and every two-track tape machine was running at fifteen inches per second. As a result I never knew whether every single cut or just some cuts wound up being recorded on a slow machine. So what happened in the final mastering cutting session was that when you put the tape on a machine that ran at a normal speed it had a little speed up to it. Some people said I did it intentionally which is totally ridiculous Why would I? There was only a downside for me and for Billy in that case.

Regardless of what happened, the music was sped up and Billy's voice, which he has never been comfortable with anyway, came through about half an octave higher then it would have normally. The album that Billy had poured his heart and soul into, and for which he had such high hopes, was a disaster.

"It's not easy for me to listen to myself," Billy said. "I'm not objective about my work."

Ripp, possibly still trying to justify the mistake today reflects on the situation and what today he might say to Billy about it. "*Cold Spring Harbor* had the faults that it had, the tape machine ran slow, but you sang high any fucking way! I didn't do it on purpose, that's part of the karma of the thing."

Whatever happened, and the answer probably lies somewhere in between both versions, the album of great material turned out to be a disaster, and when Billy heard it for the first time while sitting in his apartment in Oyster Bay, New York his reaction was predictably one of anger.

Bobby Colasanti, his childhood friend, was in the apartment when Billy came home that day with the album from the post office: "He came home to his apartment in Oyster Bay. There were a bunch of us sitting around and Billy took the album right out of the sleeve for the first time and put it on the turntable. When it started playing we just sat around looking at each other, because it sounded like the chipmunks. Oh, god, it was horrendous."

Evidently Billy agreed. After putting everything he had into the album, and having such great hope for its future, Billy was so devastated that he removed it from the turntable and hurled it against the wall where it broke into pieces. Billy knew that all the hard work would be in vain. No one would take the album seriously, the critics would pan it, and sales would be dismal. As usual, his instincts were good.

# Chapter 12

To say that at this point there was a scramble for Artie Ripp to save his investment would be an understatement. Artie knew the record business after all, and he knew that if he didn't act and act smartly then everything was going down the drain, and to make matters worse, time was against him. The album was a disaster, he knew that, but he still had the artist. He still had Billy Joel who he knew right from the start was someone with extraordinary talent. There was only one solution—Billy had to go out on the road. This way, with Artie's help, he could insure that DJs, club owners, and record company people, as well as those who bought records, would see what Artie and, for that matter, Irwin, had seen in Billy Joel right away.

Ripp says today:

> At the end of the day, I concluded that *Cold Spring Harbor* was going to introduce him. I would use the album as the calling card and I would say, "Listen, I want you to meet Billy Joel in New York, in Philadelphia, in Detroit, in Chicago," every place I could get him exposed. Bring in the radio people, bring in the press, bring in the retail people, get them introduced to this guy and have them get as excited about him and his talent as I was. And so I recognize that *Cold Spring Harbor* was like the hello card, it wasn't the end of the day card. And it was not necessarily Billy at his grown-up, mature, "I'm confident in myself, in control," it wasn't having all of the elements you wanted to have: song, production-wise and so on. It was as good as it could be at that particular time under those sets of circumstances. Fleetwood Mac had ten bomb albums in a row. Billy only had one.

The only issue was money. Ripp was already running out of money, and now with a botched record to sell and a company that was self-destructing, he knew he couldn't count on them. Somehow he'd have to come up with the money himself, even though he knew that in a sense it was throwing good money after bad, but it was the only way and he knew it.

"At that point touring made no sense at all," Mazur said. "But there was no other way to get people to see who Billy Joel was, so it happened." They had to get Billy out on the road and to get him introduced to people that could possibly further his career, and to make potential record buyers aware that he existed.

"Once *Cold Spring Harbor* was finished, then it was go out on the road and meet radio people," Mazur said. "Meet the record store guys. Meet the disc jockeys. Meet the concert promoters and so on, anything that would get his record on the air. Our goal was to get people to realize that Billy Joel was really fabulous, to think to themselves, 'Wow, listen to the way he plays. Listen to the way he sings. Listen to those amazing lyrics and melodies.'" In a nutshell that was the job that Mazur and Ripp now had if the album was going to sell at all, and if Billy's talent was going to be recognized.

Ripp came up with an ingenious plan to get his artist noticed. "I knew that there was going to be a convention for the people that booked college concerts in Kansas City," he said. "I tried to get them to let Billy play it, but no one knew who he was so I got shot down. Instead I booked a club in Kansas City and printed up a copy of *Family Scandals* that I gave to retailers in the city to give away. I also put a copy of it and an invitation to see Billy play that night in the club under every hotel door in the city where I knew bookers were staying. It worked, we ended up getting a room full of people to see Billy, and as result we created a college tour for him." One of those who attended the show was a woman named Becky Mancusco who would soon play an integral role in Billy's career.

With a college tour now in the works, Artie Ripp hoped that he'd recoup at least part of his investment. Billy would be out on the road for more then six months, well into the spring of 1972, opening for such acts as Badfinger, the J. Geils Band, and The Doobie Brothers, all of whom Billy and his hastily put together band jelled pretty well with.

Like the recording of his *Cold Spring Harbor* album, this tour was in effect a real test of Billy's professionalism both personally and musically. He wasn't standing in the background now with his organ playing or singing back up, he was now thrust into being the center of attention on stage, the leader of his own band, a role he wasn't yet intimately familiar with, and certainly after his latest series of reversals not particularly confident in himself, according to both Mazur and Ripp. Billy seemed to look at it differently, somehow despite the recent reversals, still believing in himself, if not personally, professionally.

"They'd like to present me as a dynamic and electric personality," he said in an early *Family Scandals* newsletter interview. "Well, onstage I get it on pretty well, but otherwise I'm about as sparkling as a warm beer." Regardless of whether Billy really felt this way or whether it was just an early example of his innate ability to manipulate the press, by coming up with the right sound bites at the right time, Billy was engaged in a self-awareness process like never before.

"I worked very hard to try to help Billy develop the confidence in himself that I knew was necessary," Mazur says today. "I knew Billy's potential, and I knew that I had to get him out from behind his piano and to the front of the stage so that he'd develop the confidence he needed to allow the real Billy Joel to come through."

So against all odds, and with little or no money, Artie Ripp and Irwin Mazur now had Billy out on the road playing colleges and small clubs, as they tried to create a buzz around him in order to at least get enough money from a record company to go back in the studio and record again. That was the plan anyway. Billy, meanwhile, took advantage of the situation to polish his music and his stage presence, just as Mazur had hoped he would. Always a ham, this new role of leader of his band carried with it another level of responsibility until then unfamiliar to him, but as he always has, Billy met the challenge head first and within no time had perfected his stage show to the point that audiences were as excited if not more about the performance of the opening act. Billy and his hastily put together band were beginning to create the buzz Ripp hoped for on their tour as their performance got better and better due to Billy's incredible work ethic.

Billy says:

I was doing great live, selling out 5000-seaters. We were blowing away headliners. We'd come on first and have only forty minutes, so we did what we called our kamikaze show: bam! We'd hit them with our hottest stuff and be gone. They'd say who was that guy? We became real show stealers. No one wanted to play with us. We didn't do it on purpose, but we just played our best.

Soon Billy and his band would be playing as headliners.

While things musically seemed to be going well, money was another issue. There didn't seem to be any coming in as far as Billy and his band could see anyway. He recalls:

I find myself on tour in a Winnebago, traveling all around the country, we'd have no food and we have no money, and we kept getting told, "Well just make peanut butter and jelly sandwiches." We are playing in clubs and we are not getting paid, just cigarette money and sometimes money for food, something was obviously wrong. Finally when I came back to L.A. I said, "This is not the way things are supposed to work," and I got an attorney, and I also got another person, who was also working for Family Records, whose name was John Troy—he was their record promotion man, he was the guy who brings you to the radio stations and tries to get them to play your records. And then we dug in a bit, and I realized that I needed to get an accountant, I needed to get a lawyer and I've got to realize just what I had given away.

Indeed for at least six months Billy was busy on the road and had no way to find out how the album was selling, if at all. He recalls:

I remember on that first tour I suddenly realized that the album wasn't in record stores. I never saw it in stores or even heard it getting played on the radio, then I discovered that a lot of the money from gate receipts was not accounted for and now I realize that this whole tour was nothing but a rip off. When I asked I was told, "Oh, it's all being used up for promotion."

As dark as it may have seemed to Billy then, there were going to be a series of events on this tour which would forever change the life of the as yet still relatively unknown singer/songwriter.

Elton Spitzer owned WLIR–FM, which was then the premier Long Island, New York rock radio station. Dwarfed by more powerful New York City neighbor stations, WLIR nevertheless had a large and loyal following of listeners on Long Island in the late sixties and early seventies, due to its dedication to free-form album rock which appealed to the hard core rock and roll listener of the time. In addition to playing music by bands like Crosby, Stills, Nash, and Young, Santana, The Beatles, Eric Clapton, and a long list of others, on Tuesday nights at eight o'clock, WLIR did a series of live broadcasts featuring local musicians and bands that was sponsored by Dr. Pepper soft drinks. On November 9, 1971, the Charlie Daniels Band was scheduled to be the Tuesday night guest in the Ultrasonic music studio just a block away from the radio station in Hempstead, New York. A very colorful local music promoter named Michael "Eppy" Epstein, who also ran a famous rock and roll club in Roslyn, New York called My Father's Place, was the producer of the live shows and knew Billy Joel from his days with The Hassles and Attila the Hun.

Eppy says today:

It was a great scene. Every Tuesday night we'd have forty or fifty long-haired kids sitting on the studio floor waiting for the live broadcast to begin. This week Charlie Daniels was the booked guest and he got sick. I knew Billy was using the studio to record parts of the *Cold Spring Harbor* album. He was putting his soul into that album. Anyway I asked him if he'd do me a favor. "I know you do the piano man thing and I need you to do this for me," I said. Just be yourself, play your songs. Well, he agreed to do it, and that night at eight I take the mike and say something like, "Tonight I have something very special for you guys. Charlie Daniels is sick, and the guy Billy Joel that was in The Hassles is going to play for you tonight. Next time you hear him he will be performing at the Nassau Coliseum." Needless to say, I was a little whacked.

Whacked maybe, but still right on. Billy played five songs that night mostly from the *Cold Spring Harbor* album, and closed with "Captain Jack." The concert has become a classic in Billy's career, and later on in 1971 would help to create an awareness about this "new" and "upcoming" artist who on WLIR anyway was already a hometown favorite.

Meanwhile there were still seemingly endless concert dates for Billy Joel to meet, one of them being the three-day Mar Y Sol Festival in Puerto Rico, during the first three days of 1972. With over 30,000 concert-goers this was going to be the largest venue that Billy Joel had ever played in his career. The musicians booked were a diverse group ranging from Alice Cooper to Emerson, Lake and Palmer, to jazz legends Dave Brubeck and Herbie Mann. The festival's producers envisioned it as a sort of Caribbean Woodstock, and because of the rain that fell a good portion of the three days as well as the large rural setting where it was held, it lived up to its concept. Just prior to Billy's set, he and his band and the usual list of hangers-on were sitting around in a tent away from the stage, waiting for the rain to let up when one of the festival's promoters came in flipping out and yelling with arms flailing around, telling them to get on stage. The rain had dampened the spirit of the crowd and people were starting to trickle out, and the organizers were in a panic, concerned that they were going to lose everything if people started to leave, and the revenue from Y-shirt and food concessions dried up.

"I don't care if it's raining or not. Get on the stage and play . . . or get out," he said, according to Irwin Mazur.

Not wanting to jeopardize their pay day, Billy and his band pulled it together, and got on the stage, testing their equipment in the rain, hoping that no one would get shocked or that a piece of equipment wouldn't get destroyed. Billy was sitting at his piano starting to play a little, making sure that everything was working alright when Mazur who was off the stage behind him leaned over and told him to start playing "The Letter," a top forty hit originally done by a band named The Boxtops in 1967 and then again a hit in 1970 when it was recorded by Joe Cocker and his band Mad Dogs and Englishmen. Billy lit into the song, and evidently was doing his best Joe Cocker imitation because he soon had the complete attention of the rain-soaked audience who weren't quite sure if it was Joe Cocker or Billy Joel playing as they pushed toward the stage. It didn't matter. Billy felt the electricity of the crowd who had been starved for music, and he was now "on" and before the song was over had the crowd in the palm of his hands. It was only the beginning, though, as he led the crowd and his band through 45 minutes of kick-ass rock and roll that included the Rolling Stones' "Jumping Jack Flash," "The Ballad of Billy the Kid," and "Tomorrow is Today." In what was just what the crowd needed, and was to be yet another milestone in Billy's career, he ended up getting three encores. According to Irwin Mazur, for the first time, "Billy truly took command of the stage. I was standing on the stage with my wife. I had tears in my eyes, I was so happy for him. It was a moment that I'll never forget." He had never had that kind of command of an audience before.

Billy's memories of that day echo Mazur's. "We did really well," Billy recalls. "They gave us three encores. My road manager kept coming backstage and yelling, 'They want you again.'" Then, in typical Billy Joel fashion, he answered his manager by telling him, "What? Are they crazy? What's going on? It must be the heat?" Needless to say the festival was a pivotal moment in Billy's professional career. He'd found himself as a musician/performer, and had truly come into his own. The guy who used to sit on stage at the piano with his head down, not connecting with the audience, and who so insecure about his music that he had to add impersonations and tell jokes throughout his sets, now had the eye of the tiger. He'd done it; he'd generated the magic that he'd seen so many other musicians create going back to his first James Brown concert at the Apollo Theater nine years earlier. Billy had finally mastered his art and joined those that he looked up to such as Brown, Ray Charles, Traffic, and The Beatles. Now as the hard-working perfectionist that he is, he wasn't about to ever go back again. From then on he worked tirelessly to fine-tune his art even more.

In a perfect testament to what often makes a career in the record business, luck and being in the right place at he right time, Billy was in the right place, at the right time, and fortunately for him the right people were also there. Don Heckman, a music journalist covering the festival for the *New York Times* wrote about Billy's performance which it appears generated the first true excitement in what until then had been a lackluster event because of the weather. "The first real excitement was generated by Billy Joel's gospel-tinged rock band . . . Building up a charge that was reminiscent of the work of the old Leon Russell/Joe Cocker combination, the Billy Joel group brought some life to what had been a generally dispirited environment."

Another festival-goer who was familiar with Billy Joel was Becky Mancusco-Shargo, a secretary at the time to Kip Cohen who was the head of the A&R department for Columbia Records. Becky had seen Billy perform in Kansas City at Ripp's showcase and had been impressed enough with him then to purchase the *Cold Spring Harbor* album. The Mar Y Sol Festival closed and Becky returned to her job in New York City as Billy and his small entourage left to return to the states and more club dates, unaware that the fuse had now been lit for what would soon be an explosion in his career.

About ten days after the Mar Y Sol Festival, Billy was booked to play Philadelphia, a city where, due to its proximity to New York, had a small, dedicated and growing group of Billy Joel followers. Because of a freelance producer named Dennis Wilen, Billy was scheduled to play a live radio broadcast for the FM station WMMR on April 15, 1972. Here, like at WLIR, there was also a small and select group of station listeners who had won the chance to be in the city's Sigma Sound Studios while Billy performed, and with Billy's popularity in "The City of Brotherly Love" the event was sure to be well received. Billy played a few songs from the *Cold Spring Harbor* album and answered some questions from the DJ and audience before performing a new song he'd written, but had yet to record, called "Captain Jack." It was a song that depicted the all too familiar dreariness of growing up in the soulless suburbs as Billy had. The lives that so many baby boomers were living, who as if part of some sort of religion had been led to believe that the post-World War II years would bring happiness and prosperity to the their generation, led all too often to disappointment as this increasingly disillusioned group found only huge amounts of emptiness and loneliness which because of the times was a perfect prescription to escape into the world of drugs.

"Captain Jack was a look out the window song," Billy was to say later. "I wanted to smack people in the face and say 'Whatever you have to do to escape your own life by chemical means is useless.'" This obviously was a message that Billy could speak of from experience.

The live version of "Captain Jack" that Billy recorded that night at WMMR almost immediately began to receive requests from listeners, and in a short time the tape was creating quite a sensation on both sides of the morality barometer. Most listeners, especially the baby boomers, loved the song that they could relate so easily to, while another much smaller and narrower minded group bashed the song at every opportunity because of its lines that spoke of drugs and masturbation. Because there is no such thing as bad press, the criticism of "Captain Jack" only added to its popularity.

Today Billy recalls:

I wrote "Captain Jack" when drugs were in full flower. A lot of useless, wasted deaths. Friends of mine were killed. Drugs can be fun, but they can kill too. Some guys who lived near me used to score smack from a guy named "Captain Jack", although I didn't write it to necessarily mean heroin. I meant any kind of drug you have to take over and over again.

Who Captain Jack really was has for decades been the object of much speculation. Some agree that it was the rich young heroin dealer who Billy alludes to in either "Oyster Bay" or Cold Spring Harbor, while others believe that the name is fictional. Before he died, Howie Blauvelt told friend Rich Arfin that Captain Jack was in fact the name of a fishing station on Long Island's North Shore where Billy and Howie used to rent rowboats to fish. "They never really fished," Arfin says today. "They'd bring a bunch of beers with them and hang them overboard to keep them from getting too hot." Wherever the name came from is really secondary. What was important was that in 1972 "Captain Jack" was creating such a buzz in music circles in Philadelphia and even New York City that people were beginning to hear about this new piano player named Billy Joel.

Within a month of the April 15th live broadcast in Philadelphia, word of the song had reached New York City's WNEW radio station, then the premier FM rock and roll station in the powerful New York metropolitan market. "Captain Jack" began to get airplay there too and now people in the record business, who could make or break careers, noticed.

Abe Somer at the time was a powerful music attorney from Los Angeles who had represented the likes of The Doors and the Mamas and the Papas in the sixties. He was in New York City that spring and was throwing a party for music company executives and others in the business that then Columbia Record company executive Walter Yetnikoff attended at the invitation of Columbia Records president Clive Davis. "Everyone seemed to be talking about this song 'Captain Jack,'" Yetnikoff said. "And I'm thinking to myself, "Who the hell is 'Captain Jack?'" He'd soon know.

# Chapter 13

Meanwhile Billy had to complete the tour Ripp and Mazur had booked for him. Now finished with the United States part of it, Billy was booked to play his first ever European dates thanks to Ripp's European record distributor Phonogram, which was releasing the *Cold Spring Harbor* album overseas. Billy looked forward to going to Europe for the first time, for a multitude of reasons. Because of the void he had always felt not knowing much about his family origins this trip might, he thought, shed some light on many of the stories he'd heard Phillip and Rebecca talk about, and to a much smaller degree even Karl and Howard. Also going to Europe to play his music, particularly as a piano player, gave Billy great satisfaction, knowing that some of the greatest piano players ever wrote music and performed there. Primarily, though, Billy was excited because he knew that his father was there somewhere, and he hoped that if he could somehow find Howard, that they could establish a father/son relationship, and the many years of the past where Howard's absence had left a void and pain would finally cease to exist. Billy (and also Judy and Rosalind) had been deeply wounded by his father's abandonment, as anyone would have been, and he desperately wanted to reestablish a relationship with him. All those years growing up in Hicksville making up stories about his father being in the Merchant Marine, traveling on business and even working for the CIA had been hard on all of them. Billy also naively fantasized that once his father knew of his career choice as a musician and his growing success that the acceptance and love that he so deeply needed from Howard would also fall into place.

As two people who had spent a great deal of time with Billy, both Ripp and Mazur were aware to some degree of the pain Billy held regarding his father. They thought that if they could find Howard, it would not only be good for Billy, but ultimately his career too. Selfishly they speculated that they could also create a PR event around a father/son reunion, resulting in a better awareness about Billy and his music in Europe. So with the help of an employee at Phonogram, they started looking for Howard Joel. Billy told them that he thought his father was living in Germany, and that he was pretty sure he was still working for General Electric in some capacity. Meanwhile he had dates to play, and he set out on the road hoping that his father would be found.

Family has always been an integral part of Billy Joel. Going back to his youth right until today, Billy's family is the most important thing to him, whether it is blood relatives or the few members of Billy's small inner circle of friends who are fiercely loyal to Billy. It is the only thing in his complex life that he can connect with and that causes him to be truly grounded, even more so then his music, particularly when it comes to his musically gifted daughter Alexa, with whom Billy enjoys probably the only relationship in his life based purely on unconditional love.

Because of the fractured, wildly dysfunctional family life that he lived in Hicksville and even after, Billy has always looked to that family in an attempt to ground him. Creating his own family of friends and relatives as well as desperately trying to "fix" the one he came from has always been at the core of who Billy is. He supports his mother and sister today in very comfortable lifestyles, as well as a couple of other true friends. He also will superficially acknowledge his mother's eccentricities, but always quickly turns away from the negative and ends up aggressively defending her. He is a loyal son and brother and an intensely devoted father. The other aspect of Billy's life that is essential to understanding his innermost being is the relationship, or more accurately the non-relationship, that Billy has had with his father Howard. That and its far reaching emotional ramifications have left scars in Billy that result in severe episodes of depression, self-destructive behavior, anger, and attempts to self-medicate in order to erase attempt to the pain and control his behavior.

Billy also has constantly been on a search for just who he is, while at the same time battling the many deep personal issues and resulting behavioral changes. While he is touring around the world, particularly in Europe, Billy will often pick up a phone book in his hotel room and search it for Joels in an attempt to understand where it is that he truly belongs.

Billy started his 1972 European tour while Phonogram began the search through Germany for Howard. They didn't find him in Germany, but just as Billy was finishing up his tour in Italy he received a phone call from the Holland office to say that they had found Howard in Vienna, Austria.

Billy says:

I went to Europe looking for him. I remember the last gig I did was in Italy, I'm getting on the plane in Milan, and I get a message via telex, it says we found your father, he works for GE in Austria. Now I'm on the plane from Milan to New York and I'm flipping out.

Billy returned to California and with what must have been great anticipation called his father at his office in Austria in what would be a less than fulfilling phone conversation for Billy.

"I call his office," he said. "I say something like 'Hello, I'm your son.' He says, 'Oh my God, I thought you may have been killed in Vietnam.' Now I'm thinking to myself, well you could have called or written."

Regardless, a reunion was set up and the record company flew Howard to Los Angeles shortly after to reunite with Billy. From what everyone who knew Billy then says, he was a nervous wreck as the day approached. Finally it was time to go to the airport and Billy took a few of his friends to help him get through what must have been an incredibly anxiety-ridden day. The plane landed and Billy and his group waited at the gate until finally they saw this guy who had to have been Howard coming through. Even today the resemblance Billy has to his father is remarkable. With the same deep-set dark eyes, stature, and balding heads, there was no mistaking him.

Billy was living at the time in a rented house in Malibu with Elizabeth and Sean. He took his father back to the house and tried to explain to him what he had chosen to do with his life, and that he was beginning to see some levels of success. Howard, who never had any fondness for rock and roll, could not have cared less and the reunion remained strained at best. Adding to the cold atmosphere was Howard's announcement to Billy that he had remarried a woman named Audrey and that Billy had a seven-year-old half-brother in Europe named Charles Alexander. Billy's initial reaction was one of anger and betrayal. First he was hurt because he feared that someone had taken his place in his father's life, second that Howard had really betrayed Rosalind, who had had a miserable life for the most part raising her family while Howard lived with his new wife. Today, although the anger and scars remain, Billy and Alexander, as Billy's half-brother is known, are the best of friends, very close, and Billy is extremely proud Alexander's many successes. Billy's relationship with Howard is a different story. It seems that despite trying to heal the mistakes of the past, Howard and Billy remained estranged to a large degree, and it appears that that's the way that part of the story will end for Billy. Never fully being resolved, and instead left with a legacy of anger, hurt feelings, and deep emotional wounds that may never heal for the young boy who was abandoned. "After I tracked him down in my early 20s, we communicated for a while, but there was no follow-up," Billy says. "He has Parkinson's Disease. Some days he's there, some days he's not there. It's not the kind of Parkinson's that just causes you to shake. There are different types of Parkinson's—his type affects his nervous system and his is kinda on another planet. Motor function does not work very well—some days he is completely lucid some days he is not."

Regardless, Billy continues to try to heal the past with Howard, but Howard, still the dark and emotionally detached person he was back on

Meeting Lane, can be devastatingly critical of Billy even today with his great success. Billy the world-renowned superstar is still vulnerable to Howard's cutting words and behavior, and carries the hurt within him, although closely guarded, the open and raw wounds that have yet to heal from Hicksville. Many believe that the wounds and resulting anger drive some of his greatest music.

A perfect example has to do with Billy's huge hit "Just the Way You Are," a song that was a milestone in Billy's then just starting career, and one that even today is one of his best-known songs, played at many weddings. In a phone conversation that Billy and Howard were having one day, Billy was trying to explain the success of the song and its implications on his career when Howard interrupted Billy to tell him "You've written better songs than that."

As a result of this damaged relationship that Billy has always had with Howard it is very difficult for Billy to establish close friendships usually, and in his wake he leaves countless broken ones, with both males and females, including some very desirable and beautiful women. This stems first from a deep insecurity that Billy unfortunately carries with him, and has never truly been able to come to terms with, because of his inability to allow himself to go to that place of pain and darkness inside. It's a place that he has admitted that he has discussed with therapists a few times, only to walk away when it got too personal, too real. However, inevitably when it comes time for a relationship in Billy's life to end, again in the classic sense of that abandoned child, more often then not he allows someone else to do his dirty work, avoiding at any cost and in any way the confrontation.

A perfect example was in 1989 when Billy decided to make some changes in the original "Topper" band and let guitarist Russell Javors go as well as long-time bass player, and Mean Brothers member, Doug Stegmeyer. "After thirteen years it would have been nice to have gotten a phone call from Billy," Javors said. Russell rebounded though, going on to play with The Carpenters, before starting a company that designs and manufactures large radio-controlled cars and trucks and other toys in China.

Stegmeyer's fall was much harder unfortunately. In the thirteen years that he was a member of Billy's band, he allowed his entire identity to become wrapped up in just that, despite being what many today say was an incredibly gifted and innovative bass guitar player. He found out he was out of the band when Billy returned to the studio to record the *Storm Front* album and he didn't get a call. Doug also went on to play with The Carpenters along with Javors, but had a number of his own personal demons to deal with, and used excessive amounts of alcohol and drugs to numb his pain. Unfortunately his demons got the best of him, and in 1995 he shot and killed himself.

Atrie Ripp says:

Billy is the classic control freak who uses others to do his controlling. I always felt that he was terribly insecure about the world around him, and whether the world would like him or his music and whether or not they would understand or accept him. Some of his insecurities are those that we all share like, "Am I going to be able to pay my bills? Will people like me?" and some are indicative of Billy and his career choice like "Will people like my music? Am I a good enough performer?" I don't think Billy was ever insecure about his ability as a musician. And I don't think he was ever insecure about being a composer either. The insecurities came when the finger was directed at Billy the person, rather then Billy the gifted musician that he is.

# Chapter 14

While Billy's star was beginning to rise, things at Paramount Records were not going well. The company was hemorrhaging money like never before. As a result no records were being pressed and no one, executives or artists, was getting paid. It was truly a matter of a slow meltdown over at the headquarters on New York City's Columbus Circle, and Billy Joel was in the middle of it all.

He had gone on the road for about six months to promote his album and had yet to be paid any money. You didn't need a lawyer to see that something was seriously wrong. Artie Ripp saw the ship beginning to sink too. He wasn't getting paid by Paramount and as a result couldn't pay his artists, managers, or employees either. As the Paramount ship was going down everyone associated with it was being pulled down with it.

Billy was now finished with the tour and he, Elizabeth, and Sean were living in a rented house in Hampton Bays, Long Island, where Billy went to escape and try to write music as he struggled to figure out what to do next with his career. They rented a small house on the water during the off-season, and set up house, as Elizabeth commuted back and forth to Adelphi University for some college courses.

Meanwhile the money situation in Los Angeles was deteriorating fast as the checks to Artie Ripp from Paramount stopped and as a result the monthly checks to Irwin and subsequently Billy for his living expenses dried up.

Ripp said: "Basically, I had no more record deal. My cash flow was cut off from Paramount. I had no more money. Now I failed Billy but I was failing me."

Billy's domestic bliss in Hampton Bays was ruptured and he and Irwin had to quickly come up with a plan. Both had families to support, and neither Irwin or Billy was about to let the last six months of hard work go down the drain, so they did the only thing they could do and packed up their lives again for a move to Los Angeles. If they were going to be broke, it was a lot easier to do it in LA than in New York, and besides LA was the entertainment capital of the world and they'd work something out, they thought.

"We put everything into Elizabeth's station wagon and drove across the states," Billy said. "I was going to get myself out of a bad business deal, and get myself a lawyer and different management. I knew that I'd been screwed, and the people that did it were in LA, so I figured it was a good base of operation for me to try and get out of the deal. I thought that they'd never look for me right under their noses, so I used a pseudonym."

Billy, Elizabeth, and young Sean arrived in California and set up house with Irwin and his wife and son Brett in one of those horrible and dingy Los Angeles motel/apartment complexes on the Santa Monica Boulevard, that Artie Ripp found for them.

"We all had apartments in the same complex that Artie Ripp's company put us up in," Mazur said. "It was basically a shit hole, but it was a roof over our head and we didn't have to pay the rent."

Despite Ripp's and Mazur's attempts to keep Billy's emerging career on track, there was no money coming in. The ship was sinking, and now sinking faster then ever.

For Ripp it was now a situation where he had to jump ship if he was going to save himself. With about half a million dollars invested in Billy Joel to this point, according to Ripp, it was time to bail out.

"At the end of the day when you added up the recording costs, which I bore, the tour costs, the support costs, the airplane fare, the food, the hotels, the car, the this, that and the other thing, in 1970–71 I had spent half a million bucks," Ripp says. "A huge amount of money for the time."

Billy, Irwin, and Elizabeth would be left to fend for themselves, but with Billy's extraordinary talent they would be OK, Ripp thought, whether he really believed it or not. There was no choice at this point and Ripp went to deliver the message he dreaded.

"I had become the person that he had depended upon," Ripp said. "I was responsible for making sure he had money to pay his rent, a roof over his head and he could take care of his obligations and he could have some sort of dignity and now I had to turn around and say I haven't got the money. Now I became the guy he had to escape from. I had become the father that walked out on him when he was a kid."

But Ripp had no choice; his back was against the wall. He was on the verge of bankruptcy and the banks which only months earlier had opened their coffers to him were now not returning his calls.

"I was in a situation where I had to figure out how I was going to pay my own bills," he said. "I knew that I had to somehow get out of my deal with Gulf and Western if I was going to survive."

As often happens in the surreal world of Los Angeles and the record business, Ripp in just a short time had gone from a record company wonder kid with his own label, cutting deals with perceived giants like Gulf and

Western and Paramount, to an independent producer with no outlet for his projects.

Today he claims that in order to extricate himself from his contract with Gulf and Western, he had to go deeply into debt: "In that interim of time with no money coming in, I went deep into debt, one to buy out of Gulf and Western and, two, to support Billy and his band and Elizabeth and Sean and my family and the obligations that I had as best I could."

Whether that is entirely true or not will never be known, but like all stories this one has two sides, and it is certain that Ripp did have to make a series of concessions, both financially and professionally, to get out of his contract.

Ripp continues:

I made a decision. I knew that I had a diamond—Billy—here and I now have a coffin—the contract. To me, being in Paramount though I respected and loved and appreciated Jim Judelson, who was the President, the record company was no place. So now I had to figure out how do I get out of this platinum coffin, with diamond studs in it and how do I get out of here and get Billy and the rest of my artists free and own the masters. Because I had a fucking sweet deal. I had a deal that paid me a million dollars a year.

His description of the events which freed him from his obligations to Gulf and Western, but caused him to forfeit a supposed salary of a million dollars a year, is classic Artie Ripp:

I had to absorb all of the accounts payable. So let's say there was two million dollars in accounts payable, manufacturing costs, whatever it was, I had to absorb all of those costs and I was responsible now for all of the artist obligations, and all the production obligations. So now the thing was, how do I get my child—Billy—past the Nazis? I know what I'll do, I'll get a cart, I'll fill it with straw and I'll put horse shit over the straw and I'll put my child and my jewels underneath the horse shit and the hay. Okay? And then I'll get right past the fucking gate. So I effectively put my love, of Billy Joel, underneath the hay and the horse shit to make them believe that I was a creative failure, that they had made a bad bet and that they were getting off cheap, getting out of the two years that they owed me at a million dollars a year. Because they had two million that they had to pay me plus they had the accounts payable that they would have to absorb and payout as well, and marketing costs and so on.

Evidently it worked. Artie was now free of his contractual obligations to Gulf and Western, but by no means in the clear yet. Neither was his stable of artists, in particular Billy Joel who now had no money coming in and with a partner and her son to support, he had to do something, and quickly. He hated living in the apartment/motel complex, was totally disillusioned about his management and what his next steps would be. Things were not looking good for Billy right now and he wanted some changes in his life. Luckily they were on the horizon.

Ripp says:

I rented a house for Billy in the Hollywood Hills. Then shortly after, Billy decided that he didn't want Irwin to manage him anymore. And he came to me and he said I'd like you to be my manager. I told him I couldn't do that. Billy evidently was not ready for that answer. "What do you mean you can't do that?" he said to me. I told him I couldn't do that because Irwin's your manager. Irwin's my friend. I can't take you from him. If you've made up your mind that you're going to deal with a different manager, that's not something I'm recommending, not something I'm supporting. I think you're making a mistake because the guy has sacrificed everything to get you where you are.

But sometimes, as we know, intimacy breeds contempt rather than contentment. Billy's mind was made up: he wanted Artie to manage him, and for Ripp to blow him off like that was inexcusable to Billy. But Ripp it was too much of a conflict. He knew he could never negotiate for him when he was first responsible for his production and publishing. "Could I have an arm's length negotiation with myself?" Ripp asked rhetorically.

Now Billy had been rejected by Artie Ripp and found himself in a precarious position both financially and professionally. Irwin Mazur had no well of money to draw from, and being rejected by Artie Ripp created the beginning of the end of Billy's relationship with Artie. He was fed up with what he perceived as a long list of empty promises and plans that never came to fruition, and clearly at a crisis point this fall of 1972, he did the only thing that in a situation like this he could. He split, dropped off the radar screen, or so he thought, while at the same time going out and finding himself a job.

"At that particular point Billy disappeared into the woodwork, into the Executive Lounge or whatever it was, and with my promotion guy John Troy," Artie said. John Troy worked for Artie and had become very friendly with Billy. They were close drinking buddies, and John, who had his own problems with alcohol excess, fancied himself as an advisor to Billy. So he did the only logical thing that an alcoholic would do—he left his job with Artie and got a job as the bartender at the piano bar so he and Billy would be together.

At the same time John and Sandy Gibson were working for Artie Ripp and still somehow getting paid. Sandy was Artie's publicist and John, who went on to a career as a television journalist for Fox television, was Artie's promotion man. Sandy befriended Billy and Elizabeth and, like many people then whose paths crossed Billy's, realized too that he had an extraordinary talent. She undoubtedly saw Artie's ship floundering, and knew that if she could just gain Billy's trust, that she might be able to get him the contract he needed to make him a huge star, and in the process endear herself to him, which she hoped, as anyone in that situation would, would all translate into cash.

"He was twenty-three years old and didn't even have his driver's license yet," she said. "I drove Billy to the interviews at piano bars."

Billy soon landed a job at a bar named Corky's on Van Nuys Boulevard that only lasted a short time, and by December 1972 he was working at the Executive Lounge on Wilshire Boulevard under the pseudonym Bill Martin, his first and middle names. Elizabeth also got a job there as a cocktail waitress, but kept her relationship with Billy secret from the customers because she thought it would be better for her tips. As much as some might have perceived this series of events in Billy's life as a reversal, true to Billy's promise to himself after leaving the psychiatric ward at Meadowbrook Hospital, he never allowed himself any self-pity. After all he'd already made four albums and believed in himself enough to know that more were coming.

According to Angelique Norton, who with her husband Russell owned the Executive Lounge, Billy "had a following—he was a good draw," she said. "On slow nights I'd ask him to play some of the classics, like a polonaise by Chopin, and he'd do them. He didn't really like to play requests for people he told me, and he definitely didn't like it when customers started singing along." No doubt because he felt it compromised the integrity of the music.

"I've never given myself more then two seconds of self-pity," he said. "I realized that the piano bar gig is something that a lot of people do for years and maybe their entire lives. And they're happy to have the work."

But Billy always had his sights set on a bigger goal. Soon after starting work at his new job Billy, Elizabeth, and Sean would move out of their Hollywood Hills house and up to Malibu to John and Sandy Gibson's secluded house. Shortly after the New Year John and Sandy had been approached by Atlantic Records in New York to work for them. They were promised better money and an apartment on Park Avenue as one of the "perks." With Artie Ripp still trying to emerge from the ashes completely, they jumped at the job. Now with a Park Avenue apartment to shortly call home they offered Billy and Elizabeth their place in Malibu as long as they covered the mortgage payment that was just over two hundred dollars a month and the utilities. Billy and Elizabeth took the deal, and things again were starting to look up for them.

For the coming months Billy's nights were dedicated to playing old standards for tips at the Executive Lounge and doing his classic imitations that he had always been great at anyway. He earned $225 a week, plus tips, but spent the time often in a self-described "alcoholic haze."

Feeling out his audiences was crucial to filling his tip jar, and Billy often had a number of "interesting" experiences, one night even launching into an extended version of "God Bless America" because of a group of red-neck construction workers, who found fault with Billy's long hair.

"If somebody asked for a Sinatra song, I'd get into doing a whole put-on Sinatra thing," Billy remembers. "What you're doing in a piano bar basically is playing for tips, so you try to pick out what will get you bread from the audience."

If the guy requesting the song was Irish, Billy would play him "Danny Boy." If he were Italian, he'd get something from *The Godfather*, and that's the way he would try to fill his brandy snifter each night. As the great observer of life that Billy is, he also was watching the characters that frequented and worked at the bar. Billy became the "Piano Man" for that eighteen months or so, soaking everything and everyone up that he observed, while fine-tuning his art and trying to hide out as well as he could from his obligations to Artie Ripp.

This last part of the story, like many others in Billy's long and complex history, is in fact more fiction then truth. Where Billy was at the time was common knowledge to pretty much everyone associated with him, and even though he was playing under the alias 'Bill Martin' at the Executive Lounge, Billy Joel was also performing at the Troubadour nightclub when he could, continuing to generate interest that would soon pay off for him. Artie Ripp also was not out of the picture as many today believe. He was in fact working tirelessly to try and get Billy a recording contract now that he had freed himself from the Gulf and Western/Paramount Records nightmare.

It was at this point that Elizabeth began to exercise what would be ultimately an incredible influence in a relatively short time. She must have played some sort of a role in Billy's decision to go underground. After all, she too was fed up with the way Billy was being handled, and always had an eye to emerge from the mediocrity she had been raised in. She knew Billy's great potential and in many ways was the perfect yang to Billy's yin. She is as complex and brilliant as Billy is in many ways, and also like Billy she is very tough, in fact maybe tougher. The one crucial aspect to her personality then that Billy lacked was that she was never afraid to be confrontational.

The many nights playing the Executive Lounge had been good for Billy. He'd continued to work on his music and his act, and as the nights added up his confidence grew. Couple that with his great innate talent and it was no surprise that others began to take notice of this guy Bill Martin playing the piano out on Wilshire Boulevard.

"After a while the music business in Los Angeles knew I was there," Billy said. "They'd heard that I was playing in this piano bar and they'd come down and say, 'Why don't you play your own stuff?'"

It was time for the Piano Man to take it to the next level, and Billy with his great instincts knew it.

# Chapter 15

In mid-1962 Jerry Moss and Herb Alpert both invested one hundred dollars each and formed a partnership they called Carnival Records. Shortly after, they discovered another company was using the name and changed the name of their company to A&M Records. Almost immediately they began to rack up successes with a diverse group of artists including Alpert and his Tijuana Brass, Waylon Jennings, George Harrison, and Tina Turner.

Jerry Moss was a kid from the Bronx who graduated from Brooklyn College, thanks to the G.I. Bill, and shortly after met Alpert and formed their company to promote the diverse music they both loved so much. By 1973 A&M was a powerhouse in the recording industry with offices in New York City and Los Angeles. Moss was a 38-year-old record company president, and had assimilated himself well into the laid-back LA lifestyle, yet retained that fierceness that comes with growing up on the streets of the Bronx. He was hungry to find his next star when he got a call from Artie Ripp, one of the other street kids from New York. Ross agreed to listen to Ripp's client at the Executive Lounge and liked what he heard. He offered Ripp a contract for Billy at A&M, which Ripp, despite his precarious financial position at the time rejected, soon proving that all things, despite how bad they might seem at first, happen for a good reason.

At the same time John and Sandy Gibson were enjoying their new job with Ahmet Ertegun's Atlantic Records in New York City. John was doing the promotion for Atlantic, while Sandy was doing their publicity. They hadn't forgotten their friend Billy Joel who was living in their Malibu house and at each opportunity would pitch him to Ertegun, hoping that when he was in Los Angeles, as he often was, that he would listen to Billy play. In the meantime, Artie Ripp was also still working to find Billy a record contract despite burning the A&M bridge with Jerry Moss. He was also in touch with Atlantic Records. Finally everything lined up as it should and a date was set at Ripp's LA home for Billy to play for Atlantic.

Ripp said:

I invited Jerry Wexler, Ahmet Ertegun and Jerry Greenberg to my home in L.A. They came up and met Billy and Billy played them "Piano Man" and he played them "Captain Jack" and played them a number of other songs. They loved Billy and we shook hands and basically I made a deal with Ahmet Ertegun and those guys to have Billy with the label that he chose. He wanted to be with Atlantic. Ahmet and I make a deal. We shake hands, deal's done. He's going to be an Atlantic artist, he got the label he wanted and terrific.

But was it? Simultaneously a series of events in New York City and Los Angeles were going on in the halls of Columbia Records, then run by the legendary Clive Davis. The buzz that the song "Captain Jack" had created in Philadelphia and now beyond had caught the attention of executives at Columbia thanks in a large part to Becky Mancusco-Shargo and the review in the *New York Times* by John Rockwell.

Irwin Mazur was still Billy's manager after all this and was desperately trying to find a record company for him too in early 1973. Mazur relates:

At this point I was incredibly frustrated about the *Cold Spring Harbor* album, and the fact that it went nowhere. One day I get a call from Kip Cohen, head of A&R at Columbia Records, he says, "Clive Davis would like to meet you next week at the Beverly Hills Hotel about Billy Joel." Well, to say that I thought things were looking up then would have been an understatement. I tell Billy about it, and he was as excited about it as I was, but I had no idea what was going on with Artie Ripp and Atlantic Records either.

The next week came and Irwin was driven down to the Beverly Hills Hotel by his wife for his meeting with Davis. As Mazur recalls:

We meet, and Davis is telling me that he made Janis Joplin a star, he believes Billy will be a star, I tell him I'm glad he recognizes that. "I'd love to sign Billy," Davis tells me. "Get out of the contract with Artie Ripp," he says. "Now I'm not about to fuck Artie after all he'd done, so I figure the way to do the deal is to include Artie in it. "That's not the way I operate," I told Davis. "Well, I don't talk to Artie," Davis tells me. So I'm now in the middle.

Mazur left his meeting ecstatic, but he knew he had to act quickly and to convince Ripp that it was in Billy's best interests to sign with Columbia. "I wanted Columbia," Mazur said. "They were the Rolls-Royce of record companies back in those days."

Mazur returned home and called Billy to tell him the news, only to find out about the deal Ripp had cut with Atlantic Records. It didn't matter, Billy wanted to sign with Columbia, making the prophecy come true that he'd predicted to his mother when he left high school just six years earlier.

"I wanted to be on Columbia Records because it was Bob Dylan's label," Billy said. "In the late sixties and seventies the hipper label was Atlantic. Columbia was more high-toned, but they had Bob Dylan."

What Billy wanted was the only thing that mattered to Mazur. He set out to make the deal happen, knowing that one of the biggest obstacles he had was going to be Artie Ripp and his contract with Billy.

Meanwhile Columbia was in high gear trying to sign Billy. Davis made it understood that he wanted him, and all their resources came out. A meeting between Clive Davis and Billy Joel was set up at the Beverly Hills Hotel and Davis gave it full power.

"You're not an Atlantic artist, you're a Columbia artist," he told Billy. "You'll be with Dylan, Johnny Mathis, Johnny Cash, and Springsteen at Columbia."

It was music to Billy Joel's ears.

"Billy comes home from his meeting with Clive Davis and tells me that he doesn't want to be on Atlantic records," Ripp said. "I said wait a minute, we made a deal with Ahmet. It's done, I gave him my word."

"It didn't matter," Mazur remembers. "Billy doesn't want to sign on Atlantic Records."

Ripp was now outgunned. He'd made this deal with Atlantic Records but now had to go and break it.

"I go see Artmet and tell him that the deal's off, that Billy doesn't want to be with Atlantic," Ripp relates. "Ahmet said, 'OK, what the fuck more is it going to cost—what am I being held up for?' I said, 'Ahmet, I didn't do this. I give you my word; I thought the deal is done. It is not a question of pulling a holdup on you, and saying that if you give us another fifty or a hundred grand that it'll happen, or another two points or whatever and the problem goes away. Billy wants to be on Columbia. Clive convinced him he should be with Columbia. They went behind my back.' 'Fuck 'em. Let him go to Columbia Records,' Ahmet said finally. 'I'd love to have him. I wish we would have him. He'd be a great success here.'"

Now that part of the insanity was out of the way, and in just a few weeks, Billy Joel had gone from having no record contract, to now having two major labels after him. But the contract that Artie Ripp had with Billy Joel still loomed on the horizon. Columbia had one of their attorneys read the contract to see what if anything could be done about it, if Artie could be offed somehow legally.

"There was a young attorney named Spencer Proffer on the legal staff at

Columbia working with Clive," Artie said. "He was given the job to look at my contract. He reports back, 'There ain't no exit outta this. This is a solid as the fucking Rock of Gibraltar. There is no way we can break the contract without getting sued. You ain't going to break the contract; all you'll do is buy yourself a lawsuit.' "

Evidently this was the case because it set up a relationship between Billy Joel, Artie Ripp, and Michael Lang that would last for years to come. Artie and Michael were to each receive approximately 25 cents from Billy Joel's cut for each album that he sold, insuring that each of them for many years would do very well thanks to Billy's great success, and all because of that tape that Michael Lang had heard playing in Irwin Mazur's office that day in New York City. Irwin, however, wouldn't do as well, and despite his dedication to Billy during all these years, his days were numbered.

"My deal with Columbia was for ten original Billy Joel albums and a best-of," Ripp said. "Anything that came from those albums was part of my deal. I figured that if Columbia wasn't going to give me back my half-million dollar investment in Billy that they would pay me a royalty. I know I am perceived as the bad guy, but Billy didn't have to pay it to me, the record company did."

In reality this wasn't the case, Billy was paying Artie Ripp and Michael Lang out of his pocket and would until he renegotiated his contract some years later with Columbia and got them to pay the royalty. Ripp no longer receives any money, but did very well in the meantime, generating over seven million dollars for himself. Michael Lang, who has never gotten himself into a position financially where he had to be bought out, still receives a piece of each Billy Joel album.

Before Billy signed with Columbia there was another influential person who would help Billy make his decision—one that was emerging as a powerful force in Billy's life. Elizabeth, always an astute business person, as well as a keen observer, realized that if Billy signed with Columbia rather then Atlantic, Billy's potential for world distribution of his albums was much greater. Columbia had a distribution network set up throughout Europe and therefore a much more formidable presence then Atlantic in terms of distribution and ultimately money. Elizabeth also liked Walter Yetnikoff, who with Clive Davis now gone, was beginning his unforgettable reign as president of Columbia Records. Kip Cohen signed Billy to Columbia in the spring of 1973.

It seemed as if Billy's great talent as well as years of hard work, and some of his friendships, even if there were ulterior motives, seemed to be finally beginning to pay off for him. But as is also too often the case, as Billy's star was rising, the perception that others around him had of Billy, including those closest to him, began to change dramatically. Billy now, in addition to having a great talent, suddenly had a great earning potential, and when money enters the picture, people change dramatically.

Elizabeth was watching the latest developments in Billy's life closer then anyone and from a better perspective then anyone too. She saw people jockeying for position as Billy's star rose and picked her ally wisely in Sandy Gibson. She didn't waste any time galvanizing her position with Billy and in no time changes in Billy's camp were occurring. The first to go was Irwin Mazur, despite his great loyalty to Billy all those years. It seemed strange at the time, and does even today really. Irwin didn't have any contract with Billy that paid him off for each record he sold; in fact he had no contract at all with Billy, which undoubtedly contributed to his early demise. Those in Billy's inner circle now wanted Irwin out. It was the only way that they could advance their own agendas and seal their positions at the same time. Irwin today feels that it was Elizabeth who led the lynching party, but she couldn't have done that it in all likelihood without the support of others like Artie Ripp, Michael Lang, Sandy Gibson, and John Troy, who these days was fancying himself more and more as Billy's manager.

"She was the witch that started to poison Billy's mind against me. She was the one that got Sandy Gibson on her side. Sandy had worked for Artie and it was because of that and her leading Billy that Billy gave me the heave-ho just as the Columbia deal was finishing up," Mazur said. "He did a very 'intelligent' thing of going to an alcoholic named John Troy, as a manager— an interim manager—before Elizabeth actually took over."

Any interest that Irwin had in Billy had now been bought up by Artie Ripp. "Artie made a good deal with him so that I wouldn't be out on the street," Mazur says today. "I had no royalty participation, instead I got a flat payment of say half a million dollars that was to be paid out over three years, let's say. I also had my pride in seeing my dream for Billy realized."

If anyone then that was associated with Billy was really looking out for his interests before their own, it would have been Irwin Mazur. He had now been with Billy for seven years, through the days of The Hassles, the embarrassment of *Attila*, which he stuck it out for, and then the penniless *Cold Spring Harbor* album and subsequent tour phase. Now with Billy's star rising, things were changing. People's agendas were becoming more and more self-centered, and it was now everyone looking out for what they hoped would be their piece of the success, rather then all bonding together to insure Billy's success.

"I was always looked upon as the guy who, at that time, was hanging on when in reality I was the one that carried Billy torch," Mazur said. "It was the most unjustified assassination, but everybody was looking for an angle in. The way they got an angle in was getting me assassinated. That's what happened. So when Billy and I split, Billy never had a reason. It was never you stole from me. You did the wrong things. It was none of that. I've outgrown you—he didn't even use those words."

In his typical fashion, Billy avoided being the one that delivered the message, instead leaving it to Michael Lang and Artie Ripp to do his dirty work.

"If there was one reason why Billy gave me the heave-ho it was because Billy hated Artie so much that he felt that I sold out to Artie Ripp—that I sold out Billy's interest to Artie. And, in fact, that wasn't the case. I was always looking out for Billy's interests," Mazur continues. "If it had not been for my developing the confidence within Artie during the *Cold Spring Harbor* tour the industry would have never realized about Billy Joel. It was because I had the financial commitment with Artie to keep Billy on the road. That was not in any contract. I never had the chance to explain that to Billy or maybe he just never wanted to realize it."

Regardless Irwin Mazur was out, John Troy was in, if only temporarily, as Billy's manager, and a new circle of people was beginning to form around Billy Joel, each one eager to get a piece of the money pie.

# Chapter 16

With his new Columbia contract in place Billy had to start producing. In typical fashion, Billy, who is a tireless worker, began fine-tuning some new material he had been working on, while polishing up some old songs that had been around for two years now, never making it onto the doomed *Cold Spring Harbor* album.

"Some of the things on this album are old like 'Captain Jack,' 'Travelin' Prayer,' and 'Billy the Kid' are two years old. The rest comes from about six months ago," Billy told an interviewer in 1974. "I'm not sure where I was aiming at with this album. I guess they're just songs."

The album Billy referred to would be his first for Columbia Records, and with their resources, both in money and people it would be a giant step for Billy musically. After fine-tuning his craft for almost two years now, he was up to the task. The first step was to get into the studio and start putting a band together. Time was booked at North Hollywood's Devonshire Studio, and again with Columbia's money, Michael Stewart was chosen to produce the album. To date Michael had produced only two other albums, both for his brother John Stewart, and was going into the studio with the philosophy that the best way to showcase Billy on an album was to back him up with a mix of the best studio musicians he could find. He saw Billy as a James Taylor type of performer and wanted to showcase Billy's songs and his voice, and in doing so totally missed the point that was so basic about Billy, that at his most inner self, he is a rock and roll animal. Other heavyweights like Ron Malo were tapped for the engineering, insuring that there would be no "chipmunk" sound to this album. Jimmie Haskell and Michael Omartian were responsible for the arrangements, all of course with Billy's sizeable input. Omartian also would play the accordion on a couple of songs, an instrument which Billy also was skilled at having been left one by Howard when he left the Hicksville house some years before.

Musician heavyweights such as Eric Weissberg, the banjo player responsible for the hit "Dueling Banjos" from the movie *Deliverance*, joined the group, as did Rhys Clark, the *Cold Spring Harbor* drummer that Billy liked working with, and Emory Gordy, the bassist that played on the same album.

Other heavyweight session musicians included guitar players Richard Bennett, Dean Parks, and Larry Carlton, and bassist Wilton Felder. Billy Armstrong played the fiddle, Ron Tutt the drums, and Fred Heilbrun the banjo. It was an impressive list of musicians for a relatively unknown artist's debut album, but one that would do Billy's music and lyrics justice, and which also verified Columbia's belief in Billy's abilities.

The album *Piano Man* was released on November 9, 1973. The single with the same name had been released a week earlier. At first Billy was unhappy with the album's sound, thinking the sound of his voice, which he's never been comfortable with, sounded too mushy. When the album started to climb up the charts in the first months of 1974 thanks to the title song, Billy's perspective changed, however. "This is a hit song? You gotta be kidding me," Billy said in his typical minimizing fashion. "It's just the same chorus over and over again."

The song that shares the album's title had been a concern initially to Jerry Wexler, the Atlantic Records executive, the night that Billy played it for him, Clive Davis, and Jerry Greenburg in Artie Ripp's living room just months earlier. Wexler had felt that it was too much like the hit song "Mr. Bojangles" recorded just three years earlier by the Nitty Gritty Dirt Band, and in fact had asked Billy that night "If 'Mr. Bojangles' hadn't been written, you wouldn't have written that, right?" This was not a good thing to ask Billy Joel who always has looked at his songs as his children, and additionally always has been very sensitive about being accused of plagiarism.

"I didn't steal it!" Billy answered, and with no doubt that he was telling the truth. " 'Mr. Bojangles' is one thing, 'Piano Man' is another. They have a similar structure and chord progression, but that's it."

Choosing "Piano Man" as the first Billy Joel single by Columbia had surprised Billy. Although he liked the song and was certainly proud of it, Billy found the melody to "Piano Man" a bit bland and even repetitive. The song is in fact a waltz, written in three quarter time. It draws much of its inspiration from Billy's days at the Executive Lounge, although if you listen to Michael Omartian's accordion, it may also conjure up images of a Paris bistro. It is a song where characters appear in it, characters that in this case were based on real people who frequented the Executive Lounge during Billy's tenure there. Also, like many of Billy's later works, the lyrics suggest the pain that the writer and performer feels with the line "Man, what are you doing here?" surely a question Billy often asked himself during those nights working the piano bar. Also true to Billy Joel form, his lyrics show no sympathy with the cast of characters, yet he is not overly critical either. It is a song that was so clearly autobiographical even then, that it didn't take his fans long to associate Billy Joel with the narrator of the song. "Piano Man" is also the first Billy Joel song that speaks of characters, and in so doing shows the great strength that Billy has as a story-teller, something that would become so much more apparent as his career evolved.

"I don't make my songs for any audience," Billy said. "I make my songs for me. I know that may sound self-serving, but I can't second guess an audience."

"Captain Jack," the song that stirred up such an interest in Billy, also appears on the album, as does the classic "The Ballad of Billy the Kid." The latter is a deliberately inaccurate retelling of the outlaw's life story, the singer's point being that anyone has the power to reinvent himself if he dares. It is also a complex piece of music that borders on being symphonic, and has an enormous number of ingredients that Jimmie Haskell the arranger and Billy the songwriter make work. Billy's storytelling again reflects a great sense of detail, which instantly makes the listener appreciate and like the character who we learn is unfortunately doomed with the words "under the Boot Hill grave that bears his name." With its diverse influences ranging from grade B Spaghetti Western type music to that of the premier American composer Aaron Copeland, who will also influence many more Billy Joel songs, it's easy to see that Billy's deep influence by The Beatles which was apparent on the *Cold Spring Harbor* album was now only part of his growing complexity as a musician. All in all "Billy the Kid" is the most interesting song on the album, and promises the listener much more in the form of interesting and complex music in the days ahead from Billy "the Kid" Joel. With the album *Piano Man* it is clear that the as yet unheard of Billy Joel had the necessary ingredients as a musician, songwriter, and performer to take his career to the next level, particularly if he could create the necessary synergy in the studio and on stage with a band of his own. In fact if there is one disappointing aspect to the album it is that because Billy at this point had no band of his own, and recorded *Piano Man* with studio musicians, the album lacks that gritty and more personal feel that subsequent Billy Joel albums would have. Artie Ripp agrees. "It took time for Billy to put a band together of his own, that would 'get' him and his music," he said. "When it was all done, *Piano Man* was a studio cat album."

Also indicative of what will be much more of the influence responsible for Billy Joel's music, the song "You're My Home" was written for his now wife Elizabeth as a gift prior to his Columbia contract. "I didn't have any money to give her a present, so I said 'this is for you.'" Elizabeth's response to Billy was: "Does that mean I get the publishing rights?"

Regardless, from Columbia's perspective the album was a success. With their seemingly bottomless pit of resources, they worked tirelessly for six months promoting the album.

"My first album was a nightmare. I could never find it anywhere on tour," Billy said, but with this one he knew everyone was working hard to promote it.

Their efforts paid off. The album peaked at #25 on the Billboard Hot 100 chart and hit #4 on the Adult Contemporary chart, spinning off at least two more relatively successful 45s. All in all *Piano Man* was a success. It was eventually certified gold and then platinum and convinced Columbia records president Walter Yetnikoff and other executives then at Columbia, who at this strategic stage in the company's history were dedicated to building careers for musicians, rather then spitting out one hit wonders, that another Billy Joel album made sense.

With an album out, Billy had to do what all musicians must, and a tour was set up. His first stop was as the hometown boy at Max's Kansas City in New York City. Max's at the time was at the center of New York's "café society." On any given night you might see Andy Warhol, Lou Reed, Mick Jagger, Truman Capote or Allen Ginsberg holding court. Max's had a small stage and seating for about only 150 people, but because of its high profile, numerous record company people, journalists, and others involved in the music business could be counted on to be there.

Billy and his small touring band hit the stage that night in February 1974, and as luck would have it John Rockwell, the *New York Times* music critic, was there. It was one of Billy's better performances, and Rockwell reflected that in his review on February 23, 1974. "Mr. Joel is fast developing into an important artist," Rockwell wrote. "He plays the piano both versatilely and virtuosically . . . But what is most important is Mr. Joel's songs and the way he sings them. Rockwell was impressed, although he did find some fault with Billy's performance. He felt that Billy was overly theatrical, and that his arrangements came close to being "bombastic." He also felt that Billy's lyrics tended towards the "rhetorical." All in all though it was a good review, and people now were taking more and more notice of Billy Joel.

As a result of Rockwell's review Billy was booked to open for Jesse Colin Young at his first Carnegie Hall show in May 1974. Once more the audience agreed that Billy Joel and his band was a new talent that was worth seeing. Rockwell was once more positive. "One knew that this artist was fulfilling all of his promise as a musician and a star," Rockwell wrote. *The Village Voice* agreed. While criticizing the lights and sound at Billy's performance, they nevertheless wrote that Billy's "suburban songs, showed a keen perception of the mundane and the vital."

The scruffy kid from Hicksville, who had been through the wringer as he tried to build his career, was now in just under three months a rising star in the music world. Playing Carnegie Hall was the symbol of artistic success in the music world, but Billy tried to remain grounded. When asked how it felt to fulfill one of his dreams, Billy's response was simply: "Carnegie Hall felt just as I thought it would. It felt good."

1974 was also the year that Billy would make his first national television appearance, and in typical Billy Joel fashion, he would do it on his own terms. Billy has always been fiercely protective of his music, and concerned about the manner in which it is presented to the public. As such he has always refused to play back to back with any artist whose music he didn't respect, or who he felt was tasteless, mentioning the band Kiss at one point as a perfect example. Again because he felt it diverted attention away from his music, and cheapened the musical experience, Billy has also refused to play in front of a neon backdrop that announced the name of the television show.

"If I'm going to play on someone's show, it's going to be the 'Billy Joel Show,'" he said.

But Billy was in sort of a dilemma now. His then manager Jon Troy had booked Billy for an appearance on Don Kirshner's *Rock Concert*, exactly the type of show Billy despised. Wisely, though, Billy didn't want to miss the opportunity of a national audience and sent Kirshner some footage from another regional show that he'd done titled *Made in Chicago*. He played three songs on the tape: "Piano Man," "Somewhere Along the Line," and "Captain Jack," but his performance was much less than what audiences had come to expect from Billy and certainly not the best image for potentially new fans. In the footage you see a young Billy Joel at the piano, eyes fixed on the keyboards, and never playing to the camera. It was the exact opposite of his current high-energy shows, but nevertheless the tape was used, and he met his obligation to Kirshner.

Despite *Piano Man*'s success Billy would not realize much in the form of material rewards. The album netted Billy less then $8,000, something which justifiably neither Billy or Elizabeth were pleased with, and which caused Elizabeth to announce that she would be replacing John Troy, whose drinking was now pretty much out of control, as Billy's manager. She was to soon realize that, at this point in Billy's career, managing him professionally as well as personally was too much to handle, and relinquished the responsibility to someone with more experience. Elizabeth did school herself, though, for down the road, by remaining an integral part of Billy's decision-making.

In the meantime, Jim Guercio and Larry Fitzgerald's Caribou Management was brought in to manage Billy. Under Guercio's leadership Caribou was not only managing top acts like The Beach Boys and Chicago, but also had their own state of the art recording studio in the mountain seclusion above Boulder, Colorado. With Caribou taking over the management responsibilities, Elizabeth could focus on other issues relating to Billy's emerging career including his publishing and copyrights, which at the time were a mess. It was at this point that her tenacity and steel shell began to make itself known to executives in the music business. The pretty little girl in mini-skirts looked like a pushover but, as they were to find out, she was anything but. Elizabeth soon became famous for sitting in on meetings that she insisted on, listening to the "suits" sitting in the room try to bullshit her, never thinking that she was a serious threat. When they were all done pontificating all over themselves, Elizabeth would often erupt in a tirade which would totally intimidate these executives, and inevitably result in Elizabeth getting exactly what she wanted for Billy and ultimately herself.

On May 7, Billy wrapped up the *Piano Man* tour in Cincinnati, Ohio and within months had returned to Devonshire Studio to begin recording his next album, *Streetlife Serenade*, an album that would be a reflection of the Southern California lifestyle and environment that Billy had now adopted, yet had never really felt connected to. After all Billy was a kid from Long Island and from Hicksville at that. The laid-back, mellow lifestyle of Los Angeles was alien to him, yet he was wise enough to know that he had to stick around just long enough to maintain his sanity and to insure that his star kept rising.

For *Streetlife Serenade* Billy again used Michael Stewart as his producer at Columbia's urging, although on the album jacket Billy shares credit with him for this responsibility. They also assembled another group of top-notch musicians including some from the *Cold Spring Harbor* album and also *Piano Man*, along with Tom Whitehorse, a great banjo and pedal steel guitar player, and Joe Clayton on congas and William Smith on organ. Columbia also was trying to build a team of people in the studio that would work with Billy on the road, including engineer Ron Malo and soundman Brian Ruggles, who today still are with Billy. If there was one problem with the album musically it would turn out to be the wide selection of nine guitar players used, which many feel resulted in a sort of "disconnect" with the rest of the musicians. While being able to work with such great studio talent was a testament to just how much his record company might have believed in him, it didn't translate necessarily into a guaranteed hit record, or certainly not into a band that Billy could take on the road and expect any great synergy from. It was clearly the wrong formula for Billy Joel.

"They weren't necessarily a great band. Everybody can say that nowadays as far a musicianship goes," says Billy. "But who gives a shit? The songs were great from cut one to cut end. That's what I base what I do on—it's all material, it's all writing."

If there was going to be another "issue" with the album it would have to do with the influences Billy now was experiencing in his songwriting. The gritty street kid from blue-collar Hicksville who was now firmly ensconced in Southern California, home to the laid-back sounds of the likes of Jackson

Browne and The Eagles, was trying to force himself into adopting the lifestyle. He had been on the west coast for three years now, and was experimenting with things like natural foods and "mellowing out" like many of the upwardly mobile ex-hippies he had befriended were. But, like trying to put a round peg in a square hole, it wouldn't ultimately work.

As a result the songs of *Streetlife Serenade* depict another type of suburbia than the one that Joel grew up in. Many of the scenes in the songs describe settings like the urban ghettos of Los Angeles, parties across the Mexican border, and the wide open spaces of Southern California rather then those that we would later come to expect and admire from Billy Joel's writing. In a nutshell, *Streetlife Serenade* is an album about the city that is really a suburb, Los Angeles, and for Billy, even after three years it remained an alien place in many ways.

With his package of new songs Billy entered the studio to record the album, but he wasn't truly happy with his work either.

"I wrote some horrible songs when I was doing that album," he said. "There was one called "In the Streets" that was a Bob Dylan sort of thing. The music was sticky, the rhythm was lousy, and the words were really stupid, but we recorded it. I had Michael Stewart erase it; I didn't want anybody to ever hear it."

The album was released in October of 1974 and soon after Billy started a very small tour of less then a dozen shows that would end in March of 1975. After Billy stopped touring, he returned to his house in Malibu and again dedicated his time to writing. Billy wisely felt that although *Piano Man* had been a hit and the exposure he had gotten as a result was incredible, that it had flamed out too quickly as would *Streetlife Serenade*. If he could help it, he was determined to not suffer from the "sophomore syndrome" that many musicians do by turning out a third, less successful album for Columbia, but also felt a great deal of pressure to produce enough songs to fill an album. This factor some felt caused Billy to write songs maybe too quickly, not letting them "digest" enough to then fine-tune them.

Looking back today Billy is not happy with what the album conveyed lyrically, but as the trained musician that he is first he does think the album has some interesting musical ideas.

"'Piano Man' was me," he said. Then in typical understated fashion he continued, "'The Entertainer' wasn't. The things I write have a seed of personal experience, but my life isn't interesting enough to have every song be about me."

Here again Billy's uneasiness with being who and what he is surfaces. The conflict that is at the very most inner core of Billy Joel, and one he wrestles with many times each day, rears its ugly head. He comments:

"'The Entertainer' did, however, address issues that had caused the real-life situations in 'Piano Man.' I was talking about the cold, hard business of records. The rock star as god—I hate that."

And he does, yet he loves it too. But what truly is most important to Billy, and what is at the very essence of who he is, is staying in touch with that kid from Hicksville, despite the emotional pain and many scars that come with it. Billy Joel is at his best when he is connected to that part of him, and he is often at his worst when he strays from that grounded place and embraces Billy Joel the rock star.

"I have a real cynicism about this whole rock star thing," he said. "I don't think I'm so special—I just do what I do."

Unfortunately with the exception of "The Entertainer," which peaked at #34 in January 1975, the songs on *Streetlife Serenade* were not received well by his fans or music journalists, and the album was a failure, itself peaking at only #35 in December 1974. The dreaded "Sophomore Syndrome", had indeed struck Billy Joel, and Billy was sure that he knew why, something that was only confirmed more as he struggled through the tour to support the album. Billy had to return to his roots to recapture his creative edge and he knew it; he also needed his own band. One that could understand the essence of who he was and where he was coming from, which then he knew would result in the musical synergy that he needed on stage and in the studio. He knew that his days in California were over and that he had to return to New York.

# Chapter 17

Billy was becoming disillusioned with the West Coast. Sure the weather was close to perfect and back then anyway the rent was cheap, but it just wasn't New York, and New York has always been at the heart and soul of who Billy Joel is.

"In New York if you're friends with somebody, you walk up to him and you go 'Hey stooopid!' and he goes 'Hey jerk!' and you smack him," he says. "It means 'I love you man!' But in California if I did that, they'd go like 'Oh wow. You're so hostile!'"

By now Billy had lived on the West Coast for what had been a productive three years since they fled there in Elizabeth's station wagon, but he had never intended to stay there permanently. He had gone west primarily to get his business affairs and career in order, and now that that was beginning to happen, he wanted to go home. He missed New York City desperately; after all it was his home and the people, as gritty and hardcore as they are at times, were "his" people, the people he wrote about so often.

Living in Los Angeles had undeniably been good for Billy as a musician too. Working at Corky's and the Executive Lounge had a very positive effect on his piano playing and his evolution as a performer. It also gave him that one great song which would help him to relaunch his career after the *Cold Spring Harbor* nightmare.

But on the down side Billy's writing seemed to suffer on the West Coast. With the exception of "Piano Man," most of the other songs on that album had been written in New York prior to leaving. With *Streetlife Serenade* Billy was experimenting, trying to be as eclectic as he could musically, but something was missing.

"I don't like to stick in one bag," he'd say. "I like different kinds of music, whatever's good. I don't want to limit myself to writing in one vein. I never do the same thing twice. To keep me interested there always has to be something new, something different."

Yet Billy sensed that if he were going to really take the giant steps necessary for his career to be successful he would have to return to his roots. His instincts again would be 20/20. Billy must have realized that his writing was suffering on the West Coast, that he was drifting from his roots. California was an alien place to him, and he never really felt at home there. Long Island, New York was Billy's home, and for over twenty years he had soaked up the life there. He understood it, and it was a part of him. The life of New York ran through his veins and the result was some of the best songs he'd written. California was new blood, a transfusion that never really took the way the familiar scenes of Long Island that had been burned into his consciousness. The time he'd spent on the West Coast and his observations of life there, as well as his initial feelings of homesickness, are best captured in the *Streetlife Serenade* song "Los Angelenous," which depicts Los Angeles for exactly what it is: a destination and melting pot for personalities of all sorts to live their "funky exile." Billy's exile was over. He was going home.

These were the days when New York City was constantly in the newspapers or television news because of its impending bankruptcy. The city's infrastructure was crumbling and then President Gerald Ford made the famous "Drop Dead" comment to New Yorkers that was pasted the next day on the front page of the *Daily News* and in many ways defined his uneventful presidency. Billy, who is a news and history junkie, was following this nightmare and becoming increasingly angry about the media and politicians' handling of the situation. The city he loved so much was on the brink of disaster, and because of its vulnerability it seemed everyone who wanted their names in the papers, or faces on television were taking pot shots, especially politicians. Billy's mind was made up. He had enough and he was going home. He wanted to be where he felt he belonged, and by returning to his roots, he also thought he would get the change in his music he desperately wanted. After all, he understood New Yorkers, related to them, and was one of them.

Elizabeth and Sean went first in early 1975 and looked for a place to live that was close enough to New York City to have easy access, but far enough away so that Billy could write in peace. They found a large old house in the picturesque village of Highland Falls that was for rent, and took it. Highland Falls is a small town on the Hudson River close to Bear Mountain State Park and West Point Military Academy. Elizabeth thought that with its tranquility it would be the perfect place for Billy to write, and still they were close enough to New York City so that they could be there when necessary to meet with record company executives and anyone else crucial to Billy's career.

Billy arrived after Elizabeth and Sean had set up the house, flying in LaGuardia airport and getting on a bus for the ride up Highway 9W to his new home. As he was sitting in the bus the song "New York State of Mind" started to come to him.

"It was one of those spontaneous 'vomit' things", he said. "It just popped out. I envisioned Ray Charles singing it. I had to take a bus to get up to Highland Falls, and I'm driving on a greyhound bus, the Hudson River Line, and the idea started to come to me as I'm in a New York state of mind. I'm taking a Greyhound and the music is happening in my head and I get to the house that my wife, at the time, had found for us to rent and I got in the house and she said, "What do you think of the house?" I said, "Great, great, where's the piano, where's the piano, where's the piano?" Elizabeth pointed to the staircase. "I ran up the stairs and started writing this song, and about an hour later, had the whole song done."

As often happens with Billy when he writes a song or when it comes to him like that, the music comes first and then the music will later dictate the lyrics. This time it all seemed to happen together and Billy, going with his instincts let it happen.

"I was so glad to be there and . . . there it was and I thought how you do like that!" Billy continued. "I was so overjoyed. It was one of those times when a happy feeling works. A lot of times sad is really good for writing. Happy doesn't always work. . . . Sad works good but that was one of those times where happy worked."

Writing songs for Billy has always been a deeply emotional and usually a painful process. "It's like giving birth to a child," he said. "You go through a painful hell, and then all of a sudden, when the song is finished, you experience this exhilarating feeling."

It is evidently not a great time to be around Billy either according to him. "I don't know what the hell I'm doing when I'm writing. For weeks I'm empty. I'm the worst person in the world. I curse at everything and everyone, I throw things, I think it's all over, and then I click," he said. "I don't analyze it. I don't intellectualize it. I just do it."

But within weeks after arriving Billy had written enough material for another album. He was determined that this album was going to be different. It was going to reflect who he was as a person and a musician/songwriter and his instincts and knowledge told him that he needed not only a change in musicians, but also in his life if *Turnstiles* was going to go be the album that he wanted it to be. With his last album floundering and the synergy he was looking for in his band non-existent, the last thing he wanted was another poorly received album.

"Everything is based around a hit record," Billy said. "A hit song, hit single, hit schtick, gimmick, bullshit, whatever it is. Just like the movie business was—the star thing."

Now home in New York with an album's worth of songs, he wanted to get into the studio and record, but due to some very important factors, recording the new album titled *Turnstiles* would turn into a frustrating series of false starts.

Jim Guercio and Larry Fitzgerald were no lightweights in the music business. Guercio was a one-time bass player with Dick Clark's Road Show in the sixties, who then made a name for himself in the early sixties as the producer for the hugely popular band Chicago. In 1973 he had taken some of the money he'd earned and opened Caribou Ranch. It was a recording studio that he'd envisioned high in the Rocky Mountains above Boulder, Colorado, where musicians could come and experience nothing but music. It was so secluded that the usual distractions of families, girlfriends or boyfriends, hangers-on, and the usual list of recreational pastimes would not be a factor, Guercio hoped. At Caribou musicians and their staffs would focus on one thing and one thing only: their music. All their needs including eating, sleeping, and recording were taken care of, making the experience there completely void of any distractions.

In 1974 Elton John became the first big name to use the studio, naming the album he recorded there after it. It was then that Guercio met Elton's drummer Nigel Olsson and bassist Dee Murray. He was impressed with their musical abilities and strong work ethic and later suggested to Billy that he try working with them in the studio. Billy agreed but was reluctant. Not because he doubted their abilities; on the contrary, he knew how talented they were. But Billy had often been compared unfavorably to Elton in the press, and he figured that if he used his musicians, it would only give critics a chance to further make these comparisons. In one of the few times that Billy didn't go with his instincts, he thought, "Who am I to argue with Jimmy Guercio? He's a big mongo in the music business." He agreed to work with them. His initial instincts would prove to be accurate though. For two months they worked together before Billy finally went to Guercio telling him that it just wasn't happening musically with these two guys for him. Next Guercio tried the Michael Stewart philosophy on Billy, bringing him into the studio and trying out a long list of musicians for Billy to play with. Again it wasn't happening and Billy was becoming increasingly frustrated as time went by.

He decided that he'd produce his own album and went to Columbia and spoke with Walter Yetnikoff about firing Guercio as his producer and his manager. Although talented, Jim clearly wasn't the right "fit" for Billy Joel. Fortunately for Billy, when he signed his new contract with Columbia, one of the net results was that he was able to jettison his management company Caribou without the complications that had plagued him with Artie Ripp's contract. Also Walter had always had a great belief in Billy agreed and allowed Billy to produce the album himself, but at the same time the record company was becoming antsy about not having their next Billy Joel album and also were "urging' Billy to "change managers" if that was what it was going to take. "Caribou were very 'West Coast,' " Billy said. "We were not tuning into each other."

But now, after this series of false starts with this album, and the firing of Guercio, Billy was developing the reputation of being hotheaded and to some in the business, not a particularly smart one.

Now 1975, Billy had been touring with a band that was made up of a bunch of musicians with no real connection other thsn having played with Billy in the studio and on the road. For the most part it wasn't really a band that Billy thought of as "his." They'd back him up on stage, and most times very well, but there was something missing. There wasn't that "connection' between the performer and his band that creates the energy that great performances are made of, and Billy, who for the most part, is not one to settle for anything less then perfection when it comes to his music and his responsibility to his audiences, was determined that this was going to change. That he would have a band that saw and, more importantly, felt his music the way he did.

"You've got to make the right statement with the right players on the right instrument," Billy said. "The live performance where impact is more important then detail is only once—a record is forever!"

One of the many great decisions that Elizabeth made back then was to hire Jerry Schilling as Billy's new road manager. Jon Troy had essentially self-destructed from too much alcohol and other excesses, and the spot was open. As a testament that timing and luck are possibly the two biggest factors in careers, Jerry Schilling, who was a member of Elvis Presley's "Memphis Mafia," was looking for a job away from Elvis. One night in Las Vegas he mentioned this to a friend who put him together with Jim Guercio and Larry Fitzgerald, and they all hit it off very well. The next step was a meeting with Elizabeth who asked him if he'd have a problem working with a woman boss. Jerry assured her that he wouldn't, and was hired. Now with the business aspects of his life securely in place thanks to Elizabeth, Billy could focus on putting a band together.

Once again Billy would wisely return to what he knew best, his Long Island roots, to solve the problem of having no band. At the time the bass player in Billy's back-up band was a guy from Long Island who Billy had met about four years earlier while he was playing in a bar band in Oyster Bay, Long Island, where Billy had lived around the time the *Cold Spring Harbor* album was released. His name was Doug Stegmeyer and Billy had first met him through Brian Ruggles. In a fit of frustration with Michael Stewart and his philosophy of picking studio musicians to play with Billy, Joel had called Stegmeyer from California to come out and play with him when he needed a bassist. At the time, Doug was playing in a Long Island band named Topper which had developed quite a following on Long Island. Two kids from Long Island who had grown up listening to rock and roll and playing in garage bands, Doug and Billy had hit it off in those days in Oyster Bay and Billy was aware of Doug's talent so he'd asked him to come out and play with him. Doug jumped at the chance to play with Billy even though it meant leaving his buddies in Topper. But this was one of those chances of a lifetime, Doug thought, and besides as good as Topper was they were struggling financially, and working with Billy certainly looked like a better deal financially and professionally. He left for the West Coast and he and Billy soon developed a deeper mutual friendship and respect based on their musical abilities and the similar lives they had growing up on Long Island.

Billy had always liked Topper's music and felt that Doug would be a good "fit" for his band: "He was from the Paul McCartney, less is more school of bass playing, which is almost harder to play then, say, Stanley Clark's or Jaco Pastorius' way."

From his perspective, Doug had watched through the days of Jim Guercio as Billy had been put in touch with the wide array of musicians in the futile attempt by Guercio to form a back-up band for Billy. Billy had always wanted to pick musicians like these guys, but had been talked out of it by people who wanted to use experienced session people. But now Billy was calling the shots and had called Doug to ask him to go into the studio for what once again would be an attempt to hopefully finally record the *Turnstiles* album. Doug agreed, but first they needed more musicians like themselves who would "get" Billy and his music and form the core of what would become "The Billy Joel Band." Billy wisely didn't want to go through a list of studio guys, having to audition each one. He'd been there already, and he knew that the chances of finding the talent he wanted was essentially non-existent.

He turned to Doug for suggestions and Doug suggested a drummer he knew from Seaford, Long Island, named Liberty DeVito. Liberty was also a member of Topper and already had a long history playing in bar bands. Additionally he had filled in numerous times for the high-powered Detroit, Michigan band Mitch Ryder and the Detroit Wheels on the road. They had already had a string of hits on top forty radio and from about 1965 were a very successful band with a strong national following, so Liberty was a seasoned veteran of touring too. Doug asked Liberty to come by Ultrasonic studios and he and Billy and him hit if off right away.

"Liberty used to work with Mitch Ryder," Billy said. "He is a real Italian rocker. He's got tons of energy and he's the group's comedian."

Liberty would soon become known as the "Wildman" of the bunch. Driving cars into hotel lobbies, wearing disguises on stage and changing lyrics of Billy's songs that he found boring, such as "sodomy", for "honesty." He would also be there to give Billy reality checks at times when Joel would start acting the role of the "rock star," and DeVito would break his balls for doing so. Liberty also is not one to get too much of a swelled head about his position; in fact he had a pretty good perspective about it.

"There are a lot of drummers as talented as I am," he said. "But they weren't as lucky. They didn't happen to live in the same area as Billy Joel."

Liberty and Billy would play together for almost twenty years until Liberty's mouth would put an end to their personal and professional relationship.

Now with Stegmeyer and DeVito onboard, Billy was more than optimistic about his band. He had the beginnings of the raw power he had been looking for musically and equally as important he had two friends in Stegmeyer and DeVito who were both pretty well grounded. He now needed guitar players who he could use both in the studio and on the road. The days of the revolving door guitarists were over for Billy, he wanted people who could play with him on the road and in the studio, and again Stegmeyer would dip into the talent of Topper for two guitar players and Billy would wisely go with his suggestion.

Russell Javors had started the band Topper. He was a kid from Plainview, Long Island, a town next to Hicksville. His girlfriend went to school with Liberty DeVito, and he and Russell starting hanging out when Russell was just fifteen years old. "I said to myself, this is the guy I want to play drums in my band, so I kept showing up a Lib's,' Javors said. Russell also knew of Billy and his music going back as far as the days when Billy was with The Hassles and played at My House in Plainview, and had always been a fan of Billy's, recognizing his great talent even back then. "We were all well aware of Billy's gifts and Billy's talents. The Billy I knew was the eye of the tiger." Javors said. "He is a wonderful performer and has that ability to turn a huge concert hall into a living room."

Javors was an accomplished guitarist. So much so that he had been approached by several producers, including Buddy Buie of Classics IV fame, to record an album but ultimately he opted not to record his music with studio musicians. "The only way I wanted to present my music was with my band. There were relationships that had been built between us and that was integral to my music. This was crucial. I had very definite views on that and I was not willing to compromise."

Howard Emerson, who would play guitar on *Turnstiles* too, regrets the lack of a Russell Javors release. "Topper made lots of tapes mostly down in a studio in Merrick. And, basically, Topper was Russell's band. We were Russell's band from the beginning. I maintain that Russell is one of the best songwriters ever. His abilities have never been touched at all. Never."

Javors, who is clearly talented and would go on to be an integral part of The Billy Joel Band for thirteen years had always wanted his own band since he was a kid in Plainview. Now he was being asked to essentially give up his band and turn it over to Billy, but like Stegmeyer he was able to see the bigger picture and realized that with Billy he would be able to fully realize his "vision" as it pertained to his music.

"The band that evolved and turned into Billy's band was my hand-picked band," he said. "When we played with Billy, we were an extremely focused group of individuals. The song was always the most important thing as far as I was concerned. I couldn't have cared less about the solos. Driving the song with the band like Keith Richards and John Lennon and getting under the skin of the song, not following the drums or bass was my focus, and I think we succeeded at it with Billy."

As well as Russell, everyone felt one more guitar player was needed and this time it was Russell who suggested another Topper alumnus, Howard Emerson. Howard was also a kid from Plainview who fell in love with rock and roll and, like millions of other sixties era kids, had that love galvanized by The Beatles. He had taken up the guitar as a teenager and had played with the folksinger Eric Andersen prior to joining Topper. He toured pretty extensively with Andersen at first meeting and playing with such superstars of the day as Joni Mitchell, a close friend of Andersen's. Howard remembers those days in the late sixties when Topper was formed, and music was exploding everywhere on Long Island. It seemed that every high school had at least one band that played dances and parties and rehearsed wherever they could. Then his path with Russell crossed and he was hooked.

The band was together now and they started rehearsing at Ultrasonic. Billy was producing the album himself and brought in John Bradley to do the engineering. Then one day shortly after rehearsals began, Billy mentioned to Stegmeyer that he wanted a saxophone player and Doug, who was now being called the "Sergeant" of the Billy Joel Band because of his emerging leadership, called up Richie Canatta, another Long Island kid who he knew, to come and audition.

Cannata remembers when he was asked to join the first Billy Joel Band:

I was doing a session for the television show *Sesame Street*. I played soprano sax on it. The drummer and the bass player that were on the session were Liberty and Doug. The engineer was Al Stegmeyer, Doug's brother. Al told me that, "My brother Doug is trying out for Billy Joel and they are looking for a sax player." They wanted a sax player who could play keyboards too. I was in my early 20s and making good money playing by then and I wasn't sure where I would fit in, but I said OK. I went down to Ultrasonic and they were playing "Angry Young Man," and Billy says to me, "I really want a sax on 'New York State of Mind,'" so they had come to see me play. *Turnstiles* was the first album where they used it. Then Doug, Liberty, Brian, and Billy came to see me play in a club one night and that sealed the deal."

Billy liked Cannata's gritty style so he was hired to be in the band. Billy now finally had the sound and the feel he was looking for musically. Billy's instincts told him that with these core musicians he would have the tighter, raw and aggressive style that he had been looking for, and again he'd be right. Billy has always been interested first in making records, and good ones. He believed then as he does today that if he has the right musicians with him the records success would follow. The last thing that Billy has ever been interested in is the philosophy of a bunch of record company people who too often saw making records a formula rather then a bonding experience.

As a result Billy has never been one to compromise when it comes to his music. He feels, and rightly so as he knows it better then anyone, that although he may ask bandmates and others in the studio opinions or suggestions, first and foremost his music is his, and he won't allow someone else to compromise that. However, the star thing is something that Billy has never been totally comfortable with, and today remains that way: "Yeah, I've caught a couple of good waves, but I still find this 'Billy Joel' thing unsettling at times. I'm just a rock and roller from Hicksville. I think of my self as philosopher and then I think of my self as a stupid ass piano player. These guys keep me in line. If I ever start acting like a rock star Liberty'll come over and go 'Who do you think you are you jerk?' It keeps me healthy. I don't like that arrogant 'I'm a rock star and I'm all punk and I'm great and everyone else stinks' attitude. And I can't have that attitude with Liberty watching me."

Billy, Elizabeth, and Sean left Highland Falls in late 1975 and moved into a townhouse on East 62nd Street in New York City. Living in Highland Falls had been great, but in many ways it was still like California. Instead of honking cars, sirens, rude people, and high energy, Billy found the chirping birds and whistling leaves in the trees too much like the West Coast. He wanted New York City. He also wanted to record another album, and now had the band to do it.

"Back then when Billy was building his career, Billy always looked at his band as an integral part of the Billy Joel equation," says Jerry Schilling. "He respected those guys and was smart enough to always give the band a say in the music."

Billy evidently agrees. "You've got to make the right statement, with the right players, on the right instrument."

Joel and his band entered Ultrasonic Studios in early 1976 to record and produce *Turnstiles*, his fourth album. It was released in May 1976 to widely mixed reviews, while the United States enjoyed its bicentennial. Some critics agreed that Billy Joel had matured both as a songwriter and a recording artist, but a critical backlash from music journalists was already well under way against Joel. New York's *Village Voice* ran a scathing review of Billy in their June 23, 1976 issue by critic Stephen Holden. In it Holden implied that Billy seemed spoiled and overambitious, that "his attitude was sour and further-more, that he was unlikely to develop an audience beyond the cult that he'd already attracted." Holden went on to accusing Joel of imitating Bruce Springsteen and Elton John, not to mention Neil Diamond and Harry Chapin. "Billy Joel is boring as hell," he said. And was "running full speed in the wrong direction." Holden also put his foot firmly in his mouth when he criticized Joel's "Say Goodbye to Hollywood," the first song on the album. He referred to it as a pathetic rip-off of Phil and Ronnie Spector as well as Springsteen, when in reality it was a tribute to Spector's sound. Billy would get the last laugh though because it ended up being recorded by Ronnie Spector in 1978 with Springsteen's E Street Band playing on Ronnie's version of it. Ronnie also later commented that, "When I heard the song, I said, "That's for me!' I love it, it reminds me of my marriage. It was one hell of a song for a comeback for me." Nevertheless it would seem that the often hostile relationship between Billy and the musical journalists was well under way now. The music magazine *Creem* described Joel at the time as "a Jackson Browne folkie at heart, with Elton John-like presentations"—something that surely raised the anger level in an already raw Billy Joel.

*Turnstiles* was not a success as far as the record industries measuring stick was concerned. It reached a high of #122 on the Billboard album chart before disappearing into oblivion. It was a commercial disaster to put it kindly, yet why remains a mystery to many even now, because *Turnstiles* was easily the most substantial work of Billy Joel's career to date, and without question the most entertaining. Perhaps it was the timing. Springsteen's *Born to Run* album was released about the same time and swept the country by storm. Unlike Billy, who had an adversarial relationship with the press, Springsteen was a critics' favorite, and could do no wrong. Perhaps it was an album released before its time. Regardless, its eight songs are undeniable evidence that Billy Joel is a gifted songwriter and performer of major proportions. Despite being canned by reviewers, *Turnstiles* still managed to get its fair share of FM radio play.

The last track on the album, which eerily would be played by Billy at the concert for 9/11 in Madison Square Garden after the attack on the World Trade Center, was "Miami 2017." This song was written as a vision of something very negative somewhere in New York City's future. Inspired by the precarious financial state of the city in 1975 the song was an angry reaction by Billy to then President Gerald Ford's speech saying that he wasn't going to give federal aid to New York City, and the "Drop Dead" *Daily News* headline that followed. Billy later would comment that he wrote the song after putting himself in a position of a grandfather living in Miami Beach in 2017, saying "I remember what happened in New York City when the gunboats came up and blew the whole place away."

"New York State of Mind" would be covered by Barbra Streisand on an upcoming album of hers, causing Billy to remark that only now because "Streisand had recorded it did his mother take him seriously as a musician." Soon after, it was sung by Frank Sinatra at a Carnegie Hall concert, the perfect irony for many who feel that Billy Joel is the rock and roll Sinatra.

Regardless of why, and there are undoubtedly many factors that contributed to it, *Turnstiles* tanked, which today would have been the end of the artist. Fortunately in 1976 Walter Yetnikoff was at the helm of Columbia records and a very different attitude prevailed at Black Rock. Walter wasn't giving up on Billy Joel. This was still the record business of old, committed to building careers rather then dumping artists if they didn't meet the bottom lines, and Yetnikoff believed in Billy Joel, something that was soon to become obvious.

# Chapter 18

As 1976 drew to an end Billy essentially had no real manager. Jon Troy, Billy's old drinking buddy from Los Angeles who had also been a road manager of sorts for Billy, had filled in with some of the responsibilities, but his drinking demons were getting the best of him, and it was clear to Billy and to Elizabeth that he now needed a strong manager who understood his needs. Troy did not always project exactly the right persona that Billy Joel wanted either.

"He had this galoot of a manager," according to Billy's old friend from The Hassles days, Arma Andon. "This guy was big and husky and one day he walks into my office because he had heard of me from Billy and he wanted to introduce himself. This guy was really out of central casting. I remember talking to the guy, and I think Billy was with him at the time, and I could see Billy wincing when this guy was talking. He just really had not much to say that was intelligent."

Elizabeth and others in Billy's inner circle had actually encouraged Troy's position. It gave Elizabeth the opportunity to lay the groundwork to get herself named as his manager, speculating that Troy would screw things up so much in a short time that Billy would panic and turn to her for help. It would work as planned. Billy had always depended a great deal on Elizabeth and her opinions, and next to his own, trusted her instincts the best. In December 1976 it became painfully obvious that Billy needed someone that he could trust to manage his career and who better than the woman who had been with him now for the better part of eight years, through a number of peaks and valleys in his professional and personal life. Although over the years the story has been told as a sort of off the cuff request, the reality was much different. Billy and certainly Elizabeth would never treat his career so casually. The decision for Elizabeth to begin managing Billy was one that they discussed at length and one that Elizabeth's allies encouraged Billy to make. Elizabeth felt that she had what it would take to manage Billy's career after watching others screw it up now for the better part of eight years, and besides no one had the ear of Billy the way she did, nor did Billy trust anyone as much as he trusted Elizabeth, and for Billy the abandoned child, trust is everything. The decision was made, Elizabeth would take over as Billy's manager, and in a very short time dramatic changes started taking place for Billy.

Elizabeth Weber is by no means a pushover and she has always been a quick and astute learner. During the Troy fiasco she had been taking on some of the management responsibilities anyway after Jim Guercio and Larry Fitzgerald left. She was also the only one that really had the attention of Billy Joel. In the past she had stayed clear of managing Billy, being smart enough to realize that she didn't really have a full understanding of just what the responsibility entailed. But she had always wanted the job, and as someone who always saw the big picture realized right away what it meant for her in terms of power and money, two very basic motivators for her. She has always been a quick learner and a keen observer, never missing much, particularly when it came to Billy and his career. Over the past months in particular, as she laid the groundwork for her own advancement, building allies and increasing her influence over Billy, she had kept a keen eye on developments in an effort to better educate herself. She now felt that she had what it would take to effectively manage Billy and essentially had been effectively lobbying for the job anyway at each opportunity. Besides Billy thought having Elizabeth manage him made total sense since she understood him better then anyone in or out of their circle then, both as an artist and certainly as a person. She had known Billy now since the days of The Hassles, *Attila*, the *Cold Spring Harbor* drama, and subsequently the West Coast, and his emergence finally as the talent that he was.

The decision was made. Billy and Elizabeth would take their partnership to the next level. Elizabeth jumped at the opportunity to manage Billy and the next day when Billy returned to their townhouse it was clear to him that Elizabeth was not taking her new responsibility lightly. He walked in on a scene which was now the new base of operations for Billy Joel, right in their home. In a very short time she had hired a small staff, and converted some unused space into the offices of the new Billy Joel management company. With their operations now being run out of their home, Billy and Elizabeth called their new company 'Home Run Productions,' and many seasoned record company people watched with skepticism to see how the arrangement would develop. Billy was confident in Elizabeth's capabilities, though, and having her step in as his manager would allow Billy to better focus on his artistic pursuits.

Together they were now the perfect team it appeared. When Billy isn't letting his temper get the best of him, he has always had an amazing innate ability to size up a situation and to know how to react to it. This has worked wonders for him both in his professional life with the media and music executives, and also in his personal life. He often will project the persona of a somewhat gullible and naïve guy, which leads others to believe that he has no understanding of what is going on in the room. The reality is that just the opposite is true. Billy is an extremely intelligent, streetwise, and instinctive personality who like Elizabeth has the gift of always seeing the bigger picture. He can manipulate the media and others in such a way that even they don't see it often until after the fact. Billy is brilliantly savvy when it comes to all aspects of his life, particularly when his demons aren't getting the better of him, or when his career or money are involved. He may not always focus on his business responsibilities and in his way trusts others to do it, a trait that would later get him into serious financial trouble and wound him deeply emotionally, but in reality, not much gets by Billy.

Couple that with Elizabeth's better then average looks, intelligence, instinct, and her flirtatious manner and you had a pretty lethal combination of power to deal with in boardrooms. Elizabeth more often than not had record company and other executives strutting around like roosters in a hen house until it was too late, and they realized that in fact they had become the prey. Right from the start as his manager Elizabeth was a smart, shrewd, and forceful negotiator, known for sitting in a waiting room for the better part of a day if necessary to get a meeting, then quietly sitting and listening to the often pompous and self-serving executive run off at the mouth before she moved in for the kill.

"She was a powerful woman," according to Phil Ramone, who would go on to produce seven Billy Joel albums. "She who would run around Columbia Records and people at Columbia were going, 'Oh, Jesus, she's the wife and the manager?' She pulled off some amazing shit."

Elizabeth took the time to do her homework and discover just who the people in the companies she was dealing with would be her allies. She cultivated those relationships, many of which she still has today, and in doing so accelerated Billy's rise to the top in the record business.

"She was a perfect representative for Billy; she was a cold-hearted, black and white woman," according to Howard Emerson. "That is a perfect description." Artie Ripp agrees. "Billy wanted somebody he knew and that was close to him and he felt he could trust, Elizabeth now became that person. She was now Mommy too. A bright person and a tough person as well."

Being Billy's manager also meant a whole new level of togetherness for them, something that galvanized Elizabeth's position even more within Billy's inner circle.

Meanwhile the money was not exactly pouring in for Billy but Elizabeth was busy working on that. She had renegotiated Billy's contract with Columbia, getting him more money per album prior to *Turnstiles* being released. She also hired Dennis Arfa, an old friend of Billy's who grew up in

Plainview, Long Island, and who had a background in managing bands and promoting concerts to book a tour for Billy. He'd done about a dozen or so concerts so far in 1976, but Elizabeth wanted to accomplish a couple of additional things if possible in addition of course to making money. First to try to promote the *Turnstiles* album whose sales were pretty dismal, second to test the market as far as Billy's draw was concerned. Both Billy and Elizabeth wanted to take Billy to the next level and get him out of clubs and college auditoriums, and into venues like Madison Square Garden if possible. Finally Billy had some new material he'd written in New York that he wanted to test on his audiences to see how they'd respond, and a tour was the only way to accomplish this.

They had also moved the Home Run office out of their apartment over to West 57th Street and, under her leadership, it quickly became an umbrella corporation embracing video, magazine, and music publishing. The little hippie chick from Syosset was quickly making a name for herself as a shrewd and hard-nosed businessperson.

"People never expected me to be as smart as I was, and they would be totally frank because they didn't realize I was building my empire," she said. "Money is the bottom line of everything." A lesson she wasn't soon to forget.

Within a short time of taking over her husband's business affairs, Elizabeth had launched a flurry of lawsuits on Billy's behalf. Billy, she agreed, was "a lousy businessman," something that isn't rare for musicians. She was determined to find out where all his money was going and why. Without a doubt the most important thing that Elizabeth did for Billy at this point in career was to call the producer Phil Ramone and ask him to come and see Billy play Carnegie Hall.

By the end of 1976 Billy had been on tour for five months promoting the *Turnstiles* album. He was in a pretty good place musically, having put together a band that "got" his music, and even at times was responsible for filling in the holes creatively for Billy when his famous writer's block would hit. Even if *Turnstiles* sales weren't something to be excited about, the tour that Dennis Arfa had put together was a success, and Billy was now the top billing on all stops having made the decision just a year or so earlier that he would no longer be an opening act for anyone, after being paired so often with bands whose music was so radically different then his that it often was embarrassing.

"You know, you are making a living on the road, you are having a great time with your buds, you're meeting girls, you're getting to see the country, you're opening for Electric Light Orchestra, Yes, and The Eagles, Janis Ian, Linda Ronstadt, Jethro Tull, and it's great." Billy said. "But then they might have me open up for Olivia Newton John. She is the Sunday school girl wearing the white gloves so instead of doing stuff like 'Captain Jack' we do our 'sweetheart set.'"

These were dates that would sell out time after time with requests for additional tickets, making it clear that Billy would soon be ready for bigger venues.

# Chapter 19

As 1976 drew to a close Billy was in the place he wanted to be musically, despite the dismal lack of success encountered by *Turnstiles* and what the critics might be saying. He had a band that understood and "felt" his music, and the synergy that the two would soon create was undeniable. This first became apparent to Billy and the band members at Caribou Studios when they assembled there for the first time to work on tracks for *Turnstiles*.

"The vibe was so good, it was right you could tell, our thing was about vibe," said Richie Cannata about that first session together. "It was a huge step for Billy, he had a band that was his age and we were all from the same Long Island area code—516." This was an important aspect of the band's understanding of Billy's music. When it came right down to it, Billy was hanging out again with his buddies at the Village Green or soda shop, instead this time it was at the recording studio, and they were making music together.

Jim Guercio put them all together first to record the album. But they were clearly in an environment, that although beautiful, was alien to a bunch of guys from suburban Long Island.

"We didn't know what to do, here we are, a bunch of New Yorkers, and the air was so clean," Cannata continues. "All we wanted to do was smell a bus, or trip over some garbage, and here we are at Caribou. Caribou was a place where we were fish out of water . . . We just had fun, lots of girls up there, we got them in a bunch of trouble, hippy chicks, Ivory soap girls, we got them to come out with us, and drank in the bars with us and we had fun."

Russell Javors agrees. "I look back and I am very grateful for the opportunity that Billy gave us, you know it's kinda like playing on the Yankees, every so often you get to play with some guy who is really at the top of their game, and they are all on top of it and all focused, and every so often the sparks and the stars fly and great things happened. He worked so hard at his craft to achieve his goal, and you know I felt we were part of that and I felt that we really achieved that too."

Meanwhile with an album out Billy had to go on tour to support it. In

June 1976 he and his band did a live broadcast over New York's WNEW-FM from the Bottom Line in Greenwich Village, and then set out on an ambitious 108-show tour that Dennis Arfa had booked and which was to end with four sold-out shows at the prestigious Carnegie Hall a year later, which would be a huge turning point in his career.

After this recording, Howard Emerson departed. A loner, he never liked life on the road. He'd rather go back to his hotel room and read or play his guitar than to party or indulge in some of the activities that bands on the road are so well known for.

Walter Yetnikoff rose to the presidency of Columbia Records in May 1975 as a result of Clive Davis' firing. Walter was a kid from Brooklyn whose father was a housepainter, and whose immigrant tailor grandfather, who always kept a needle pinned in his lapel, had tried to influence Walter against a career in law telling him that essentially Jews are people who are always in flight, and that his fancy diploma would do him no good in Lithuania. Walter followed his own instincts and ignored his advice, graduating from Columbia Law School. He eventually found his way to the culturally Jewish Columbia Records led by the consummate WASP want-to-be William Paley, the son of a Jewish cigar salesman who spent his entire professional life presumably ashamed of his Jewish origins.

When Walter started at Columbia he was a shy and unostentatious lawyer who rose through the ranks of the company where he was regarded as a superb negotiator. He formed his alliances carefully and subsequent to Davis' firing they paid off. Walter now held one of the most powerful positions in the entertainment industry, a position that he himself referred to often as the "Fuhrer's job," and turned it into his own personal fiefdom of sorts complete with his stable of Gentile girlfriends who he called his "shiksa farm." With his new job came a drastic change in Walter's personality. The once unassuming lawyer evolved rather quickly into a hard-drinking tyrant whose tantrums are still legendary today. Yet underneath the tyrant, whose mere presence was enough to cause many of his subordinates to break out in chronic anxiety attacks, lay a "mensch," a supreme Yiddish compliment which translates into one who is noble, generous, and upright. This was the real Walter Yetnikoff in the heady days to those who really knew him, and who today, now sober, remains the same person. Although certainly a lunatic at times Walter was also a boss who couldn't even fire his driver, even though the guy was not showing up for work, and who upgraded an employee who had wrenched his back to a first-class seat on an airplane at his own expense so the guy would be more comfortable.

Walter had "inherited" Billy Joel from Clive Davis' regime, and always thought of Billy not only as a musical genius, but also as a wonderful human being who shared many of Walter's better (and some not so good), personality traits. He believed in Billy as he did in many of his other artists, and had a large personal investment in insuring that they reached the success that Walter felt they could.

About two-thirds of the way through the *Turnstiles* tour, Yetnikoff received a phone call from Elizabeth asking him to come and see a Billy Joel concert at the Hollywood Bowl. Elizabeth had two reasons for the request. One, she wanted Walter to listen to some new material that Billy was trying out on the tour, material that would be used on the next album, and that Elizabeth told Walter audiences were responding to in an incredibly positive way. Two, the tour would be out of money quickly and despite her pleas to executives at Columbia, they had turned off her chance of any more funding, and the tour was in danger of ending prematurely.

The tour was losing money primarily because of Billy's refusal to be an opening act for any other bands. As a result Billy was forced to play some new and much less lucrative venues that caused the money budgeted for the tour to be used up much quicker then anticipated. Places like the Cellar Door in Washington, DC, the Bottom Line in New York City, and The Ritz in Memphis were all great places for Billy to showcase his music, particularly because there were usually members of the media in these clubs. But this had been Dennis Arfa's and Elizabeth's plan from the start, to try and get Billy as much exposure as possible.

Consequently, because these clubs only sat a few hundred or so people, and the other venues were small too, the money to keep the tour going just wasn't there. Elizabeth was in a panic. She obviously believed in Billy, and now on tour she saw the way that the audiences were reacting to Billy's music, especially the new and unrecorded stuff. But without the money to keep going she was looking at a disaster that conceivably could also be the end to Billy Joel's career. She had to do something and quickly. In her typical ballsy fashion she called Walter Yetnikoff in New York.

Walter has always been a sucker for a good-looking woman, and although his preference is clearly blondes, Elizabeth was a hard one to ignore. Add to that the fact that she was aware of her looks and appeal and knew exactly how to work them, and you had a pretty lethal force to deal with back then.

"Billy was struggling," he said. "The business side of his life was in total disarray. His copyrights were scattered all over the place and his career had stalled after the release of *Turnstiles*. He was in serious trouble. Anyway I went to the show and I spent the bulk of the time watching the audience instead of listening to Billy's music. I knew Billy was talented, but when I saw how the audience was reacting to his material, it only confirmed my belief in Billy."

After the show Billy, Elizabeth, and Walter all met backstage. Walter told Billy how much he loved what he heard and saw.

"I love it too," Billy answered, "but we're cancelling the rest of the tour."

"The money is running out," Elizabeth interjected. "I called Columbia and asked for another eighty thousand dollars, and they laughed."

"Call again tomorrow," Walter said. "Take my word for it. No one will laugh."

The long and short of it is that Elizabeth did call the next morning, and the money was waiting.

Now with the additional funds the tour could continue and Elizabeth and Dennis Arfa started strategizing on how to best exploit some new avenues for Billy, namely his international visibility. While he had toured Europe with Irwin Mazur and Artie Ripp briefly, this time they had a better name recognition to draw from as well as more material. Additionally, with Columbia Records strong presence overseas and Walter Yetnikoff's connections there, Billy, Elizabeth, Walter and Dennis Arfa knew it made sense to test the waters. First, though, they had to finish up the US end of the tour. Billy and Elizabeth also knew that after the dismal showing of *Turnstiles* that his next album had better be successful or that his albums might end up in the discount rack at the record stores, with Billy back playing venues like the Executive Lounge instead of Madison Square Garden, which now was his goal. They had to find a top producer who would understand Billy's music the way his new band did, and who could translate that raw power and emotion onto a record. Never one to shy away from a challenge or settle for anything less then the best, Elizabeth phoned George Martin, The Beatles producer, and asked him to come to a concert at Glassboro State College in New Jersey to watch and listen to a show. Billy and Elizabeth hoped that George would see the influence that The Beatles had on Billy's music and go on to produce the next album. George showed up that night in May and later met with Billy where Billy tried to sell him on becoming his producer. They discussed Billy's goals and his music with Billy, explaining to Martin that his song "Scenes from an Italian Restaurant" was Billy's mini version of The Beatles' *Abbey Road*. The song which Billy wrote about an Italian restaurant in Syosset, New York, named Christano's, where he and Elizabeth often ate, describes the reality of Long Island teenagers in the fifties and sixties. Originally titled "The Ballad of Brenda and Eddie," it is an accurate assessment of the tackiness, restlessness, ill-conceived marriages and partnerships, low aspirations, and feigned toughness that were such an integral part of that American dream that Billy Joel was both a product and observer of.

To Billy's disappointment, George ended up passing on producing Billy's next album. He didn't like Billy's band, but Billy who did wasn't about to compromise, not even for someone like George Martin. It was a strong vote of confidence from Billy. After all Martin had produced spectacularly

**LEFT**
Howard and Rosalind,
Billy's Parents, circa 1947

**RIGHT**
Howard, Billy's father

**LEFT**
Howard and Rosalind,
circa 1947

**RIGHT**
Rosalind, Billy's mother

**ABOVE**
Billy and his sister, Judy, circa 1947

**LEFT**
Rosalind and Billy circa 1953 at home in their Hicksville, NY backyard

**ABOVE**
Billy and sister Judy at the Hicksville house

**ABOVE**
Billy in his school band uniform aged fourteen

**RIGHT**
Fourteen-year-old Billy, outside the Hicksville house

**LEFT**
Billy, his grandfather,
Phillip Nyman

**RIGHT**
Billy aged fifteen,
playing whiffle ball

19 61

**RIGHT**
Billy and his mother
Rosalind circa 1967 in
Hicksville, NY

**BELOW**
Billy and his best friend, Billy Zampino on motorcycles in Hicksville, NY

**ABOVE**
Group shot of The Hassles, prior to Billy joining

**ABOVE**
The Hassles, circa 1967 at the Barge Club, Westhampton, NY (Billy and John Small in front)

**BELOW**
Billy and John Small in a publicity shot for Attila

**LEFT**
Vicki Chicollo, referred to in the song as the redhead in the backseat of the '57 Chevy. Although 'it' never happened there. 1963

**RIGHT**
Vicki at Billy's home in Hicksville, 1963

5/67

Sun. night

# THE BARGE
**P.O. BOX 29, EAST QUOGUE, L. I. • DUNE ROAD AND TRITON LANE • 516 653-9863**

Dear Vicki,

How do you like my paper? If you want
some you can have it. I am writing this letter
in desperation. This last week has been the worst
week I've ever had. I can't sleep and I can't eat, (really!

I told you about those other girls so you know
how I feel about it. You must think I'm really a ____
fool because I'm writing this. This is the second time
I've come crawling back to you. But I have no pride.
I would do it again and again. I don't know what I
will do if I lose you. You meant more to me than
anybody in my life. Maybe this sounds like a
lot of played-out horse crap but I don't care, that's
how I feel. I know I took you for granted before, but
you see whenever I felt down, I always felt a little better
because I could say "But I still have Vicki." I may not
be the best looking guy around but I always felt so proud
to walk next to you somewhere and watch all those other
guys stare at you. If you think I'm writing this to
make you feel bad, you're wrong. I'm writing to ask you
to try to understand how I feel. Maybe I did treat you
pretty rotten and it must have been hell sitting around
doing nothing on weekends while I was working. But you've
got to understand that I want to be somebody. I want
to be able to walk tall among all the nobodies. I want
to be able to provide a good secure home for a family.

**ABOVE AND OVERLEAF**
Notes Billy wrote to Vicki Chicollo from the Barge Club in Westhampton, NY in May 1967.
They were breaking up and Billy described back then how focused he was on his success.

You see, I grew up without a father and my mother had to break her back to make ends meet. I had to watch my mother get old and bitter while she was still in the prime of her life.

You may think my mother is a lot of laughs, but you don't know what goes on behind that happy front she's putting on. I've made up my mind to make a name for myself so my kids will never have to know what hunger is. You see I never told you this, but when my father left, my mother had no money and no food. My sister and I lived on crackers and water for a month because my mother had too much pride to ask the neighbors for anything.

So you see my life hasn't been all peaches and cream. I'm only worried now that you don't have much respect for me for begging you for another chance. But I miss being able to say "My little Vicki, mine! M-I-N-E!!" You always say 'it will never work out' but I'm willing to try to work it out as long as there are differences between us. You say your father would stop you sooner or later from seeing me but you're almost eighteen years old and that's when a girl is considered an adult. I think you have the right to choose who you want to go with and you should assert that right.

This summer I won't be working that much and I'll be off a lot of nights (with a car) and you can go out on summer nights.

If you want to try again you will have to take me with all my shortcomings and that is why I don't think you will. I can promise you more appreciation but I can't promise five feet, 10½ inches, and a pontiac. So whether you take it or leave it I will always hope and love you forever,

Billy

# THE BARGE

P.O. BOX 29, EAST QUOGUE, L. I. • DUNE ROAD AND TRITON LANE • 516 653-9863

Dear Vicki,

Okay, so now I know where I stand. You're right to make your own decisions about having your freedom. But I will always be your friend. If you ever have any problems don't be afraid to ask me. Maybe someday I will find somebody else, but they will never replace you. This isn't going to be one of those mushy, whining letters either.

Just remember if you're ever lonely or you want me back, I will <u>always</u> be your guy. I guess maybe this is a good way for you to find out what it's like to go out with other guys and to see if we were really meant for each other.

So if you change your mind, no matter <u>when</u> you do, I will always be waiting for you.

Until then –
Love,
Billy

**RIGHT**
The tree Billy hit in
Sag Harbor, NY.
January 25, 2003

**BELOW**
Billy on tour in 2006

**ABOVE**
Billy on the beach in Cuba

**BELOW**
Billy at Madison Square Garden 'Homecoming' concert

**BELOW**
Billy doing what he was born to do!

successful albums for The Beatles who without a doubt had made the largest impact on Billy's music to date.

"He thought they were too rough," Billy said. "Too street rock and roll and unpolished. It was kind of disappointing, but once again I had to stick up for the band."

After the meeting with Martin, Billy went to see the band who were waiting with great anticipation. They too were really excited about the possibility of having a heavyweight like George Martin produce their album and Billy couldn't tell them the truth. Instead he made up some lame story about how scheduling wouldn't allow it to happen.

Not one ever to accept defeat Elizabeth pressed on. The tour would be over in just about one month and time was an issue. Billy was scheduled to go into the studio in July and producing the album himself this time was not an option.

Prior to making the *Turnstiles* album Billy had mentioned to Elizabeth that he would like to work with Phil Ramone sometime on an album. He admired what he referred to as Phil's "efficiency" in the studio and besides Phil's reputation as a producer was, even then, legendary. He had recently worked with Paul Simon on the hugely successful *Still Crazy After All These Years* album, and also had produced Chicago, Kenny Loggins, Barbra Streisand, and Phoebe Snow. Phil was familiar with Billy's work. He had seen him just months earlier play a 45 minute set at a Columbia record convention in Toronto and was blown away by the raw intensity of the performance.

During that three-month period Elizabeth phoned Phil and asked him to come see Billy play at Carnegie Hall. She told Phil that Billy was interested in having him go into the studio with him and produce the next album. Phil accepted the invitation, and was at the June 2 show, as was Don DeVito, an A&R guy from Columbia, who brought a recording truck to tape the concert. Phil watched the show and was hooked.

"What I saw on stage is what I wanted to have in the studio," he said. Phil was immediately sold on that raw, street sound of the band that he saw on stage that night, and he didn't want to change them at all like other producers had.

Phil had lunch with Billy, Elizabeth, and a couple of others from Billy's camp at a small Italian restaurant across from Carnegie Hall. Their conversation that day galvanized Billy's determination that Phil was the right guy to produce the album.

"I told him that I'd listened to his albums, and that truthfully I thought that they were too glitzy, too shiny, and that they didn't represent the performance that I saw in Toronto or Carnegie Hall," Ramone said. "I told him that I wondered why his previous records didn't capture the energy that his live shows generated. Obviously I said the right thing."

Phil's love of Billy's band also gave those guys the confidence that they needed and as a result they worked their asses off for him in the studio. They felt how much Phil loved them and for once they didn't have to "prove" anything to a producer. They could just be themselves, which was all Ramone expected from them.

"Don't play any differently than you do on the road," Phil told them. "Be the rock and roll animals that you are."

Billy was psyched. He'd finally hooked up with a producer that he felt would do his music justice. Equally as important Billy realized that Phil was exactly what he and the band needed to draw the best possible work out of them. His unassuming and low-key manner of producing was one of true support.

"I never left the studio, and I think Billy liked that," Ramone said. "Also the band was an integral factor in the way Billy performed, and I always thought that was critical for him."

Billy and Phil entered A&R Recording Studio in New York City during the early summer of 1977 to record the album.

"I didn't know I was going to call it *The Stranger* when we went in," Billy said.

Unlike the previous horrendous experiences that studio work had sometimes been for Billy and his band, this album was going to be anything but. They went in with just three songs ready to record, but there was so much synergy there between Billy, his band, and Phil, as well as guys like John Bradley, the engineer, that everything just seemed to fall into place.

"It was inspiring," Billy said. "I didn't have a concept for the album, and we never took a long time agonizing over the perfect take or the right way to do it." They just went with it and it worked. Billy and the band worked with Phil putting pieces of songs and music together, improvising, with Billy either writing songs in the studio or bringing in songs to be worked on. Here Ramone's responsibility would be to walk that fine line between helping support Billy and trying to be a part of the creation process.

"Billy needs time to hear things when he's in the studio in the middle of a struggle," Ramone said. "If he were stuck he'd turn around and seek support. I'd often give him a piece of crap lyric line just to piss him off and he'd say, 'What are you crazy?', and I'd say, 'I thought you were the writer.'"

"He's got spontaneity," Billy said of Ramone. "He's as crazy as I am, as nuts as any other musician." But what is undoubtedly the most important aspect of Phil's gift as a producer and the one which really sold Billy on teaming up with him was Billy's observation that Phil "doesn't go for technical perfection, he goes for the feel."

Always, the decision about when a song was "done" was a mutual one. There was clearly enough of a mutual respect between the two that Billy, who guards his songs like a parent does a child, was comfortable enough with Phil Ramone's abilities to allow that power over his music.

"I don't make records that aren't mutual," Ramone said. "To do it any other way would result in no objectivity."

The classic example of this is the song "Just the Way You Are," which was recorded ten different ways and today remains Billy's most covered song. Phil told Billy that he would continue to record it in different versions but that "I'm only doing this for you out of respect. I hate this song."

A lot of people hated that song, including Liberty DeVitto, who in a fit in the studio was said to have thrown his drumsticks at Billy, proclaiming, according to Billy, that, " 'I'm no damn cocktail lounge drummer,' because we couldn't come up with a drum beat. So Phil came up with the samba beat that Liberty ultimately played."

The song which was originally titled "Don't Go Crazy" almost never made it onto *The Stranger* album, and may not have if it hadn't been for an unplanned visit to the studio one day by Phoebe Snow and Linda Ronstadt. Billy said: "They hear the song and they go, 'You've got to put that on the album.' We said, 'Really?' And they said, 'You're not going to put that on the album?' And we said, 'We don't know.' And they said, 'You're stupid guys.' And so we thought okay. Phil was for it and we were fighting with Phil about putting it on. So, that's how it ended up on the album."

After it was agreed that the song would be on the album, Billy still worried about the effect it might have on his career. Particularly the perception by the music media about just who Billy Joel really was. That image like everything else in Billy's career to date had been hard fought for and Billy didn't want to jeopardize it.

"Everyone thought it was too goofy and sappy," Billy said.

"Billy didn't want to lose the rock and roll image that he was looking for," Phil said. "The rock critics never gave us a break. Never." Phil continued. "It took us seven or eight years to get a review in *Rolling Stone* that was OK."

In the end, like it or not, they got one of the best wedding songs known to man, and one that many also feel is one of the great love songs of all time. It also to a great degree carried *The Stranger* album into the mass popularity that none of Billy's albums had ever reached previously, ultimately becoming the best-selling Columbia album up to that time. What many don't know about the song is that Billy gave it to Elizabeth as a birthday gift, causing her to ask in typical fashion, "Does that mean I get the royalties too?" Which indeed she did for many years until Billy ended up buying the rights back.

Elizabeth also was playing a role in the studio, although a much more minor one then, working behind the scenes as Billy's manager, as she shook up record executives, concert promoters and anyone else who might have to do with Billy's career. The days of overlooking details or giving away more money then necessary to a promoter or record company were clearly over for Billy, his financial future along with his career were looking better with each passing day.

Ramone said: "She'd come around the studio sometimes on a Wednesday night, saying I really think we should play a couple of those on Friday for the marketing guys."

Another time during *The Stranger* studio sessions Elizabeth wanted to rush a record to the radio stations. It was a copy of "Just the Way You Are" and her determination and innovation paid off once again.

"I remember we had to get this single out. This is the second single of "Just the Way You Are," Ramone said. "She took a helicopter to the company that was pressing the record and she brought some champagne for the crew to work overtime on a Saturday. The guy who ran the factory didn't care if the record wasn't finished until Wednesday, but Elizabeth wanted them in the DJ's hands on a Monday, and they were."

Being a record producer is also a multi-faceted job with wide-ranging responsibilities, some of them not directly related to making the record, but ultimately so. So in the studio Phil found that he also had to act as an administrator of sorts, particularly because of Billy's non-confrontational manner. It was another fine line to walk, but one that Phil felt was absolutely necessary if they were going to maximize the unnatural experience of being in the studio for extended periods of time. It's obvious from his work that Phil has an extraordinary gift for drawing the best out of his musicians, and he wasn't about to allow anything such as chronic lateness by band members to jeopardize that.

"All of these guys either drove in or took the train from Long Island so I had to create a system for those that were late," Phil said. "I was the sole judge in the studio so I would fine them. At the end of the week we'd have a bowl filled with ones and fives along with a bunch of excuses for being late from their girlfriends or mothers. Things like 'Please excuse so and so for being late. The TV blew apart and blew out his glasses so he had to go to the doctor for new ones.'"

It worked, and although it never eliminated the lateness completely, Phil's policy did confirm his level of responsibility in the studio, which was in many ways equal to Billy. From Billy's perspective, he welcomed Phil's role as the disciplinarian. It was a role he has never liked, and it allowed him to focus totally on the writing and performing process.

"He never voiced anything about the tardiness," Phil said. "But I could feel the discomfort. For Christ's sake we were starting at two, and if you couldn't get there by then, it's pretty sad."

Whatever they were doing worked. Billy eliminated overdubbing his voice to the music, and this time recorded the vocals live at the piano. The album was recorded in just seven weeks in a studio atmosphere that Billy had never before found so relaxing and inspiring. It's clear that the experience of recording *The Stranger* was one that agreed with Billy. His voice is stronger then on any other previous albums and the sound of his band is full of the energy that Ramone captured in its entirety. Billy and his band were out of the studio by mid-August and preparing to go on tour.

With *The Stranger* album done and now in the hands of Columbia's distribution and marketing people, Billy pretty much had the month of August to himself. Other than rehearsing for the upcoming tour, there were no real demands on his time and he was free to do one of the things besides music that he does best—hang out.

Billy was still living on New York City's East Side and with his growing hometown boy celebrity status was quickly becoming the "darling" of New York City nightlife, which was a scene that then was the epitome of excess. Studio 54 had opened that spring and was the focal point of New York City's nightlife. Fueled by celebrities who made it their home away from home and some would say the decadence of Rome, complete with open sex, back-room orgies, and drugs. Unlimited amounts of drugs, particularly cocaine. It wasn't Billy's thing, though.

Billy has never been a follower, and although he certainly was familiar with Studio 54, he hung out in more down to earth places such as J.P.'s, a restaurant on New York's East Side. Although nothing like Studio 54, J.P.'s had its share of partying going on downstairs in what was their version of a VIP room. Mountains of cocaine and other drugs passed through the place, and Billy was curious about the drug.

"There was an exorbitant amount of drugs," said Arma Andon, the former Columbia Record Company executive and friend of Billy's since the mid-sixties. "And because of my relationship with Billy, which was, I think more unique than just anybody that he had at Columbia Records, whatever we did stayed with me. Unlike a lot of executives who came back to the office bragging, "Man I got fucked up with Billy Joel." Whatever he did, he knew would stay there. We were in the cellar many times together."

And everything pretty much did stay with Andon. And again, this is a perfect example of how those who befriend Billy border on being fanatical about protecting him, and it's not just because they are in awe of being in his presence. It's because Billy at his core is truly a good soul who has been handed some really shitty cards in life, but there is a fiercely strong sense among his inner circle and even outside of it that he should be protected from prying eyes.

Billy spent a lot of time that summer at J.P.'s, and not all of it eating. He was down in the cellar the evening of August 16 when J.P. came down from upstairs to give them the news that they were announcing Elvis' death on the evening news. Needless to say everything downstairs stopped and everyone rushed up to the bar to watch the unfolding news. Dumbfounded, they were standing there in various states of shock as newscasters announced the death of the King of Rock and Roll, when suddenly Billy turned and walked over to the piano in the dining area and sat down to play an Elvis show.

This impromptu concert by Billy is legendary in some circles. For some reason there was a tape of it that was later destroyed, but not before Jerry Schilling, Billy's former road manager and Elvis' former bodyguard and member of Elvis' "Memphis Mafia," got to hear it and agreed that it was 45 minutes of high energy Elvis that the King himself would have been flattered by.

*The Stranger* album was released in September 1977 when the disco phase was taking the United States by storm, and whose music dominated much of the airwaves. The Bee Gees and Donna Summer albums were the primary choice of a large portion of the buying public, and to add salt to the wounds, Columbia Records initially marketed the album horribly. They were still trying to sell Billy as the sensitive, singer-songwriter, instead of the rock and roll animal that he is. A perfect example is the ad copy for the album which followed its release: "*The Stranger*. He's the one that sits down next to you at a bar or on the plane or in a restaurant, and he tells you stories about somebody vaguely familiar . . . somebody you suddenly realize is yourself."

The album included four songs that would go on to be big hits in the United States: "Just the Way You Are," "She's Always A Woman," "Movin' Out (Anthony's Song)," and "Only the Good Die Young." With Billy's popularity now stretching beyond the shores of the United States, his reputation was now firmly established, something that the album would only reinforce.

Although Billy would be playing bigger venues such as the Nassau Coliseum on Long Island during this tour, and now having acts open for him, the music critics were now in the beginnings of what would be a long adversarial relationship with Billy and his music. Many of them still looked at Joel as a second-rate artist and they weren't about to give him the big lead reviews in *Rolling Stone* or other magazines that he would get later on in his career. Consequently reviews of the album, which without question was his best work to date, were found deep inside the magazines. *Rolling Stone* is a perfect example. When writing about *The Stranger*, the review that was placed four or so pages into the section totally missed the point, although they did have praise for Phil Ramone with whom they enjoyed a much less adversarial relationship. It read: "Billy Joel would probably still be only a cult figure, idolized in concert, but poorly represented on record, if he hadn't found the perfect studio collaborator in producer Phil Ramone."

The Angry Young Man was angry. He'd recorded what many felt was his best work to date and the reviewers were still up his ass. Yet the album was selling and selling strongly, fueled by the release of "Just the Way You Are" as a single which was getting strong airplay that fall and early winter of 1977. By New Year 1978, *The Stranger* was certified gold and Billy had "Movin' Out" reissued as a single, which became an immediate top twenty hit. Billy was now on his way, and his international reputation was firmly established. From 1977 through 1985, *The Stranger* was Columbia's best-selling record ever. Its sales today exceed 11 million copies. Because of the disco craze that was sweeping the country it would only peak at number two, behind *Saturday Night Fever*. It vaulted Billy to the highest level of a recording artist and suddenly his face and words were everywhere. He had become a star of the highest magnitude, one that even Billy could never have imagined, but with that stardom came a very large downside and the beginnings of the conflict that lies at the core of Billy Joel. The one that he wrestles with constantly: the Billy Joel that grew up walking and hanging around the streets of Hicksville and who dreamed of making it as a musician some days, versus Billy Joel the rock star who has the world at his fingertips. It's something that Billy struggles with daily and in which at times he seems to find a middle ground, only to lose it again, particularly in his days of excess.

With the success of *The Stranger* he had the money and success he'd wanted, but people who were Billy's friends, particularly in places like Hicksville, began to look at him differently. Some of those he grew up with began to look at him in awe instead of as the guy they'd kicked around with and it was unsettling for Billy.

"I try to go back to Long Island and just talk to people, but they talk to me like I'm superhuman," he said at the time. Billy was discovering that indeed you can never really go back . . .

# Chapter 20

With a huge amount of energy behind it, *The Stranger* tour kicked off in September 1977 shortly after the album's release. Billy's multi-faceted talents were now undeniable and this tour would be the biggest to date. Arenas were booked from September until just before Christmas, and when he wasn't playing concerts there was now a long list of requests from magazines and television for interviews and appearances to take up any free time. For those in Billy's camp there was now no denying the feeling of Billy building success.

As was often the case then, with the success came excess, and plenty of it. Cocaine use at the time was sweeping the world. With the vast and seemingly endless coca plantations in South America, coke had become cheap enough so that it was no longer just a rich person's drug. In the backrooms of clubs and bars, as well as the living rooms of suburbia and the backstages of concert halls, coke seemed to reign supreme. It was everywhere and people of all types, many who never had even smoked grass, were trying it. Although Billy's true drug of choice would always be alcohol until he went to rehab in 2005, there was no escaping the availability of cocaine. Heroin was also always sort of around in those days, but spoken in much less hushed tones than the popular cocaine, although it would be a drug that Billy would experiment with briefly later on, and from which a song would be born.

The other dynamic which comes with a rock star's success, and just as much in excess as the drugs, were women. Now that Billy was enjoying a unheard level of success, the class of groupies that could be found backstage, or waiting anxiously to be chosen outside the arena, had been upgraded dramatically. Not only were there seemingly endless numbers of beautiful women around at each tour stop, but Billy and his band couldn't go to a bar or restaurant afterwards without someone offering their services to them. Downplaying his role in what is an undeniable and inescapable part of touring, that life where the unsaid rule of "what happens on the road, stays on the road," Billy says.

"It takes a lot of work for me to get laid on the road, I was the bait and the band worked that. They would follow behind me and pick up the wake; I left the chum. We'd go to a bar and the girls would be like where is he?"

Partying is also a large part of touring for bands. The boredom of touring, the endless hotel rooms that all seem to blend together, particularly when you're touring, as Billy was then, nine months a year. You begin to burn out of all the seeming glitz and glamour of being a rock and roll band on the road, and end up doing things like gluing furniture to hotel room ceilings, trashing rooms, or, in Liberty DeVitto's case, driving a car into a hotel lobby.

There is also a sort of "disconnect" from the real world where you lose touch with what is going on outside your bubble. This is what was happening to a degree with Billy regarding the early success of *The Stranger*. It was taking a while for the growing success to become a reality out on the road.

"We were seeing younger kids come in and older people, and all sorts of people," Billy said. "They were recognizing the new material much quicker then people had picked up on the older stuff. That's when we recognized that something must be going on. I guess it was sort of a surprise."

The other things that were happening for Billy that were beginning to pay off in spades was the performance he did of "Just the Way You Are" on February 18, 1978 on *Saturday Night Live* for an audience of twenty-plus million people, causing him to miss his tenth high school reunion, scheduled that night in Hicksville, which he regretted. The decision paid off, though, fueling even more albums sales for *The Stranger*. Now enjoying the huge wave of success and with a tour scheduled to go to Europe and then Australia in March, Billy went back into A&R Studio with his band and Phil Ramone to begin work on the new album that he would call *52nd. Street*. Billy wanted to take advantage of the momentum that he was enjoying now, but wisely he also realized that this was a somewhat precarious time professionally for someone who was enjoying the success that Billy was with *The Stranger*'s sales and his resulting growth in popularity. Where *The Stranger* was clearly a make or break album for Billy's career, *52nd. Street* carried with it an equal burden in the sense that it had to be successful, yet could its success equal the monster that *The Stranger* had become? Very few albums ever have. When an artist has the success with a record that Billy just had, the record companies will press a million or more copies, meaning that the artist can actually have an instant gold record, but lose tremendous amounts of money if it doesn't sell. It has happened to many artists, but perhaps the best known is Peter Frampton, who after the hugely successful *Frampton Comes Alive* album, shipped his next album as a multiplatinum one only to see it sell less then 400,000 units. It was essentially something he never recovered from, and Billy was determined that this dynamic wasn't going to happen to him.

What he had going for himself was that Billy then was an artist who was never content to just rest on his past success. He felt an incredible amount of pressure to constantly reinvent himself in order to prove to himself and the music industry as well as, to some degree, his fan base that he was indeed a true musician worthy of what now was growing amounts of praise from everywhere. He was the "golden boy" who seemingly could do no wrong after *The Stranger*, but Billy has never been one to rest on his laurels. Then he was a tireless worker always focussed on what was the next goal. He easily could have followed what other artists had done and released a *Stranger II*-type album but would never have compromised his art that way.

"That would be boring," he said. "I wanted to explore my potential."

And that's exactly what he would do with Phil Ramone again in the studio with him. *52nd. Street* is a much different album than *The Stranger*. It has a harder edge to it, and unlike his previous albums much less of the gentle singer-songwriter that the record company had cultivated as part of Billy's image up to *The Stranger*. Also *52nd. Street* has a consistent tone and feel to it, where the songs seem to be in just the right order and none of the tracks seem to clash with each other. It was the album that undeniably introduced the rock and roll animal that Billy is to his audience for the first time.

*52nd. Street* was named after the block in New York City where great jazz clubs used to be located and where the CBS Records headquarters was. It wasn't his first choice for the album's name. Billy had initially chosen "Stiletto" after one of the album's songs, but on giving it some thought he decided to change the name because the song was about "a bitch wielding a stiletto," and also about "masochism and castration." He decided that it was unfair to taint the entire album with that type of image and instead, the historian that he is, decided to pay homage to New York City's jazz heritage. The album was released in October 1978 a little more than a year after *The Stranger*'s debut. "My Life" was chosen as the first single to be released from the album and rose to number three on the Billboard charts, although the album would be Joel's first to reach the coveted number one spot. The song "My Life," more than any of his others possibly, has become Billy's signature song, certainly until that point. It's a song about self-assertion and independence and was written as a "bar song" by Joel.

"I pictured a bunch of people sitting in a bar and turning around, raising their glasses and going, 'I don't care what they say anymore this is MY LIFE!'" Billy said.

The song would result in the first of a long line of plagiarism suits for Billy Joel. A guy named John Powers from Reno, Nevada sued Billy, claiming he'd stolen the song from one that he'd written titled "We Got to Get It Together." Billy was livid. He knew he'd written the song, and on top of that he'd never met this John Powers or for that matter ever heard of him. Powers in his defense claimed to have sent the song to Columbia Records for consideration, and although they rejected it, he claimed that Billy must have heard it there.

The situation brought Billy's anger to a new level. He wanted blood. There was no way he was going to settle for anything less then total vindication. Elizabeth, however, who was much more rational about the situation, hired one of the most successful women attorneys in the music business, Ina Meibach. Together Meibach and Elizabeth were a formidable team and they were able to finally convince Billy that settling made the most sense. To fight the guy would cost untold amounts of money and bring a bunch of bad publicity down on Billy. He didn't need a situation like that now in his career. It was too risky and, although they'd certainly prevail, the bad publicity might taint his career and, eventually, courts being what they are, he'd have to pay something anyway to settle. Eventually they were able to negotiate a settlement of just over $40,000, plus admitting no liability. Powers wasn't satisfied, though. He took out newspaper ads inviting people to compare the two songs which only infuriated Billy more. Billy went off on Powers in a *Playboy* magazine interview where he asked the interviewers if they wanted to go with him and "beat up" the guy. Seeing another pot of money this resulted in Powers again suing Billy for defamation of character. That case dragged on until 1988 when the judge made a decision that Billy today remains unhappy with. In his decision the judge stated that, "The reader should be put on notice that many if not all of Billy Joel's statements will be nothing more then his opinions. His sought after opinions as a leading singer–songwriter should not be chilled by litigation unless he's lying outright."

The entire situation left a scar with Billy that today remains close to the surface, and which soured him on the possibility of ever helping young musicians or songwriters to get ahead. Where he once would consider helping young musicians he liked, today is a different story.

"If I see somebody coming at me with a tape, it looks like a subpoena," he said of the situation then.

Billy has always looked at his songs as his children, and to have been accused of plagiarizing one of them, essentially suggesting that it was illegitimate, brought out the worst in Billy during the Powers' lawsuit; it also tainted the song forever for Joel: "It is a song that turned sour for me . . . just like some of your kids turn into bums," he said. "Some grow up to be doctors and lawyers, and some grow up to be drug addicts and drop outs. But I love them all for different reasons."

On September 26, 1978 the *52nd. Street* tour kicked off in New Haven, Connecticut. Again this tour would be made up of mostly arenas and the first leg of it would go on until they hit New York City and Madison Square Garden for five nights in mid–December. Then it was a month off to spend with their families over the holidays before starting again at the end of January in Spain for a two-month European tour before returning to New York and then traveling to Cuba in the beginning of March for the controversial Havana Jam at Karl Marx Stadium.

But first the 21st annual Grammy Awards were held where Billy won his first Grammys. He received his first two for Album of the Year and Song of the Year for "Just the Way You Are," the song that almost wasn't recorded and may not have been if it weren't for Linda Ronstadt and Phoebe Snow.

Back from Europe and fully rested, Billy, Elizabeth, and his band flew into Havana on a chartered airliner with a bunch of other musicians that included Steven Stills, Kris Kristofferson, Rita Coolidge, Bonnie Bramlett, Weather Report, Stan Getz, and the ever popular CBS Jazz All-Stars in late February 1979. They had all been OK'd by the State Department who were nervous about the concert and wanted to try to send musical acts that would pose the least threat. The last thing the US government wanted was to cut loose a bunch of rock and rollers in a Havana hotel room, smashing furniture, throwing TVs out windows or driving cars into swimming pools. With their carefully researched list, which included Billy and his band, they felt they'd made the safest choices. Cuba had also handpicked a group of their musicians to also play that included the saxophone great Paquito D'Rivera and trumpet player Arturo Sandoval, among others. The "Cuban Woodstock" was scheduled for March 2nd through the 4th, and was CBS record company's idea to spread the music of both cultures to the masses. By all accounts the pilgrimage there by CBS and its artists was a traveling circus of sorts, combined with a drug induced "Magical Mystery Tour."

But also it was not entirely a goodwill tour on CBS' part either. In their best capitalist manner the company planned to tape and film the concert for a later release, something that evidently they never quite made clear to Billy. They were investing over $300,000 in the three-day festival that would be held at the 4,800 seat Karl Marx Stadium in Havana and, like the good capitalists they are, they wanted to make money on their investment. When Billy found out about this, he was already in Cuba, and as the most popular act on the tour scheduled to close the concert. Needless to say, Billy, whose politics have always been somewhere between socialism and capitalism, was livid. Sure he loved money, but he also would never forget the struggle that he watched his mother go through in Hicksville raising them. He had come to Cuba primarily because of his father's past history in Cuba and because he wanted to play music for the people he told them. Nothing else.

CBS was disappointed to say the least. Billy was by far the biggest star on the bill and to have him not cooperating in the film or album meant that their sales could possibly be dismal.

"I'm not down here on some capitalist venture," he said at the time. "I'm here to play music for these people."

And that's exactly what Billy would end up doing. But first Cuba and its legendary nightlife and friendly people awaited. Cubans were not all together in the dark about Billy Joel, having listened to him in many cases on radio stations that they could get from Florida. "This is the most important thing to happen in twenty years," one concert-goer said of the event. It was not a comment that would go unnoticed by the media, as just twenty years earlier Fidel Castro had seized power of Cuba.

Because of budget constraints, CBS had also insisted on keeping the entourages small, dictating that they be made up of just the musicians and the smallest staff possible. Rita Coolidge was there as her husband Kris Kristofferson's manager as was Elizabeth Joel, and they were the only two wives that did travel to Cuba, which for many of the male entourage was like turning a kid loose in a candy store. The Cuban women's reputation for beauty and sensuality preceded them. To make matters even better for the unescorted males on the tour, the Cuban officials wanted to show off their country, taking them one night to the legendary Tropicana Hotel, one of the few hold-overs from pre-Castro Cuba complete with its famed dancers in their revealing outfits that caused Liberty DeVitto to ask no one in particular at his table, "Hey, is it horny in here or is it just me?"

Billy and his entourage also got a sense of the other side of life in Castro's Cuba when they were turned away from entering one of Ernest Hemingway's hangouts because, as Billy said, "they said we looked like hippies."

Drugs also were rampant in the musicians' camp although carefully not rubbed in Cuban officials' faces. There's one great story from the tour that has to do with a set of speakers belonging to one well-known American guitar player being stuffed with cocaine prior to leaving the States so that a private stash would be there for him. It worked.

Although Billy didn't exactly sit in his hotel room during his stay in Cuba, he was still pretty well-behaved compared to others. He really had wanted to see Havana as his father might have, feeling that in some way it might "connect" them better. But he also spent time on the beach talking with his Cuban fans about music and reading Harrison Salisbury's huge historical work on Russia, *Black Night, White Snow*.

Politics were a touchy issue at the festival too, as most of the audience was made up of high-level Cuban officials, their families, and those with connections to them. Oblivious to this, Stephen Stills got into a long-winded rap about socialism on the stage that drew a cold response from the audience. Billy didn't want to make the same mistake and stayed clear of that subject, wisely sticking with the music.

The first two days of the festival were pretty non-eventful. The American musicians that did play were not known as rock and roll animals and their performances generated little if any enthusiasm from the crowd. In fact those days were primarily days when the Cuban musicians rocked the crowd and when the Americans played the audience often would go to get food or use the facilities. The State Department and CBS had been too careful in their planning it seemed.

Billy was scheduled as the last act on the last day of the festival and was noticeably nervous all day prior to it about the huge responsibility that this meant. He was scheduled to go onstage at 11.30 pm that night, but due to the inexperience of the people who were putting on a show of this magnitude it wasn't going to happen. Elizabeth, in her typical undiplomatic fashion and always one to test the limits, as well as to insure that everyone knew she was in control, threatened to cancel Billy's appearance all together. In this case she wasn't up against a group of record executives drooling over what might be hidden underneath the mini-skirt outfit, she was dealing directly with Cuban government officials, who told her in no uncertain terms that Billy would play when the time came. Sensing their seriousness she backed off and Billy went onstage that night at 1am. Unlike the festival in Puerto Rico years earlier, that morning no one had to push Billy out onto the stage. He channeled all that nervous energy and went out and blew the place apart right from the beginning. It was something that didn't go unnoticed. John Rockwell, the music critic from the *New York Times*, was there to cover the historic event and wrote: "Mr. Joel's presence at the three day festival . . . the only American pop performer here whose career is in full tide, lent the proceedings a legitimacy they might have otherwise lacked. He drew the most fervent response of the entire festival."

Billy walked out on stage and announced to the roar of the audience, "No hablo Espanola," before ripping into "Big Shot." From there he pounded on the piano and pranced around the stage, playing hit after hit, and at one time even ripped a broken piano wire from inside the instrument and hurled it into the audience, causing the chanting crowd to charge the stage, much to the annoyance of the Cuban Army security force. When Billy started playing "Just the Way You Are," the crowd leapt to their feet and started singing along in often broken English. It was an emotional moment for Billy who, now totally pumped, launched into a set of rock and roll songs for the remainder of the 60-minute set allotted by the State Department. He bounced and strutted around the stage, shaking hands with the audience and working them even more into a rock and roll frenzy. It was without a doubt the most hard-driving rock and roll show that the audience had ever seen, and they were fully caught up in it. The "Bay of Gigs," as it became known, had been a success and the greater part of that was because of Billy's raw and powerful rock and roll set.

Nigel Joseph at the time was a young engineering student in Havana and a rabid music lover. He was there at the festival primarily to see Billy Joel, who he was first introduced to on his friend's shortwave radio picking up stations from Florida and other Gulf Coast states.

"When Billy came to my country it was something you can't believe," he said. "I never danced so much in my life! When Billy played "Rosalinda's Eyes" every student in Cuba went crazy for him."

"Rosalinda's Eyes" is the musical opposite of the hard-hitting "Stiletto." The song is named after Billy's mother and has a heavy Latin influence. Its festive Caribbean sound is due largely to Hugh McCracken's nylon-stringed guitar which makes every note crisp and precise sounding, and also the soprano recorder work of George Marge. Together with the lyrics it projects a very simple and romantic Latin story about its subject who yearns for the life of stardom and an exotic life in Cuba, and ultimately only gets to see it in his lover's eyes as he is sadly destined to a life of relative obscurity in New York's Spanish neighborhood.

Billy's show had been a huge success. He had gone there to play his music, hoping that, as rock and roll does, it might work its magic and bring the masses together, and it had worked. *People* magazine wrote in an article about the festival that "Over the past twenty years the only other person who has moved a Cuban audience with such charismatic intensity has been Fidel Castro." But perhaps the *New York Times* said it best when they wrote that "in the right context rock and roll can still be subversive."

After the success of the Cuban festival it was back to the States for Billy. He had more 34 more shows to play including one in Honolulu before resting up a few days and then heading to Japan and then returning for a concert at Long Island's Nassau Coliseum to benefit Charity Begins at Home, one of Billy's favorite causes that distributed food and aid to the needy on Long Island.

Life on the road seems like paradise for some, especially those who haven't been through it and experienced the loneliness and repetitiveness when you are doing it night after night for months on end. It can become unbearable and desperate band members were often forced to break the monotony with practical jokes. One of the better ones was played on Billy by guitarist Russell Javors in a city in the Midwest whose name no one can remember. It was at the end of the tour and cities, as they often do, turn into one big blur. Russell recalls:

We used to open the show with "The Stranger" in those days. Russell said Billy would always whistle "The Stranger" intro. He would lean into the mike with his eyes half closed and his lips puckered up, and Liberty would often yell 'Duck Lips!' at him to try to make him laugh."

The show always started off the same way. We would walk onstage in the dark as an intro tape of "Mexican Connection" played. The tape would end and a pin spot would hit Billy's hands as he started playing "The Stranger" intro. He would then pucker up and lean into the mike to whistle and, as he did, the spot would open to show his face. At this point Billy's eyes always crossed mine as he would look over at Lib for time, and that was because Liberty was always behind me on a riser.

Well, that day I left a pack of Blackjack chewing gum on my amp during sound check. That night, as the show was about to start, I chewed up a piece of the gum (which was black) and covered my front teeth with it. The pin spot hits Billy's hands, then it opened to show Billy puckering up to whistle. Like always, his eyes passed by me. But this time I looked him and gave him a big toothless smile. Billy's eyes opened really wide in a panic, and instead of whistling, he yelled "GET THAT SHIT OFF YOUR TEETH!" Needless to say, Liberty and I were laughing our asses off.

The next show I went into Billy's dressing room before we went on. I went over to his mirror and started combing my hair with my mouth shut real tight. Billy came over to me and said, "Open your mouth. Let me see. Lift your tongue." I said, "Look, there's nothing in there. Nothing to worry about." I even emptied my pockets. Of course, I had my roadie put another stick of gum on my amp right before the show. That night I got him again. After that, he couldn't even think of whistling "The Stranger" intro without laughing. We actually wound up dropping the song for a while.

Billy would have the last laugh, though. Soon after on April Fool's Day 1979, Billy and his band were playing in Richmond, Virginia. The concert started as usual and this time there was no gum stuck to Russell's teeth. Billy played "The Stranger" in its entirety, then stood up and walked off the stage leaving his band and audience completely dumbfounded. He returned shortly afterwards, and this time had the last laugh on his bandmates.

As 1979 came to an end Billy had just experienced his best year yet professionally. His audiences, which were growing and more enthusiastic each night it seemed, were made up of a cross-section of adults who liked Billy's music because they felt he got what things like love, work, and life were all about. They sensed that he had gone through many of the same struggles that they had, and had the gift to translate them into music. But in looking out over his audiences Billy also saw a good cross-section of college kids, high schoolers who were fans because of his combination of raw energy, a message in his lyrics and also the messages of his love songs. His fans were dedicated on a level that today remains obvious, resulting in sold-out concert after sold out concert. Billy remained calm and cool about it all, although privately he was much more enthusiastic as he rode this wave of success, a wave so big that he could never have imagined it as a kid playing in The Echoes or The Hassles. Throughout it all, though, Billy never lost touch with who or what he is.

"Billy is basically a regular Joe at his core," said Dennis Arfa, his booking agent. "Today he's the same guy he was before all the success and he has the same attitude today as he did back when he was 19. He's always been driven by that same integrity, and it ultimately wouldn't have made a difference to him whether he'd had the success that he has or not. He projects that, and people feel that about him, which is why he is perceived as such a regular guy. Billy has always been true to his own beliefs."

Billy would modestly agree. He told Dave Marsh in an interview that he felt he'd been successful since about 1969 when he was first able to support himself as a musician.

"There are very few musicians that can support themselves just being musicians," he said. "So that's success."

As a result of Billy's success, others around him benefitted. The people on his staff who had been with him from the start, such as Brian Ruggles, were now paid more, as were his musicians.

"The only difference that success means financially is that I can pay these people who have been working for me a long time, who weren't able to get peanuts in the old days and are now getting a financial return," Billy said. Then, not forgetting his audiences, he added: "Or we can put it into production and have a better show. That's all I'm interested in—it does make a difference."

As a result Billy and Elizabeth purchased a new apartment on 57th Street in New York City with a 360-degree view of Manhattan and also a modern glass-fronted home on a hill in wealthy Oyster Bay, Long Island. It was in one of those areas that Billy used to drive around with his mother as a young teenager, one of those beautiful North Shore places they would go past after a day at the beach or the park, and he would sit in the car saying to no one in particular that he would own some day. His predictions were beginning to come true.

# Chapter 21

The album *52nd. Street* certainly had been another success in terms of sales and in 1979 would go on to earn Billy two more Grammy Awards for Album of the Year and Male Vocal Performance of the Year for the single "My Life," a great irony for Billy who has always been uncomfortable with his voice, which he often makes fun of.

"I don't like my own voice," Billy says. "I'm always trying to sound like somebody else. I'm trying to sound like Little Richard, I'm trying to sound like Ray Charles, I'm trying to sound like The Beatles, I'm trying to sound like anybody but that little schnook from Levittown. I don't like his voice."

Billy decided to not attend the ceremonies in Los Angeles that year because "it was too Vegasy," and it would mean putting on a tux "and thanking all the little people." Instead Phil Ramone sat in for him. The show that year was right in the middle of the disco craze that was sweeping the country and artist after artist when accepting their awards all ended up thanking God for their talent. Finally it was Phil's turn, and standing at the mike on the huge stage he injected a much needed breath of fresh air and humor when he said, "I guess the Lord must live in New York City." It was the dry and witty humor that Billy and Phil shared and which prevailed in the studio, making the surreal experience of recording often bearable.

"I found his humor to be great. It's either absolutely below high school level or somewhere where nobody gets to," Ramone said. "We seemed to always be floating around in some oddball place by ourselves. There were many times we would laugh at each other because neither one of us had said anything that made sense."

As 1979 drew to a close many changes had occurred for Billy. Elizabeth, who had taken the reins just a few years earlier and had been instrumental in not only getting all the loose ends of Billy's life and career straightened out, but also of being an integral part of his success today, was no longer managing him. She was burned out on the responsibility yet secure enough that her marriage to Billy, which was beginning to show signs of stress, was enough of an insurance policy that would guarantee her financial independence for life even if they did separate. With Billy Joel now a cottage industry of five separate divisions Elizabeth had indeed "built her empire."

She stepped aside gradually, though, still keeping her hand in Billy's affairs at least temporarily until she was sure that the machine that she so carefully had built was in good hands and not about to tumble. Here was where she would make her first big mistake. A mistake that ultimately would cause her little if any harm, certainly not financially, but in just a decade would put Billy in a very precarious financial position.

In order to keep her hands in the pie so to speak, Elizabeth brought in her brother Frank Weber, who previously was working for a Long Island, NY defense contractor in their marketing division. It wasn't an easy sell for Elizabeth either with Frank and his family or Billy. Frank and his wife initially turned down the offer to work for Billy, but as usual Elizabeths perseverance paid off and Frank finally took the job. Billy also had reservations about hiring Frank, but from her bargaining perspective, Elizabeth convinced Billy that it made more sense than trying to bring in someone from outside of their world. After all, family made the most sense particularly when it came to Billy's affairs. Family were the ones that could be counted on to keep secrets and to always make the best choices, or so it should be, and Billy who has always felt family was more important then most anything else was finally convinced to give Frank a chance.

"I had questions about somebody's brother coming in," Billy said. "Because she brought Frank in I thought it would help to preserve the marriage by having someone . . . handle the management and the business for me."

In another attempt to hold his marriage together, Billy also signed his own post-nuptial agreement splitting his and Elizabeth's assets right down the middle. Again, Elizabeth had prevailed.

Frank Weber gradually eased his way into the operations at the Home Run office as he familiarized himself with five companies that made up the Billy Joel machine. These ranged from his merchandising company Roots Rags, Inc. which handled his lucrative T-shirt and merchandise sales, to the Home Run Agency which was Billy's in-house booking agency, to Impulsive Music/Joel Songs, the increasingly lucrative music publishing part of Billy's music. Additionally, Billy Joel Tours now handled the tour production in-house, including staging, lights, and sound. Last but not least was Home Run System Corporation which was Billy's personal management company. By the end of 1980 Frank Weber was working at the Home Run offices on a full time basis. As he took on more and more of the responsibilities, he began to like the job and its perks even more. He and Billy were spending more and more time together, and sensing the growing gap between Elizabeth and Billy, Frank began to show his true colors when he started questioning many of Elizabeth's past decisions to Billy in an attempt to further galvanize his position. As a result Elizabeth's role continued to diminish as did her marriage to Billy. Never one to be counted out, though, she continued to stay just involved enough to keep an eye on her interests. In a relatively short time, Frank was calling a lot of the shots and bringing in some people of his own including Rick London, who was married to Elizabeth's and Frank's sister, Mary Sue. Rick was an accountant who also within a decade would play a role in Billy's precarious financial situation. Rick joined Jeff Schock who was brought in by Elizabeth before she stepped aside to market Billy Joel to the press. Schock would go on to become a member of Billy's then inner circle, yet not get caught up in the legal mess that was a decade or so away. Finally in a move to further improve his position, Frank dismissed attorney Ina Meisach, a close ally of Elizabeth, and hired Mike Tannen, Paul Simon's lawyer, who was an archnemesis of Walter Yetnikoff. Tannen's role as Billy's lawyer would be short-lived, however, as Yetnikoff let Weber know in no uncertain terms that he was prepared to give Billy Joel a better deal in upcoming negotiations with Columbia Records if Tannen were out of the picture. Weber, who was still a little unsure of himself and also looking to insure a good bottom line for himself, agreed and took Walter's suggestion that he hire Alan Grubman, whose legal practice Yetnikoff accurately takes credit for single-handedly handing to him one client at a time. Now with Grubman representing Billy, Walter had just what he wanted, an attorney who was so beholding to him that he wouldn't think of turning on Yetnikoff.

"I never had to worry about Grubman suing me," Yetnikoff said confidently.

Now with Billy Joel as a client, Grubman instantly became "the" lawyer to have in the entertainment industry, while Tannen's practice began to fall apart. Within a year Grubman would have to show what he was made of as contract negotiations with Columbia began, but first there was music to make and a world that still wasn't really aware about Billy Joel. Much damage had been done to his image over the years by critics who he'd pissed off and those in his camp decided that it now made more sense to attempt to compromise then to continue to battle. After all, good reviews translated into better album sales and more concert tickets, and although Billy certainly was doing just fine now in both areas, there was always room for improvement, all agreed.

Howard Bloom was the public relations spinmeister to have on your payroll in the seventies and eighties if you were a musician and your image needed to be authenticated to the masses, and he was just what Billy needed at the time. With his company the Howard Bloom Organization, which he founded in the seventies, he had successfully transformed and launched the careers of many rock stars including John Mellencamp, Kiss, Hall and Oates, AC/DC, Run DMC, and soon Billy Joel. He was hired by Columbia with Walter Yetnikoff's blessing to make Billy Joel more media friendly.

Howard was not totally in the dark about Billy Joel either. Bloom's path had crossed Billy's back in the days of Artie Ripp and the *Cold Spring Harbor* album. At the time Howard was briefly head of publicity for Gulf and Western's music division, so Howard had been part of that effort to bring Billy to the masses which unfortunately had failed not because of Howard's efforts, but because of the rudderless ship that Gulf and Western had become at the time. As a result he had some knowledge about just who and what Billy Joel was, as well as some of the professional issues surrounding him.

When Billy came to Howard this time he was in the unenviable position of having an incredibly adversarial relationship with the music press. Some of it was his own doing. Early on, the press had loved Billy. Then he had essentially dropped off the radar screen as his career went through the numerous changes after the Artie Ripp break. Suddenly Billy was back, and back as a major star with two hit albums behind him, and he had essentially done it all on his own without the help of the music reviewers. This was something that irked the music journalists like nothing else. In their elitist manner they couldn't accept the fact that someone had risen as high as Billy had without their assistance. It was an unwritten law in the music business that people, no matter how talented, weren't supposed to make it without their help, and Billy had broken that law too now. Consequently, with Billy's blatant antics such as ripping up reviews on stage and bad-mouthing music writers in public, he had pretty much alienated most if not all of the writers, including Timothy White who wrote a scathing piece called "Angry Young Man" attacking Billy. So the energy that could have been spent helping Billy's career now seemed to be used to undermine it.

Another example was a two-part article in the *Los Angeles Times* at the time by Robert Hilburn that featured both Billy Joel and Bob Seger who then had a red hot career. The first part dealing with Seger touted him and suggested that because the author loved him, the fans should too. On the other hand the piece about Billy was essentially just the opposite and suggested, if subtly, that readers should not pay any attention to Billy Joel.

Howard Bloom knew that if he were going to succeed in bringing Billy Joel to the public in a positive way he'd have to take music writers to lunch or dinner and massage them on the virtues of his client, but words wouldn't be enough and he knew that too. He'd need real substance. At the time Howard had Elaine Cooper working for him. Elaine became Howard's publicist on the Billy Joel project with an issue that right out of the gate created an obstacle for Howard—Elaine was not a Billy Joel fan; in fact she despised him and didn't even want to work with him at first. Elaine was supposed to not like Billy Joel because no one else in music journalism did. So in reality the first obstacle on the Billy Joel case for Howard was going to be in-house. Gradually Howard did prevail, using the same logic and facts that they would soon use on the journalists, and Elaine was converted to the Billy Joel camp.

Now the two of them had to focus on how best to get to the writers and turn them. Howard had identified the one common thing that all writers share and that they could then use as their selling point on Billy Joel's talent—a love of words. Simple as that. Howard believed that if he could get the writers to really take a look at Billy's lyrics they would have to see the extraordinary gift that Joel had in putting words together to form his music, his stories, and it worked. Howard's theory paid off.

At the time, Elaine was living with an editor at *Rolling Stone* magazine named Jim Henke who today is a curator at the Rock and Roll Hall of Fame, so she had a great "in" with music journalists, many of who were her good friends. Together she and Howard hatched the plan to sell Billy purely on the merits of being himself and it worked. They made the writers really read and study the lyrics to a couple of Billy Joel songs which started the walls of resistance tumbling. The writers soon realized Billy's extraordinary gift for putting words together to tell his stories and they began to warm to Billy's talent. Then Howard and Elaine took Billy on a whirlwind tour of all the influential music critics and just let him be himself. Under her watch, Elizabeth had pretty much kept Billy from having to socialize because he hated it, but in reality Billy is a great communicator on a personal level. "His social skills are brilliant but he also hates it," Phil Ramone confirms. So Billy, who has never been known as much of a social animal, when in reality he is, totally charmed the journalists and won over the vast majority, but importantly the ones that mattered like Timothy White who just a year or so earlier had written his piece "Angry Young Man." Not only did Tim change his thinking about Billy in the days ahead, but they ended up becoming good friends before his untimely death in 2002.

Elaine too benefitted from the rounds of interviews, and not just professionally. At one of the meetings in Howard's office Elaine met her first husband Jeff Schock who had come with Frank Weber and Rick London to do some publicity brainstorming. They were going over the plan on selling Billy to the journalists when Elaine noticed Jeff writing down what she thought initially were ideas for the publicity plan. She learned later that instead Jeff had been drawing her legs. Although she was still living with Henke, Schock eventually prevailed.

While Billy's growing army of behind the scenes people were touting his many gifts, Billy was as usual thinking about making music. So in the fall of 1979 Billy and his band went back into A&R studios with Phil Ramone finishing up what would be another major musical surprise for not only Billy's fans, but the critics too. Billy and Phil had decided once and for all to capture Billy's ability to do rock and roll, and once and for all to put to bed that image that many had of Billy as the laid-back singer/songwriter that had followed Billy from the beginning. It was a calculated risk of sorts on their part. Billy obviously could turn out great melodies and love ballads like the best of them, but it was rock and roll that touched that spot deep inside Billy.

This was also a weird and, some would say, almost schizophrenic time in the music world. Punk and New Wave music arrived from Britain and, like The Beatles in 1964, had taken a large part of the record-buying music audience by storm. Suddenly bands like Boston and Rush, whose strengths were certainly not in their songwriting or music, but instead always primarily in their overly produced, self-indulgent stage shows, were being cast aside by true rock and roll listeners who had suffered through this eight-year complacency on the part of the music industry. Also many of the older more established rock bands around at the time, who incorrectly thought that they'd have their audience and wallets of their fans forever, discovered that they too were feeling the heat of the new emerging bands. The Ramones, The Clash, Elvis Costello, The Sex Pistols, and a long list of other bands led the way into this musically uncharted area, and their music was clearly changing rock and roll in a major way. The days of the mellower singers and songwriters would never disappear, but rock and roll was irrevocably changing, and as change usually is, it was ultimately going to be for the best.

Joel's next album, *Glass Houses*, was released in February 1980 and would put to rest once and for all Billy's image as a pop stylist. It would also pretty much end the unofficial truce between Billy and many of the music critics after Billy blew up once more after its release. The cover of *Glass Houses* immediately began numerous debates about its meaning. The reality is that the image of Billy dressed in a leather jacket, jeans, and sneakers, ready to throw a large stone through the large plate-glass window of his modern Long Island house, was Billy's way of "throwing a rock at the image people have of me as a mellow balladeer." On the back of the album cover is a photo of Billy dressed in a jacket and tie looking at the hole that he'd made. "It was a very deliberate statement," he said.

The album immediately ruffled the feathers of some music critics who were offended by the lyrics of the opening song, "It's Still Rock and Roll to Me," which questioned the validity of what was going on in the music world and paid homage to the music that Billy and many others loved. The review by Paul Nelson at *Rolling Stone* was venomous. He awarded Billy a trophy for "a polyester record" that he hoped would "go away." He also added sarcastically that "what Billy's defenders say is true: his music's catchy. But then so is the flu." Needless to say Nelson wasn't the only critic that felt that way.

Billy wasn't fazed by it at all. He loved rock and roll, being weaned on it since a kid, and was one of its biggest cheerleaders. But people were offended by it because to many the perception was that Billy wasn't about rock 'n' roll, he was about pop. But as Billy would point out time and again, he had always played rock 'n' roll, it was the perception that journalists wrongly had of him that many people bought into. Certainly "Big Shot," "My Life," or "Say Goodbye to Hollywood" were not ballads, and Billy rightfully so points out that "When The Beatles did 'Yesterday' did that mean that they became an adult contemporary group suitable only for dentists' offices?" So when Billy sings that "It's the next phase, new wave, dance craze/It's still rock 'n' roll to me," he's only saying that he likes rock and roll music, simple as that.

"We've been playing rock and roll for years, years, years," he said at the time. "This album is hard rock heavy," he added. "Jazz went away and never came back, but rock and roll every fifteen years refreshes itself . . . and I think that's really good."

Then Billy in his typical in your face manner told Timothy White that indeed he did like Donna Summer music and that, yes, some of his earlier work had been overly produced, over-indulgent, and overly-hyped. Also that he felt New Wave music was "good and necessary," but also that "the whole damned industry" could use "an enema" and that it made sense to "jam that tube right up its rear end."

As for the song itself which generated all the drama, "It's Still Rock and Roll to Me," Billy explained that it came to him the same way that most of his songs do. First he gets the fragments of it in his head. Then someone in the band will pick up on it in the studio, pressuring him to finish the song and he does.

"I wrote it on the way to the studio," he said. "I was sitting in the back of a car with Doug Stegmeyer and I'm going, "Da, da, de, da, da. But it's all rock and roll—no it's just rock and roll—no, I had just the way you are. It's only rock and roll—no. The Stones did that—it's still rock and roll." And Doug was going, 'Nah, it still doesn't make it.' But I stuck with it."

In the end *Rolling Stone* magazine was so offended by the song that they created their own survey so that they could vote "It's Still Rock and Roll to Me" the worst song ever written about rock and roll. Bizarrely these were the same people that praised "I Love Rock and Roll" by Joan Jett but she hadn't taken on the rock critics as Billy had, particularly with the line "you can't get the sound from a story in a magazine," which obviously struck a nerve.

Despite all the bullshit from the critics, with *Glass Houses* Billy also pays due respect to his band who had reached the next level in not only the studio, but the bigger venues that Billy was now playing with his growing success. On the album's inner sleeve the band is pictured without Billy in a show of respect, a bold statement by Billy as to their importance. He purposely did it as a statement to his listeners saying that although he was the singer/ songwriter, "we" had made the album. A rare tribute to a band such as Billy's where he was such a powerful front man. Yet even behind the scenes, Billy took care of the band in those days. Paying them a better then average wage and, equally important, allowing them great input into the music. Although things would change in the days ahead, at that point they all felt the respect that Billy had for them, and also just how they individually were part of an important puzzle.

Since *Turnstiles* Billy's band had continued to evolve into one of the greatest back-up bands in rock and roll. The multi-talented members of the band who had been initially pretty much hand picked to audition for Billy by bassist Doug Stegmeyer now consisted of Doug, Liberty DeVitto, Richie Canatta, and Russell Javors. In addition, David Brown was there for his first album with Billy. He was brought in to play lead guitar and in doing so would give Billy's music that extra reach that it needed for the Colosseum-sized venues that they were now playing.

"David Brown used to kick my ass on the guitar," Russell Javors said.

"David joined on the second album . . . I remember he was a very young, cocky guy. Billy kind of looked at me and he wanted, he needed, to let him know in the best possible way who the boss was," Phil Ramone added.

But Billy has always also had a kind of love/hate relationship with guitar players in his band. Not on a personal level, but as they pertain to his music.

"I used to call it guitar-ria, what happens often when two guitar players get together," Ramone said. "And Billy would say, 'Do I have to go through that?' "

The new aggressive musical support that Billy had in his band now was critical in keeping Billy's music fine-tuned. "They were there when I was nothing," Billy said of them at the time. "We all grew up together, personally and musically . . . Their presence gives me an invaluable sense of perspective on my work . . . They walk in and go 'Shut up schmuck. I know you; don't give me that dopey garbage.' They are not impressed by Billy Joel one measly bit."

Some of the band members and stage guys also became part of a very elite group of Billy's fans. In testament to how they had been influenced by growing up in the suburban world of Hicksville, NY in the fifties and sixties, Billy and Doug Stegmeyer, Brian Ruggles, Liberty DeVito, Steve Kahn, and Max Loubiere, Billy's long-time tour manager, formed a gang of sorts called "The Mean Brothers," complete with their own satin jackets, with names on the front and a Doberman pincher dog surrounded by "The Mean Brothers" text on back. Billy of course was MB-1. Their role was to "lay down the basic tracks. Then the guitars and the horns come in and do their thing," according to Billy.

"We were the elite corps, and we'd give the other guys, especially the guitarists, 'the ear,'" Billy added. "We'd sit there like Cheshire cats while they tuned up . . . making taunting comments like, "Go ahead pal, play with your toys. We're waiting . . ." And they'd be frantic, fiddling with their chords and buttons, trying to shape up. We could really be mean."

But obviously it was all done in fun, and again a throwback to the days of greasers, West Side Story, and Hicksville's West Village Green where Billy and his friends all had explored the limits of suburban society just a few years before—things that added up to who Billy had become by that day.

# Chapter 22

Billy Joel has always had a remarkable gift for class and great taste. Maybe it comes from the days of riding through the roads of Long Island's North Shore and dreaming about living there one day, maybe it is another of the many gifts that Billy was blessed with at birth. In all likelihood, it is a combination of those and many more things. Regardless, Billy's taste is impeccable.

Now with an apartment in New York City and the Glass House in Oyster Bay, Billy spotted a beautiful waterfront home in Lloyd Harbor, New York that was for sale. It was located in another one of those North Shore areas that Roz used to drive her children through on their outings, and the stone and brick home, which was surrounded by a wall, had once been the gatehouse to one of the huge estates nearby. Billy was rich now, and he'd loved the house since he first saw it as a kid, so he bought it and moved there, selling the Glass House.

Like a kid who had just won the lottery, he saw The Dakota apartment building on New York's Central Park West one day, and also decided that he and Elizabeth had to live there. Actually at the time, with his marriage in a really precarious state, he was more interested in buying it for himself, yet somehow hoping against hope that maybe the change might also save his marriage.

He discovered that an apartment in the building which was also home to John and Yoko, Roberta Flack, Lauren Bacall, and Gilda Radner was for sale. It belonged to the ultra waspy Dr. Frederic Pratt Herter, a surgeon who was also the son of the late Christian Herter, a former governor of Massachusetts and Secretary of State from 1959 to 1961. He and Herter agreed on a price for the apartment and all Billy had to do now prior to moving in was to be OK'd by the Dakota's board. This Billy felt was going to be pretty much a slam dunk, because unlike other stuffy apartment boards in New York City that might have had an aversion to show-business or rock and roll types, the Dakota had a bunch of them living under its turreted, gothic roofs, including the biggest of them all, John Lennon.

The meeting was scheduled for Thursday June 26, 1980 and Billy and

Elizabeth were to be "presented' to the eleven-member board which unfortunately did not include any of the show business tenants, just a bunch of stiffs. Elizabeth and Billy were in town anyway for Billy's five-night sell-out of Madison Square Garden so at the scheduled time they showed up at the Dakota. At first everything was smiles and handshakes, as members of the board met Billy and Elizabeth, with one even bringing the *Glass Houses* album for Billy to sign for his daughter, which Billy was glad to do. Then it was down to business, and the atmosphere turned cold.

Billy had recently talked in an interview about trying marijuana. Not being a chronic user as other tenants at the very least certainly were, but just "trying" it, and that shortly became the primary issue from which other obstacles would then arise.

It seemed the board, even the one who had asked Billy to autograph his daughter's album, had a problem with Billy's "marijuana use." They also were increasingly touchy about the issue of the John Lennon groupies cluttering up the sidewalk on 72nd Street where the tenants came and went each day. There was a growing feeling that there were already enough "celebrities" living there, and another, particularly of Billy's stature, was just too much for these shallow-minded hypocrites to deal with. Billy and Elizabeth were rejected by the board, which not surprisingly infuriated Billy to the point that he raged about it the next night at Madison Square Garden, tearing up an article about it that had appeared in the *New York Times*.

"I was turned down . . . because I was an admitted drug user," Billy said. "I admitted to once smoking a joint before going onstage, and that came up in the meeting with the Dakota board. We were looked at as undesirables, when in truth we were duller then those bankers."

The hypocrisy of the entire situation was what primarily had raised Billy's anger, and rightly so. Then just about six months later, with the event still fresh in Billy's mind, John Lennon was gunned down by a madman as he returned home that night from a recording session with Yoko and one of the great voices of our generation was silenced.

Billy had a long-time aversion to doing a live album. Many musicians use the live album as filler between studio albums to honor their contract obligations. Billy didn't want to just do the usual "Greatest Hits" thing and release songs for various concerts which he felt in a way were a rip-off to his fans. If he were going to record live, it would be done in a different context.

Luckily for the fans, Phil Ramone had just the idea: "We were talking about the previous songs that had never been recorded right and about going to go back into the studio and doing them over."

"If I'm going to do a live album, it's gonna be something special, something unique," Billy said at the time.

Billy's primary concern about recording live initially was about the quality of the album, particularly the sound. "It doesn't come out the same as the actual performance. When you're live, there's only one guy who's got his hands on the volume controls, and that's the sound man," Billy said. But as he and his soundman Brian Ruggles worked more and more together this concern fell by the wayside. Brian is also a kid from Long Island who first hooked up with Billy in the early seventies back in Oyster Bay and who today remains his soundman. He also did the sound for Billy's Broadway show *Movin' Out* and additionally has done sound work for such giants as The Eagles, Paul Simon, Fleetwood Mac, The Who, Elton John, and a long list of others on tours. Billy wouldn't think of going out on the road or in the studio without Brian.

"Brian has a different kind of enthusiasm for what he does and why he gets the sound he wants in the halls and stuff," Phil Ramone said. "It's different from what I do. For me it's the instinct Billy never has to explain it to me and that's a major advantage in our working relationship. I don't have to do anything about explaining, 'what does that mean' or 'why are you doing that?'" For Phil working with Billy was always exciting from many perspectives. The studio was certainly always a wonderful place to be with Billy, but also the contrast and rawness of live shows were exciting for Phil musically.

Billy, Phil, and Brian decided that if a live album were going to be made, and Phil had now argued his case successfully that instead of being a "Greatest Hits" rip-off compilation of music from Billy's previous three platinum albums, it would be a reintroduction of Billy's earlier songs, the songs from the *Cold Spring Harbor* album that had been such a disaster. This way artistically Phil and Brian would satisfy their artistic yearnings and Billy, while always doing the same with his music, could also introduce this music, which he still felt had substance, to his old fans in the way it was meant to be played, and to the newer fans that possibly were not even familiar with the songs. He was excited about playing these older songs with his new band instead of a conglomeration of studio musicians, and particularly because Phil Ramone would be producing the album. Making the album which was released certified-platinum was just one more great career decision for Billy.

Billy, Phil, and Brian set out to match each song that would be on the album to a specific concert hall or club that they were playing, where the acoustics would best enhance the sound.

"Ambience was essential," Billy said.

This was a much different tack then other musicians use where the album is done in three days or so, with a giant recording truck plugged into the venue, but Billy was determined to capture the essence of each song.

An itinerary was planned that ranged from such places as the 15,000-seat Madison Square Garden in New York City, to Toad's Place, then a well-known 300-seat club in New Haven, Connecticut. This again was not the usual way to do a live album, but Billy was adamant that it was going to be done the way he wanted and Phil and Brian were smart enough to trust his instincts and decisions. They set out to record the album which was released in September 1981.

Included on *Songs in the Attic* are now well-known pieces such as "Miami 2017," "Captain Jack," "Summer," "Highland Falls," and "She's Got a Way," a classic love song that until then had been largely overlooked. The album begins with "Miami 2017," a song about an apocalyptic vision of New York City, that in some ways would come eerily true in September 2001. It is aptly recorded at Madison Square Garden and the hometown crowd in the packed arena that night captured the "gothic reverberation of a vast railroad terminus" as Joel had hoped it would. The level of intensity that the crowd brings to Billy's playing that night enriches the lyrics and gives it a magic that transcends any other cut of the song.

"She's Got a Way" was, until its release on *Songs in the Attic*, a largely overlooked Billy Joel song. After its re-release it reached number 25 on the Billboard charts in early 1982, and today is considered one of Billy's most famous ballads. The recording for the album was made in Boston's Paradise Club, and the version, done solo, eliminated any doubts people may have had about how well Billy may have done as a solo-performing artist, had he chosen that career path.

*Songs in the Attic* was a success in terms of sales although nowhere near Billy's three previous albums. From Billy's, Phil's, and even Brian's perspective, though, it succeeded in doing what they'd set out to do and, in classic Billy Joel style, it succeeded on its own terms. It not only brought these songs back to be heard the way they had been written to sound, but in doing so gave them a more cohesive style that they also deserved.

While his career continued to grow in success, things at home were deteriorating fast. Billy and Elizabeth were separated in early 1982 and Billy was living alone in the old gatehouse on Lloyd Neck.

Many reasons were given for the split from both parties and a long list of others, but for those around them at the time, it was clear that being on the road for months at a time, and all that offers, as well as simply growing apart as people, were big contributing factors. Elizabeth, like Billy, is easily bored and now that she had accomplished what she'd set out to do and created her "empire" it was on to other goals.

At the time there were many stories about infidelity by both of them. One famous story had Billy refusing to play in France for a while because of a relationship Elizabeth was said to be having with a record company executive there. While at the same time, Elizabeth vetoed any concerts in Germany because of a German society girl that Billy was bedding. Whatever the reasons, one of the great partnerships in the music business was now over and all that remained of it was to settle what each would walk away from it with. Again, Elizabeth would not be a pushover.

In the meantime, Billy was enjoying the single life of a rock star, dating primarily models, including Elle McPherson, for whom he would write a song describing their loving but doomed relationship. But it can't always be all glitz with Billy Joel, he also needs to have that quiet part of his life, where he just hangs with friends, many from the Hicksville days, including best friend Billy Zampino. These are the grounding times for Billy, the opposite of the insanity of the road. During these times Billy and his buddies would cruise old haunts and new ones, and spend inordinate amounts of time on Billy's other passion, motorcycles.

He'd amassed quiet a collection of bikes including BMWs and Harleys that he kept garaged at his waterfront home and could often be found blasting around Long Island on one of them, either alone or with friends.

On April 15, 1982 Billy had been out riding and about 5.30 that afternoon was on his way home on New York Ave. in Huntington Station on his way home. He'd just gone through a red light when a car driven by elderly Cornelia Bynum, who lived nearby, ran her red light and plowed into him. Billy was thrown off the bike and hurled about 100 feet in the air before crashing down on his back.

"I felt absolutely helpless," he said, but eventually he got back on his feet. In what must have been even a slight case of shock, he tried to pull his totaled motorcycle off the road only to realize that his left wrist was "the size of a grapefruit." He also noticed that the thumb was split open to the bone and a bunch of "red junk' was hanging out of the mess.

Billy was taken by ambulance to Huntington Hospital and eventually flown by helicopter to Columbia Presbyterian Hospital in New York City where he was operated on by Dr. David Andrews, a reconstructive specialist. There were some justifiably tense hours when many people, including Billy, were concerned about what lasting effects if any this injury was going to have on his career. But, as the hand began to heal it became apparent that the surgery had been successful and that, with a routine of physiotherapy, Billy would regain the use of the hand and fingers. Once again, luck was on his side.

"I learned from the accident, that just when you think you have all the control in the world, someone runs a red light," he said in typical Billy Joel humor.

Meanwhile, when the police had arrived at the scene, they noticed who the injured guy was right away without seeing his driver's license. In talking to Cornelia Bynum, the investigating officer asked, "Do you know who you

just hit?" She didn't have a clue, although with the help of an accom-
modating lawyer, she'd soon realize that she'd hit what may have been the
motorcycle rider to lay her golden egg.

In what was an amazingly quick turn around, Mrs. Bynum went from
being mortified and scared to death of being sued, to the one doing the suing.
A lawyer who she went to consult convinced her that if she sued Billy that
he'd have to settle with her to keep his name off the headlines. That's just
what she did, filing a multimillion dollar lawsuit against Billy for hitting her.
The lawyer was right, though. Billy, who was justifiably angry, did settle with
her for an undisclosed amount to put the incident to rest once and for all.

During the recuperation period and resulting physiotherapy sessions, Billy
took the down time he now had to fine-tune the material for his next album.
He had set out again to write something really special and, as his own biggest
critic, had forced himself to really stretch his creative reach. A huge fan of
The Beatles as a kid, Billy wanted to write his equivalent of *Sgt. Pepper* this
time.

"He worshipped The Beatles," said best friend Billy Zampino. "After they
broke up he said to me, 'It's a shame that we won't be hearing any more
songs from them. Maybe I'll write one myself to cheer me up,' and then he
did."

Although the album would not spin off a number one single, it did reach
number seven on the Billboard charts. More important to Billy, though, he
had succeeded in writing what was his most musically elaborate and until
then the most controversial record of his career. It was nothing at all like
*Glass Houses*, but then none of Billy's albums have ever been carbon copies
of the previous one. It hadn't come easily, though. *The Nylon Curtain* was at
that point the most difficult album Billy ever sat down and wrote.

"I felt like I almost died making it," he said. "It was going to be my *Sgt.
Pepper*. It was going to be my masterpiece."

But after almost seven months of painful labor, the Promethean process
ended, and the album was birthed.

"The piano is this big black beast with 88 teeth," Billy continued. "You
have to lay your guts on the table and go through them 11 times on the
album. 50,000 packs of cigarettes later, you start getting it. You're horrified
that it won't come, but it did."

*The Nylon Curtain* would show fans and writers for the first time that Billy,
who had opposed the Vietnam War in the sixties, indeed did have a social
conscience. He just never wanted to force it on his audiences.

"My politics don't mean a damn thing to people," he said. "I'm in a
trusted position and I don't want to abuse it."

The album's name came from an image Billy had of American society.

"We talk about the Soviet Union . . . the iron curtain. And you picture a kind of image," he said. "When I think of the West, I think of a nylon curtain. It's soft, but still a barrier . . . sort of a rose-colored isolation. It's a stream of consciousness thing for me."

The album was finally finished in July 1982 and released the following month. It blew everybody away, many of whom expected much less than the powerful social statements that two of the songs from the album, "Allentown" and "Goodnight Saigon," were to strike with the socially conscious as well as to gain the hearts and minds of Billy's biggest adversaries—the music critics. There was now no denying any longer that Billy's arrogance, which always left a bitter taste in the mouths of critics and others, was at least to some degree justified. This was an intriguing and serious album of the highest degree, and from now on through the years Billy Joel and his music would be taken a lot more seriously.

On a humorous note, Billy, who was obsessive about not only the musical content of his "masterpiece" but also its "look," had envisioned the album's cover in a very esoteric way, with a genderless body covered up by a large piece of fabric. He got the idea from remembering the covers of books by Michener and Ludlum that he'd read. When he excitably showed the concept to Walter Yetnikoff, Walter burst his bubble by telling Billy that his cover idea wouldn't do, that it was too "artsy." In typical Yetnikoff fashion he told Billy that "I'm not in the shmatte rag business, I'm in the business to sell records." Walter prevailed.

As 1983 approached, there was a lot going on in Billy's world. This new album which was blowing everyone away was out, Billy loved the life of the rock star and all the perks that meant, and his marriage was now over, so he and Elizabeth set out to get divorced. While that part of his life was over, Billy was never blind enough not to understand what an integral part of his current success Elizabeth had been. Because of this, and other reasons, he wanted to do right by her. Besides, he thought, he was in the prime of his career, and had many more years ahead of him to make any money up that he'd give Elizabeth, and more.

Their lives these past fourteen or so years had become intertwined in the most complex personal and business ways imaginable. Elizabeth had always kept one eye towards the future and the way their affairs were structured so that if/when a divorce became a reality she would be well represented in every aspect of Billy's life. Elizabeth is also an honorable person, and although she can be cold and calculating she, like Billy, had a certain degree of integrity. She wasn't out to screw Billy; on the contrary, she wasn't driven by anger or revenge as many are in divorces, nor was Billy. Elizabeth simply wanted what she felt she was due, and she'd get it.

Billy did make one big mistake in the whole process, though. He used an attorney that Elizabeth had introduced him to named Ron Williams. "I sat with him and he explained what every paragraph meant," Billy said. That was fine, but what Williams never did do while representing him was to attempt to negotiate the post-nuptial agreement in his client's favor. Instead Billy ended up giving Elizabeth half of everything that he had earned since their marriage, which although undisclosed was a considerable sum conservatively estimated to be in the high seven figure range. She also ended up with half of all future earnings that were generated from intellectual property created prior to their marriage breaking up, another equally large amount, and on top of that three million dollars for what was estimated to be her share of his song copyrights, prior to 1984, which included her royalties for "Just the Way You Are."

Billy ended up getting hammered financially. "I shouldn't have gotten married," he said one day. "But she said either we get married or our relationship is over, so I said OK."

If all this weren't bad enough, and in a sign of things to come, Elizabeth's brother Frank who was now running the entire operation, convinced Billy to sue his own sister for 25 percent of money that Elizabeth had earned during the time Frank and she had both been running the Billy Joel businesses. Weber had endeared himself to Billy, accompanying him on the trip to Haiti for the final divorce, and following him around like a well-trained pet. Elizabeth eventually settled with Frank for an undisclosed sum, but like an elephant, she was not one to forget.

Billy would never look back, though. Although on some level disappointed that the marriage failed, Billy is a big believer in family and the institution of marriage, plus he had his music and that after all would always be his true love.

Billy and his music had grown up, and *The Nylon Curtain* was making waves and not storm-strength ones either for once. From the halls of Congress to the cellars of suburbia listeners and fans were being influenced by the wide range of music that Billy had written as a testament to the growing concerns and attitudes of his generation—the baby boomers. The album was Billy's favorite and one that he felt accurately portrayed the disappointments, guilt, fears, and pressures that they had coming down on their shoulders.

In fact, then congresswoman Barbara Boxer of California would say that the song "Goodnight Saigon" helped her to make her decision to sponsor the legislation compensating Vietnam veterans for Agent Orange related disabilities. Additionally Frank McCarthy, then the president of the Vietnam Veterans Against Agent Orange, wrote that "Goodnight Saigon" was the first song to accurately express the experiences of the soldiers who survived Vietnam's battlefields.

Billy had researched the song by spending many hours with old friends from Hicksville who had been to Vietnam. Many nights of sitting around a table, smoking cigarettes, both legal and not, drinking beers and talking had opened Billy's eyes and mind to the experiences these guys had shared there.

"They were never encouraged to talk about it. They were really shafted," Billy said. "I think they had something to say . . . to teach us." Indeed they did, and for the first time Billy brought the horrors of their experiences and subsequent alienation back home to listeners.

But it was the song "Allentown," a study of the effects of the collapse of the steel industry and subsequent unemployment on the people of the Pennsylvania town, that generated the most interest from the album that struck the nerve of not only America but the world.

*The Nylon Curtain* was written during the era of Reaganomics, of Springsteen's *Born in the USA*, a renewed interest in flag waving, and a rediscovery of the American spirit. "Allentown" had originally started as "Levittown." Billy's initial concept was to write a song about the shattered American dream from the perspective of those born from suburbia, but eventually became influenced by what was then going on in the country, and the precarious economic state of regions like the Lehigh Valley that was home to the once burgeoning steel industry of America. Now with the steel mills shut, and the towns all but boarded up, Billy wanted to draw attention to what had once been another part of America's heart and soul.

"Allentown is a metaphor for America," he said at the time. "It's like 'Our Town.' "

Another cut on the album, "Scandinavian Skies" has generated years of debate regarding just what it's about. At the time, when Billy was asked about the song, he told an interviewer that it had taken a long time to write and was just a "stream of consciousness thing." Then when asked if it might have fit well into the *Sgt. Pepper* album, Billy suggested that in fact *Magical Mystery Tour* would be a better place for it.

The truth about the song's origins is that the idea came from a plane trip while on tour in Europe, when he experienced heroin for the first and only time.

"Until the end of seventies I never really got into anything heavy," he said. "Then I tried heroin when I was in Europe. I wrote a song about it called "Scandinavian Skies." No one knows what that song's about. But it's about a heroin trip one time when we were all on a plane listening to the blues, going 'Oh my god, now I get it' . . . A guy on the plane did it for us, he cooked it up and shot it in our arms. We were taking a flight from Amsterdam to Stockholm and we were stoned out of our fucking skulls. It was a Robert Johnson tape and we were all plugged into the same set. 'Scandinavian Skies' . . . It makes sense to me and the guys I was with as well as others who have had similar experiences."

More important, though, musically Billy had succeeded in creating an album that he was really proud of. He had set out to begin where The Beatles had left off, to create an album that was a powerful sociological statement, but also one that had musical texture, was richly complicated, and that you "could put on a set of headphones and listen to it." With *The Nylon Curtain*, Billy's fans got just that. In the end it was generally recognized as a major achievement, and even generated some favorable reviews from critics that previously had been very tough on Billy music. *Village Voice*, a notoriously difficult customer when it came to reviews, called it "easily Joel's best." *Rolling Stone* called the album a "masterpiece." Perhaps the best indication of the album's impact came from the city of Allentown itself where, after playing a sold-out show on December 27. at Lehigh University, the mayor presented Billy with a key to the city. In typical understated Billy Joel fashion, when Billy accepted the award he told the crowd of 6,000: "I just wrote a song. I'm not Thomas Edison. Let's not blow this thing out of proportion."

After the Lehigh University show Billy only had two more concerts to do before wrapping up the short tour, and both of them to hometown crowds: one at Nassau Coliseum on Long Island, the other a New Year's Eve concert at Madison Square Garden, where he rocked the crowd with a 23-song set, including two encores before taking some well-deserved time off.

# Chapter 23

Billy Joel is undoubtedly one of the most brilliant self-promoters in the music business. In typical waspy, "less-is-more" fashion, he has often made sure that the perception was that others in his camp were responsible for the promoting of his career and marketing decisions, not him. He often is perceived as almost disconnected with that aspect of his life, when in reality Billy, who has an incredible instinct when it pertains to the manipulation of the media, is in fact always in the forefront of decisions.

One of the few errors Billy made regarding promoting himself was back in the seventies when music videos first began to be used as marketing tools. Billy felt that these new "concept" videos, which translated his music to a visual medium, robbed the listeners' imagination. In other words, that once someone had seen a video associated with a song that was going to be the way that they would perceive the music from then on. Billy felt that the "meaning" of each song should be interpreted by the listener, thus making the experience of listening to music that much more personal.

However, Billy was also keenly aware of the power that these videos would have on the artist's bottom lines and testing these waters, in 1980 wrote and directed a video to accompany the single "Sometimes a Fantasy." He also continued to do some live performance videos, which until then had pretty much been the norm, one of which was the performance that he had done for *Saturday Night Live* in November 1981 from Media Sound Studios. The song "She's Got a Way" was taped and then used subsequently as a music video, but again this was an old school solo piano performance and not a concept video.

Then in the summer of 1981, Billy watched with great interest as MTV hit the airwaves and music videos emerged to be used for the first time in selling not just bands, but primarily records for the recording artists. There was now no denying which way the industry was going and Billy knew that he would evolve with the times. Music videos were becoming increasingly more powerful in artists' professional lives, and Billy immediately saw the power that they had in making or breaking careers and also in increasing the royalty checks.

Some record company executives were initially worried about Billy making videos. They were concerned that his voice wouldn't translate well to videos and equally concerned that Billy, who never has been known as a guy with looks that kill, would not be sexy enough for watchers. Unlike some rock stars then, like the pretty boy band Duran Duran, or even Mick Jagger who looked good no matter what, Billy was short and dark, with stubby legs and oversized eyes. Like it or not he didn't have a lot going for him in the looks department, they felt. Couple that with the fact that Billy is anything but flamboyant, especially when put up next to his friend Elton John. While other rock stars such as Elton are known for their outrageous appearances on stage, Billy is more comfortable in a jacket, jeans, and sneakers. But, as he'd done before, Billy proved these people wrong. In spite of his looks and voice, Billy became one of the most popular rock stars on MTV because of the innate warmth and humor that Billy has, coupled with his incredible instinct and imagination. That combination would go on to translate into many great videos and many dollars through the years.

At first he recorded just more performance videos such as the ones he did for "You May Be Right" and "It's Still Rock and Roll to Me." These became immediately popular on MTV and by the time *The Nylon Curtain* was released Billy was now fully convinced which way the wind was going to continue to blow on this new marketing medium. He'd have to make videos for his songs and in typical fashion, if that was the case, they were going to be the very best possible.

He first teamed up with award-winning Australian director Russell Mulcahy, who did the "Allentown," "Pressure," and "A Matter of Trust" videos for Billy. But then Billy's hometown loyalty kicked in and he called on his old friend Jon Small, who now had established a well-respected video company. Together with another award-winning director, Jay Dubin, they would go on to make a long list of Billy Joel videos together and remain close friends, while in the process continue to make Billy an even bigger star.

On the "Allentown" video Billy and Russell tapped into the socioeconomic situation in the region that was then experiencing almost 14 percent unemployment. Using black and white clips of food lines, unemployed workers and Depression-era shots of railroads, the video featured Billy strumming a guitar in perfect Woody Guthrie fashion. For "Goodnight Saigon," Billy was presented in a place where he is most comfortable, on the stage, singing the song as the song then is intercut with pictures of Vietnam, soldiers in battle and in camp, and other wrenching scenes of Vietnam, including death. It, like the song itself, was a powerful statement about an unjust war.

Then, as 1982 was coming to an end, Billy enlisted Jon Small to record what would be his first full-length concert video. It was recorded at Nassau Coliseum on Long Island with a fanatical Billy Joel hometown crowd. The video starts a little slow as the concert did that night, but by the end Billy is dancing around the stage and completely in control of his audience as they roar enthusiastically almost on cue. Small managed to accurately capture the energy of a live Billy Joel show and in doing so laid the groundwork for what later would be some of his best visual work.

With 1982 wrapped up and his career better then ever, Billy wanted to take some time off for a well-deserved rest. He hung around New York for a while dating more women, and enjoying the life of the single rock star, but Billy is at heart a homebody and this life soon was getting old for him. Yet he was still comfortable enough in his own skin that things were OK.

"People were calling me at the time, going 'Are you OK? Are you lonely?' And I would tell them, 'No man, I feel good.'"

Paul Simon had rented a house on a small and then relatively unknown island in the Caribbean and was telling Billy about the place on the phone one day.

"It's great down here," he told Billy. "It's real quiet. Just take a break."

So Billy decided to do just that. He flew down to the French/Swedish island of St. Barthelemy in the Caribbean which was then just beginning to become a sort of Manhattan south during the winter months. St. Bart's then was still a sleepy little jewel of an island with some great beaches that had the added appeal of hosting nude bathers, and a little bar in the island's main town Gustavia, called Le Select, where islanders and tourists alike gathered every afternoon to drink and swap stories, and which served the best cheeseburgers on the island, resulting in Jimmy Buffett, then a part-time resident to write the hit song "Cheeseburgers in Paradise."

On the flight down you get off on the island of St. Marten to board a small plane for the quick rollercoaster ride to St. Bart's. Here in the tiny terminal Billy first spotted Christie Brinkley with some friends also headed to St. Bart's where they'd share the ride over.

"I saw Christie . . . I recognized her immediately," Billy said. "I wondered if she knew who I was." So in an attempt to attract her attention he did what any normal rock star would do.

"I tried to look like me on an album cover," he said. "I gave it every angle I could. She didn't recognize me from a hole in the wall."

It was a pretty non-eventful flight over except for the landing. When you fly into St. Bart's you come into the airport over a big hill, and then the pilot in order to make the runway has to put the plane into a forced "slip," which causes it to drop almost vertically from the sky to the paved runway, putting your stomach up in your throat. After safely landing on St. Bart's all the plane's passengers were transported to the very exclusive and very private Taiwana hotel in a van by staff members.

Christie was going through her own stuff at the time. She had just split up with her long-time boyfriend and fiancée, the 27-year-old, Oliver Chandon, of the Moet et Chandon family, who she'd met at a Studio 54 party promoting her first major pinup poster. Her first reaction had been to withdraw from the world and return to her parents' home in southern California for some time to reflect, but instead she had decided to plunge headfirst into her work, and took a modeling assignment on St. Bart's.

That first night after dinner in the lounge of their hotel overlooking Flamands beach Billy sat down and started playing requests on the piano for guests, successfully attracting the attention of not only Christie, but also Whitney Houston and old girlfriend Elle McPherson.

"I was making believe I was Humphrey Bogart in *Casablanca* as I was playing 'As Time Goes By,'" Billy continued. "Eventually . . . Christie was sitting next to me. And that's how we met. I looked like a bloated puffy lobster. I had this incredible sunburn."

It was a totally unexpected turn of events, not only for Billy who was there to just relax and have fun, but Christie as well.

Now 28 years old, Christie was at the top of the modeling world. A smart businesswoman, she was earning upwards of well over a million dollars a year in endorsements and modeling fees which started at $1500.00 per half-day. Her pictures in bathing-suit spreads were legendary and she also oversaw a growing cottage industry of Christie Brinkley businesses.

"We started out as friends, and then fell in love, which is the best way," Billy said.

Billy was clearly hooked, but Christie was still caught up in her own drama with Chandon and didn't want to jump into another relationship. They didn't see much of each other again on St. Bart's and both returned separately to New York City. Billy was living at the St. Moritz hotel on Central Park South and Christie in an apartment close by on 67th Street and Central Park West. He was dating Elle McPherson now and one day in March saw in the papers that Oliver Chandon had been killed in a race car accident in Palm Beach, Florida. Billy knew that Christie would be devastated so he got her number and called.

"Look, I know you're going through a hard time," he told her. "If you need someone to talk to I'm here."

"Billy was a strong support for me," Christie said. "It's his heart and soul . . . that made me want to marry him."

They started seeing each other much to the delight of the press, who had a field day with their relationship, referring to it harshly with headlines such as "Beauty and the Beast" and "Opposites Attract." Both were initially hurt by it, but Billy played it cool and was there to support Christie when she needed it. After all the rock star and the supermodel was the stuff papers were sold of and the two of them wisely played it to the fullest, at each opportunity, despite both of them insisting that they were "just good friends."

Billy is the type of person that needs constant intellectual stimulation, and many from Billy's inner circle who bought into the stereotype of Christie as the dumb blonde model were blown away when they met her. She clearly was anything but dumb, having micromanaged her career to huge success. But at first some were reluctant to accept Christie, suspicious of her motivations, and feeling that it was just too much of a marketing dream for her and that Billy might possibly be hurt. Billy was hooked, though, and there was no turning back. In Christie's defense, he told the press that, "There's something beyond her looks, she's a very sweet person, and she hasn't got that snotty attitude of some models." Also that Christie "was not skinny, and that she's nicely rounded which is very important in bed." The press predictably ate it up.

Christie from her perspective told friends that she thought the 34-year-old Billy was "cute," and that Billy was also "a strong support for me" after her loss of Oliver Chandon. She also made it clear that she had a problem at first taking anyone with the name "Billy" seriously, so she always called him "Joe" instead.

Within fours months of returning to New York, Billy and Christie were a couple, spending time at Billy's Lloyd Neck house and also his apartment on New York's Central Park South, overlooking the park. But their nights were no longer spent as Christie's had been previously at clubs like Studio 54. Instead Billy and Christie preferred the company of mutual friends, often over dinners in old haunts.

"My wife and I had dinner with him, when he just started taking out Christie. We were at J.P.'s," Arma Andon said. "I remember Christie and my wife got up to go to the bathroom or something and I look at Billy and ask, 'Oh man, Billy how did you pull this one off.' He said, 'Thank god I'm rich and famous . . . I remember getting her in my bedroom the first time. "I played a few bars of Frank Sinatra, boom that was it.' "

Besides the obvious perks of dating a supermodel, and from Christie's perspective a rock star whose "town" was New York, the relationship seemed to be very beneficial for Billy's creative juices. As is the case with Billy, he writes his best music either in times of conflict or love and as relationships often are, these first months were a whirlwind blur of idealism. Of the promises of a love that would last forever, of finding a true soulmate, and for Billy that would soon translate into more songs, He told the publicist Howard Bloom shortly after their relationship exploded that his relationship with Christie was vastly different then anything he had ever been involved in previously. "I met this girl, I could talk to her," he told Howard. "She was intelligent, and we talked until four o'clock in the morning." Then Billy handed Howard a notebook that Howard opened to find a complete album's worth of songs that he wrote in just seven weeks. Songs that had just poured out of him. His relationship with Christie, in addition to everything else had opened the creative floodgates for Billy. This was the same Billy Joel that used to agonize over the songwriting process, but this time the valve of creativity had opened and there was no stopping it. On every one of Billy's albums he strove to adopt a different type of character.

"The character on this album is sort of a sweet person who is in love and feeling good," he said. "It's a guy enjoying the courtship rituals of making out, dating, slow dancing, and the insecurities that go with it." Billy had set out to have as much fun as he could writing the songs. He wanted people to understand just how good he felt things were in his life. "I discovered that you can be just as crazy when you're in love in your thirties as you can when you're sixteen," he said.

Being in love also made Billy associate the feelings to those of his youth in the fifties and sixties when songs by groups such as Little Anthony and The Imperials, The Drifters, The Four Seasons, Dion and The Supremes generated music with romantic feelings in a much simpler era. He felt that that type of music best conveyed the romanticism that he was now engulfed by. The album *Innocent Man* was released in September 1983, and would undeniably capture the lighter side of Billy's youth, but also clearly add a touch of Billy Joel for good measure. But there was also a selfish motivation of sorts behind the album, and in his typical way Billy addressed this. In the song "Innocent Man" there is a very high note that Billy sings which generates the same type of emotions that a song from Ben E. King or someone else from that era of music might have.

"I had a suspicion that was going to be the last time I was going to be able to hit those notes," Billy said. "So why not go out in a blaze of glory?"

The first song on the album titled "Easy Money" was written for Rodney Dangerfield's movie with the same name. Rodney had met Billy within the past year or so through Dennis Arfa who represented him until his death and he and Billy hit it off right away. Rodney would later appear in Billy's video "Tell Her About It" and when Rodney died from heart disease Billy was pretty crushed.

"Tell Her About It" was released as a single. It was a testament to Billy's new feelings about romance. "You should communicate your feelings to somebody you're in love with," Billy advised at the time. "Despite the insecurity that brings."

But Billy wasn't feeling insecure about his new romance then or his career and the record soared up the Billboard and Adult Contemporary charts as did "Leave a Tender Moment Alone," a song, like "Tell Her About It" was about relationships, as Billy elaborated.

"You say something really tender and affectionate and a part of you thinks 'I don't believe I said something that corny,' so you've got to make some kind of humorous comment to cover yourself."

The video for "Tell Her About It" was a major production for its time. Joel is featured as a Jackie Wilson-type character on *The Ed Sullivan Show* singing it. The shooting cost over $100,000, at the time a substantial amount for a music video and had a technical crew of over forty people, with a cast of 35 backed up by 600 extras. Billy clearly had made up his mind about the importance of music videos.

He hadn't enjoyed the ritual of courtship at this level anyway for about sixteen years, since he and Elizabeth first started hanging out seriously in Hicksville.

"I never thought that I'd fall in love again," he said. "Now I've learned that you're never too old to fall in love, and it can be just as wonderful."

The public found the album satisfying too. Its lyrics were relatively simple, so no deep listening process or attempts at interpretations of songs were necessary. You just put the album on and listened to it. *Innocent Man* became a huge commercial success not just in America, but Europe, Japan, and Australia too. In Britain, Billy had always had a strong fan base, but the song "Uptown Girl," a Frankie Valli-sounding song that echoed the sounds of The Four Seasons during the sixties, took that to the next levels hitting number one as a single, which was his first top ten hit there. It ended up selling well over two million units and took the album as high as number 2 on the British charts. It too was propelled in many ways by another of Billy's $100,000 videos, this one perhaps Billy's best remembered one, and in doing so effectively announced Billy and Christie's relationship to the world.

In the video Billy plays "downtown" gas jockey, a role he wasn't entirely unfamiliar with, having briefly pumped gas in Hicksville as a teenager to survive. He ends up winning over the "uptown" girl Christie Brinkley and in the process not only sings but ends up doing some dance steps thanks to the work of choreographer Michael Peters, who had initially talked Billy into doing it and then after he saw just how poorly Billy did dance, wisely kept the dancing to the bare minimum.

In her role as Billy's "uptown" girl, Christie, dressed in a skirt and "fuck me" pumps, leaves the shop with Billy, giving hope to all the other "down-town" souls watching that, yes, there may be a chance for them someday too.

Both videos were shot by Billy's old friend Jon Small, who would go on to produce many more for Billy and countless other well-known performers. These two videos showed that in the subsequent years since *Attila*, when Billy and Jon were last paired, that Jon had suffered no loss of talent himself. In addition to being a talented musician, he also was a gifted presence behind the camera.

With another successful album out, Billy was ready to hit the road once more for what would be his most ambitious tour to date. Dennis Arfa had once again done well by Billy, booking him into a long list of dates in the United States and additionally England and Japan. The tour would last seven months, during which time *Innocent Man* would be nominated for a Grammy for Album of the Year, with "Uptown Girl" nominated for Best Pop Vocal Performance by a male. The tour finished up with an unheard of seven-night sold-out shows at Madison Square Garden in which Christie could be seen sitting each night front row center watching her man whip the crowd into a frenzy. Things were good for Billy now and it showed. He was even getting some good reviews from music critics.

When it was all over *Innocent Man* had been another huge success for Joel, selling over seven million albums, opening him up to new audiences around the world and spinning off six top 40 singles in the process. He was now a star of the highest level, certainly beyond anything he could have ever imagined playing dances and clubs back on Long Island.

Billy had to be wondering at this point where the next level was, if it were possible to exceed the success and happiness he now felt. But first it was time to spend some quality time with Christie, because in just nine months another milestone in his life would occur.

# Chapter 24

1985 was going to be one of those years when Billy had few if any regrets. He was now engaged to marry Christie having popped the question first in a Texas hotel room and then a couple of weeks later at home in New York.

"I got her this diamond ring and I had this whole candle-light dinner planned," he said. "But I couldn't wait. Christie was upstairs painting . . . and the ring was burning a hole in my hand. I ran upstairs and put it on her easel table. She broke up, and she said 'Yeah, let's get married.'"

At the time Billy was taking some time off from recording and touring to focus on his personal life. He is one that never has taken marriage lightly and now was determined that he wasn't going to blow this one up by running around with other women behind her back, or any of the other vices that had contributed to the demise of his marriage to Elizabeth.

He'd now been together with Christie for about one year and unlike the stereotypical rock star/supermodel they were spending all of their time between homes on Long Island and New York City, and not partying until all hours in places like Studio 54. They enjoyed quiet times together with close friends and some family members and things seemed during this time to run fairly smoothly for the new darlings of the press, who if there were any problems in their relationship were more often then not caused by the press's incessant invasion of their lives. In their infinite wisdom, they questioned one time why Billy had not been at a show celebrating the introduction of a new swimsuit line that Christie was heading up. Billy for his part tried to explain rationally that he'd stayed home because he hadn't wanted his presence to take away from Christie's day. The press, as they do, twisted the story to appear that there was jealousy between the two and that a break-up was inevitable.

Then tenants in Billy's apartment got up his ass too. They called the fire department on him for keeping a motorcycle in his apartment and succeeded in getting that removed, and then tried to evict him by claiming that he was behind some scheme to take the building co-op. Further, they stated that Billy was not really a tenant because he was rarely there. What they didn't take into consideration in their suit was that Billy toured seven months the previous year around the globe. Needless to say, Billy prevailed.

With his new high-profile star status Billy was asked to participate in a fund-raising effort to try to call attention to the incredible famine that was being experienced in central and eastern Africa as a result of a drought that was plaguing the region. Not one to really ever lend his name to a cause, he felt that this one was not only worthwhile, but that as part of a group of celebrities it wouldn't backfire on him and result in the media adopting it as "Billy's" cause.

The "We Are the World Sessions" were held in Los Angeles on January 28, 1985 at A&R Recording Studios. The song was written by Michael Jackson and Lionel Richie and the session was produced by Quincy Jones. The concept came from Harry Belafonte who had been impressed with Bob Geldof's Band Aid effort and thought that by holding it on the same night as the American Music Awards the most amount of recording artists could participate. It worked: almost forty people were part of the recording including Billy, and the record would go on to earn over three million dollars for the cause. Billy's contribution was singing the line "And the truth's you know love is" solo, and then with Tina Turner "All we need." Not very aggressive, but it was for a great cause and Billy had done it just for that reason.

"It wasn't an ego bath," Billy said. "It was just spiritually uplifting."

It also wasn't bad from the perspective of acceptance in the industry either for Billy. Being asked to participate finally made Billy realize that he had been accepted by his peers as well as his growing fan base.

"There is nothing like peer recognition," he added. "It made up for every bad review I've ever had."

After the "We Are the World" sessions it was back to New York. With a wedding date now set there was a shit load of planning to do.

Billy and Christie wanted to keep their wedding as private as could be expected from two people with their star status. They wanted to get married on their terms, without tons of press and gawkers around to disrupt their day. As a result they decided that on Saturday, March 23, 1985 they'd get married on a boat off Manhattan Island. Not just any boat, but again in a fitting testament to their status they chose one almost one hundred and fifty feet long named Riveranda that they rented for the occasion.

Christie, a former art student in Paris and an amateur artist of sorts, had designed the invitation herself. On its cover was a likeness of she and Billy standing on a boat in New York Harbor as they are serenaded by two violinists. The words "We've been waiting to do this for the longest time" are written across the face, while inside is the invitation.

Christie had told the press that they chose the boat because of their mutual "love affair with the ocean." Billy on the other hand was a little more believable when he told the press that "The reason we're going on the boat is to get away from the press."

But Billy much more so than Christie has always been a private person, one of the many things that would go on later to end this happy union. In an interview just a day before the big day, Billy made it clear that "the wedding is not something we want to go public about . . . We don't think of ourselves as royalty. We happen to be working people."

The day arrived and it was rainy and raw cold as March days in New York often are. The 150 guests boarded the boat now decked out with a thousand white tulips and lines were cast off as the boat headed towards the Statue of Liberty. Here a visibly nervous Billy Joel tortured some guests by asking questions about how he looked, over and over again. Finally with everyone in position, as Christie arrived from down below on the arm of Don Brinkley, her father, Billy turned around to see his soon to be bride and a huge smile broke out on his face. As she arrived at his side he took her face in his hands and gave her a huge kiss. Then it was Judge Shirley Fingerhood's time to share the spotlight and in a ceremony of less then ten minutes, that had each promising to "humor and respect" each others "goals and ambition," they were married. Immediately after in the usual "first kiss" Billy grabbed Christie and as he gave her a big hug and kiss the DJ onboard fired up James Brown's "I Feel Good' on the turntable.

Billy Zampino, the kid who Billy had found thirty years earlier when his mother Rosalind "gave him a quarter and told him to go find a friend," served as the best man. But other than that it appeared that very few of the guests were friends of Billy's. To many it looked like Christie's friends primarily with a touch of Billy's great taste.

"The wedding was odd: if you counted Paul Simon, there may have been eight people there who knew him," said Chuck Arnold, Billy's high school music teacher. "I just remember before he got married he was really nervous. We chatted with him, to make him feel better, and we all went upstairs, where there was a string orchestra playing Bach and Schubert. It was a very traditional ceremony; the partying was done later at the restaurant. At the ceremony, which was very low key, he tried to make it as nice and intellectual as possible."

After the ceremony the yacht set a slow course towards Queens, New York and the Water's Edge Restaurant which had been rented for the evening. As fans and photographers strained from behind barriers to see the couple emerge, Billy and Christie disembarked the yacht and headed inside. There guests were served swordfish and Billy and Christie danced to a Strauss waltz and mingled with the guests before feeding each other pieces of the five-tiered wedding cake.

Billy's mother Rosalind was in her usual form, bragging to anyone that had to listen about her son and how far he'd come. She loved Christie, though, at least then, and thought she was a "sweet person." Billy for his part was genuinely happy, quipping that: "A lot of people have told me that I'm so happy. I feel happy. I must have been a real drag at one time."

The partying went on until about 11 p.m. for Billy and Christie, who then made their exit, complete with the thrown rice and good wishes. They entered a limo to be taken to a secret location, and then the next day to a "sunny" location, according to Billy.

The fairytale wedding was over and the couple that came from entirely different backgrounds set off on their life together. Christie said at the time that Billy had given her "substance and security" after her two crazy years with Chandon. Billy, who in hindsight said that the couple hadn't been "looking to fall in love," had his "uptown" girl now and he was genuinely happy and determined to make the marriage work and to raise a family. Christie had her rock star who she truly loved, but also knew would be great for her image. "She feels Billy is a big star," a close friend said at the time. "She thinks she's marrying a highfalutin' guy, while he thinks he's marrying the most beautiful girl in the world." It was going to be an interesting eight years ahead for both.

The honeymoon was a great success as evidenced by the birth of Alexa Ray Joel on December 29, 1985, just over nine months later. Alexa's name is the feminine version of Alexander, the name of Billy's half-brother in Vienna.

"I like the fact that Alexa has a particular rhythmic patter and sound," Billy would observe in typical musician manner. The "Ray" was after Ray Charles who Billy held in the highest regard.

Billy now had the life that he'd wanted since he was a kid in Hicksville: a good marriage, and now a child of his own to go with it. While he has always loved Sean, Elizabeth's child with Jon Small, and treated him as his son in many ways, Billy now had his own child, the one person in his life that he could give his unconditional love to, and Billy was determined not to make the same mistakes that had been made in his house as a child. Towards that end Billy would take off most of 1985 and half of 1986 with the exception of some charity work for an organization he started for the needy on Long Island. Charity Begins at Home was started by Billy to raise money for Long Island families which would then be given back to people in precarious financial positions like he had been brought up in or worse. It is something that Billy continues to support quietly, without a lot of attention to the fact that he is involved. But as a rock star of his magnitude, his friends and peers often were calling on him too to lend his support to their causes. Billy knew that in many cases he had to accept, and besides they would then owe him, and if he needed them to help with one of his causes, they'd be there.

Farm Aid started as an idea at the Live Aid Concert when Bob Dylan said on stage one day, "Wouldn't it be great if we did something for our own farmers right here in America?" Willie Nelson, Neil Young, and John Mellencamp agreed that family farmers were in dire need of assistance and decided to plan a concert for America. The first show was put together in just six weeks and was held on September 22, 1985 in Champaign, Illinois before a crowd of 80,000 people. It raised over $7 million for America's family farmers thanks to the efforts of performers like Bob Dylan, Billy Joel, B.B. King, Loretta Lynn, Roy Orbison, Tom Petty, and many more.

Billy had become involved because he remembered the farm behind his house in Hicksville where he played as a kid. He remembered that when it was sold, it quickly turned into a bunch of tract houses as his father's land had and like countless thousands of others on Long Island. He'd always felt a sadness about seeing these people go, and wanted to do anything he could to see that not only the farms but the families that ran them stayed intact.

"The reason I did Farm Aid was that I'd seen farmers leave and I saw the texture and standard of life change," he said. "That has always stayed with me even though I'm always strongly identified with New York City."

But there were two other reasons too for Billy to become involved, both of them close to him, and by becoming involved it gave him an opportunity to give back.

"I toured for many years playing agricultural colleges in small communities," he said. "These were the children of farmers who came to see me when I was struggling, and I wanted to give something back."

The other thing that concerned Billy was what was happening to the farmer in terms of their political philosophies. Some of the White Supremacist groups that were surfacing in the United States were reaching the farmers who, in their desperation to make sense of what was happening to them, were starting to buy into their hate-based rhetoric. Billy had called John Mellencamp to discuss this after seeing a piece about it on 20/20 one night on television. John told him that by making Farm Aid a success he felt that they were "presenting an alternative point of view" to the farmers. That they would be showing middle America that "people from New York do care about their problems." Billy was sold and called his buddy Randy Newman to ask him in typical Billy Joel humor to participate too.

"Randy, I'm an East Coast Jew, you're a West Coast Jew, let's get in there and show them that we're not responsible for this one." Randy accepted.

*Innocent Man* had held its own on the charts and in the stores until June 1985 when Billy's *Greatest Hits* Volumes 1 and 2 were released. A move that many saw as an effort to buy time until Billy's next album, they nevertheless had a good selection of Billy Joel hits that Billy had selected himself and two new songs: "You're Only Human," a song about the trials of teenage years and suicide that reached the top ten, and "The Night is Still Young," a love song that reached the top forty. Billy would go on to receive commendations from both President Ronald Reagan and Mario Cuomo, the then governor of New York State, for "You're Only Human," whose proceeds Billy quietly donated to causes tied to preventing teenage suicides.

Billy's paternity leave had not been totally free of writing as one would suspect. The seeds of songs were still popping into his head and as usual there was the piano overlooking Long Island Sound or Central Park to sit and work through ideas. Eventually Billy had enough of them written to return to the studio again. In the first few months of 1986, Billy called Phil Ramone to let him know it was time to do their sixth album together and had the band members alerted that it was time to return to work. They assembled at New York City's Power Station studios where it quickly became apparent to the band members that changes were on the horizon. Some attributed it to the new influence that Christie had over Billy, while others just felt as Billy did that he was moving on in another direction that may not have places for all the current core band members. Billy as is his usual way avoided the emerging drama within the band. He is never one to initiate confrontations, leaving it instead, like a good Godfather, to others to do his work.

*The Bridge* was "not a happy album" according to Billy. "I wasn't simpatico with the musicians, some of whom I'd been working with a long time." Billy also admittedly was not one hundred per cent happy with the material he wrote and felt that the record company put too much pressure on him to get the album out in a certain amount of time. "I sort of gave up caring," he said, "which for me was unusual." Indeed, for someone known to have an incredibly strong work ethic and to obsessively micromanage his art at time, this was not business as usual for Billy Joel.

With *The Bridge* album Billy had set out to write an album that was not a "concept album." However, he would soon go on to admit that in fact the name for the album which came to him about two-thirds of the way through making it in the studio had indeed been because of the many connections that were made on the record.

Steve Winwood was an old hero of sorts for Billy who had loved Traffic as a kid and he plays the Hammond organ on the cut "Getting Closer" for Billy. "I've always admired Steve for years and years," Billy said, "so there's a bridge."

The same philosophy pertained to Ray Charles' appearance on the album, where he does a duet with Billy on "Baby Grand." In a message that took a complicated path, Ray Charles had heard through Quincy Jones that Billy had named his daughter after him. As a result Charles sent word to Billy that he would be interested in recording a song with him, if they had the right material.

"I was so excited that very night I sat down and wrote 'Baby Grand,'" Billy said.

The experience of recording with Ray Charles turned out to be important to Billy on another level too.

"I found out that I could hold my own as a singer," he said. "I'm not a great believer in my voice." But it hadn't started that way in the studio at first for the two of them.

Billy was at first intimidated to be singing soul across the studio from the master of it.

"I can't do Ray Charles because there's Ray Charles," he thought. So instead he started singing like this little kid from the suburbs and when Ray heard Billy he started singing the same way. Phil Ramone would save the day, though.

"You've got to go after him, kid," he told Billy. "You know, get Ray to sing like Ray, because he's following your cue." As usual it was great advice from Phil Ramone.

Another curious thing happened during the recording of *The Bridge* for Billy. Since he'd emerged as a star, Billy was known as an artist that had never written a song with another collaborator. That had ended back in Hicksville during his days with Attila the Hun and Jon Small. Since then Billy had written everything on his albums, a rarity for any artist.

But as the album was wrapping up Billy found himself with one unfinished song that was driving him crazy. "I'd gotten to the last song and I had terrible writer's block," he said, unaware that soon fate would raise its head and save Billy from totally coming apart.

One day he was sitting in the Power Station studios trying to finish the song when Cindi Lauper, who was recording in a studio below Billy, walked in on him.

"You look like you're going out of your mind," she said to him. "You're climbing the walls." Which indeed Billy was.

"I can't get this song I want to write," Billy told her.

"Sit down at the piano and play," Cindi instructed Billy, as she grabbed a legal pad and pen. "I'll write down the words that you throw out." And she did.

Billy sat and played and Cindy wrote. Between the two of them, Billy and Cindy Lauper came up with the title "Code of Silence," which in the process stimulated Billy's imagination enough that the words came as together they put them in their proper context.

In another humorous turn of events, Billy had also gotten stuck writing a song in a studio he'd set up for himself downtown.

"I had a writing studio down in SoHo, in this place called the Puck Building, a big, gigantic old printing building," he said.

The floor Billy was on was about ten thousand square feet, an immense space. In it he had a bunch of recording equipment set up along with his piano and a desk. But even with this massive space Billy only really used a small corner of it to work.

"I could see this whole gigantic room," he said. "When I got stuck I'd pace the room, but sometimes I'd leave the building and walk down to Little Italy to get a little food, wine, and espresso."

On one of these walks there he got the idea for the song. He imagined himself as this character as he walked from his studio to lunch in Little Italy, and the more he fantasized about it, the more the song came together.

"I just kind of invented this character who thought he was Mr. Cool," Billy said. "The character is really kind of nebbish, but in his mind he's the king—the King Of Mulberry Street. I had fun writing that song."

With *The Bridge* released in July 1986 Billy set out on a tour to support it in September that would take him around the United States until May 1987. Then it was over to Japan for June, and a return home to rest briefly before heading to England in July for a mini-tour that would precede another milestone in Billy's career: his six concerts behind the Iron Curtain that would end up costing him a pile of money and seeing him throw a temper tantrum that now is famous, but also gaining him another huge audience of fans.

# Chapter 25

In November 1985 Presidents Ronald Reagan and Mikhail Gorbachev of the Soviet Union held the U.S.–Soviet General Exchange Summit in Geneva, Switzerland to try to hammer out the many issues that faced the two superpowers. Buried in the overly ambitious agenda was one issue that was understandably dwarfed by the necessity to scale down nuclear weapons arsenals as we tried to put the final nail in the coffin of the Cold War. It was an effort to reaffirm the importance of contacts and exchanges between the two superpowers and to attempt to broaden the understanding between the people of the United States and the Soviet Union in the areas of education, science, sports, and culture primarily. And after all, like it or not, rock and roll is culture.

So in May 1987 Billy's management announced through *Billboard* magazine that Billy and his band would be traveling to Russia to play three nights of rock and roll in Moscow and then three in Leningrad. Billy would be the first American rocker to pull this off and, not surprisingly, it became big international news. Billy once again had scored a great media coup.

The cost for the tour was then estimated at just under three million dollars and would be paid for by Billy out of his pocket and not Columbia Records. Billy, who is a voracious student of history, felt that being part of this milestone was far more important then the money, and at least initially said as much. At first the tour was planned to be one of just rock and roll shows— Billy hadn't even planned to release an album of the concerts—but Billy is also a very savvy businessperson, and that idea would soon change in an attempt to recoup the money spent.

These days when Billy and his entourage took to the road there was an entirely different vibe backstage then there had been before he and Christie had married and she had become a big part of the touring circus. Now with Christie and baby Alexa in the picture and their marriage still strong, Billy wanted to spend as much time together with his family as possible, and that he knew meant an immediate change in the backstage atmosphere. Word went out that the days of hedonism behind the scenes at the concert venues were all but over, and at the very least it better be curtailed enough so that the obvious wasn't obvious at all. As a result the backstage experience became much more family oriented, and, for the first time, others associated with the crew and band felt comfortable enough to bring their families, if even for short times, out on the road.

Christie, to her delight, became the focal point of the backstage life for many, with hangers-on and others constantly asking as to her whereabouts and when she and Billy would appear. It was made very clear by management at Billy's request that drug use and groupie sex had better not be seen, and as a result all these activities were forced quickly underground with band and crew members coming up with some incredibly innovative ways to participate in both.

Billy of course knew on some level that is was still "business as usual" backstage, but wholesome Christie, who wasn't as familiar with the decadent lifestyle of touring, remained pretty much in the dark, except for the obvious alcohol and marijuana consumption, which at times even bothered her.

After all and to a degree she had a good point: not only was she now part of Billy's traveling circus, but from both Billy's and her perspective, so too was baby Alexa, and both parents were obsessive about making sure that she was brought up in the best possible environments, whether backstage or home in New York.

So for the first time, on *The Bridge* tour, a nursery area of sorts had been set up backstage at each venue for the children of the band and crew. It was complete with games for them to play, people to watch over them, pinball machines, and other kid-friendly stuff. The change made it easy now for others associated with Billy's tour to bring their children, and as word of it got out other touring bands even implemented the same concept. This new kid-friendly experiment in rock and roll touring would also go behind the Iron Curtain with Billy and his band, making it easy for anyone who wanted to bring their families on what would truly be a historic event in rock and roll.

In late July 1987, after a brief stop in London to perform, Billy and his entourage landed in Moscow and set up shop. Christie, who has always been an anti-nuclear activist and equally concerned with health issues surrounding nuclear contamination, was, to put it mildly, afraid of the possible health effects the Chernobyl reactor meltdown just over a year earlier might have on her and Alexa. Her solution was to bring an ungodly amount of bottled spring water to not only drink, but also to brush teeth with and to even use to wash her and Alexa's hair with. She also brought a supply of canned goods and other safe foods such as fruits and vegetables because of her concerns about radiation contamination.

Billy, on the other hand, was as much focussed on the historical perspective the concerts would have as well as the music and potential money-making aspects of the tour. He'd managed to get the band members to do the tour for essentially what were expenses only, with the promise of more if and when the trip made any money. That would never happen, though, and the hard feelings between Billy and some band members would continue to escalate as a result. "Jesus, we did Russia and we never got that money," Russell Javors said. "When we did Australia we were going to split the money, and all this other stuff . . . I saw Billy at Liberty's brother's funeral and he says, 'Oh, don't worry we are going to straighten it all out' . . . but he never did." But the band members were excited about the possibility of making rock and roll history and signed on to do the six shows. Upon arriving in Moscow, they became totally captivated by Russia, and the bad feelings that were starting to raise their ugly heads in the band were temporarily at least put to bed.

"The Russian tour was fascinating," Russell continued. "You know real rock 'n' roll only exists when it is a response to repression. Russia was just opening up at that time and the musicians we met there were hungry for any input we could provide."

Indeed, that was the case. Billy, who had an interpreter with him at all times, wanted to explore the music scene there as much as time allowed. He was curious about the long reach of rock and roll and just how it was influencing the youth of Russia. He'd stop and talk to musicians whenever he could, amazed at the wonderful reception he got, a testament to the universal language of rock and roll.

"I think they were just thrilled to have a rock star from the west," Billy said. "I mean they even applauded the equipment."

The shows also became an international media event of sorts. Newspapers from around the world were there to report on the concerts and events, especially those that had to do with Billy and Christie, whose presence overshadowed the tour at times. For the fans back in the States that couldn't be there, Billy agreed to do two live radio broadcasts from Russia that would set up a number of technological challenges for techies on both sides of the Atlantic.

The first broadcast was to be a one-hour call-in show where Billy would be interviewed and then answer questions from callers, his first of this type. The other, the simultaneous broadcast of a two-hour concert that Billy and the band would be doing from the Lenin Sports and Concert Complex. It was another rock and roll history-making event, being the first time that a rock concert was broadcast via satellite from the U.S.S.R.

Peter Kauff, a successful concert promoter, who at the time was in charge of distributing the concert to the 300 broadcast stations around the United States, was caught up in the great significance that the show would have.

"We did it because of its artistic and promotional merit," he said. "It had true event status."

Peter was also impressed that Billy was reaching into his own pockets to finance the six shows.

"Not only was Billy willing to delve into his own pocket to do the tour," he said. "He wanted people to listen, and he was willing to make that happen."

With the idea gone of not trying to recoup expenses, the plan was to now tape and film the concerts for an HBO special and a video that would be released. Also a live album was now planned. Billy's management had convinced him that all this was a good idea, although in reality they were now just trying to cover their own asses by bringing in more money for reasons that Billy still was in the dark about. But, nevertheless, Billy had put his trust in his former brother-in-law Frank Weber and because Frank liked the idea, he was now determined to get the money he was spending to tour Russia back.

The concerts turned out to be blow-away successes. Billy played to packed houses each night, and gave his audiences shows like nothing they'd ever seen before. The rock and roll music which had changed America just decades before and which Communist leaders in Russia had banned for years because of the fear they had about how it would affect their youth was now in the veins of Russians where it would remain forever. Billy's concerts proved conclusively that when it comes to rock and roll there are no barriers—it is truly an international language, and one that motivates great change often.

Billy's performances were powerhouses of energy. He was determined to play his best each night and to give his Russian audiences the best possible rock and roll experience. This happened except for one well-known event that was beaten to death by the press. One night during his show, Billy had asked the person in charge of the venue's lights to turn them off numerous times. He sensed that the crowd was intimidated by the well-lit complex, and wouldn't really cut loose because of it. He knew that if it were dark things would change and with it the energy inside, but the crew that was filming the show wanted the lights up and ignored Billy's repeated requests. Finally things came to a head, and Billy snapped, yelling to turn the lights down and throwing the piano and mike stand into the crowd. It was one of rock and roll's great moments, and one that years later Billy looked back on in a somewhat mellower light, but still as the champion of his fans.

"It was a real prima donna act, but I have to protect my shows," he said. "The people in the audience want to be in the dark. They want to cut loose."

Billy was also amused by all the hype the press gave the episode: "I've thrown by piano twenty times in the states and none ever said a thing. All of a sudden I do it in Russia and it's an international incident."

On one level Billy knew the value of the press coverage of his tantrum and how it would later translate into album and video sales, but rationally Billy was disappointed too. The real story as far as he was concerned was that he'd gone to Russia and, with the help of rock and roll, conquered it. All the rest of the "news" about the trip, including the temper tantrum and Christie washing her hair with bottled water, was bullshit as far as Billy was concerned.

Now that an album was going to be made Walter Yetnikoff decided to join Billy in Russia. Besides Walter also felt that, as President of Columbia Records, and a Russian Jew, he could hopefully influence the political process there as it pertained to the refuseniks. These were the families of Russian Jews who had been refused emigration visas to leave Russia for Israel. As a Russian Jew whose family had immigrated to the US just two generations previously, Walter was sympathetic to their plight and wanted to help. Billy's tour and the media attention it was receiving was a great platform from which to call attention to the plight of these people. In one well-choreographed event Walter met with one family of refuseniks in their apartment to attempt to draw attention to the issue, something that infuriated the Russian political hierarchy.

But besides having his political agenda, Walter was always a big supporter of Billy Joel and wanted to be there for Billy at the shows to watch the crowds' reaction to Billy's music as he had done over a decade previously at Elizabeth's request. They blew him away.

"Billy rocked the place," Walter said. "In fact he rocked it harder then they wanted him to. The authorities made it clear that they didn't want any encores, but Billy ended up doing seven one night and singing 'Back in the USSR' which ripped the place apart and caused the group to rush the stage."

Not everyone that night was so happy about the seven encores though. Billy's tour manager was so afraid that they were all going to be thrown in some Russian prison that after the show he actually hid in the men's room, afraid that they were going to be carted off by the KGB.

When it was all over a video and an album titled *Kohuept*, the Russian translation for "In Concert," were released the following October. Also HBO presented a concert special on October 24 of one of the Leningrad shows. Unfortunately neither the video or album ever really sold well for reasons that today baffle people, but Billy's appearances in Russia had been a success from a social perspective and did much to squeak open the Iron Curtain a little bit further. The tour would later cause Billy to admit that, "Ever since we played Russia, everything has been kind of anticlimactic. We felt like we'd hit a pinnacle."

In addition to verifying that indeed rock and roll is a universal language, Billy also knew that he had some other more personal issues to deal with after Russia that had to do with band members. While Billy had been ecstatic about doing these shows he felt that others in the band hadn't shared his enthusiasm and were in fact more focussed on the financial aspect of the Russian tour then anything else. It was a situation that Billy felt was beginning to affect the music, and that was one thing he wasn't going to tolerate.

"It separated the wheat from the chaff," Billy said. "There was no money. . . . It was a real test of 'How much do you want to play?' . . . I wasn't getting that any more from this band. I was getting, 'We're in double scale now.'"

After Russia, the band traveled to Australia, another home of rabid Billy Joel fans. And then back home to Madison Square Garden for the homeless children's Medical Benefit, a one-night gig in mid-December, before going their own ways for the holidays. Although the year ahead would be uneventful as far as music was concerned for Billy, it would be a wake-up call for him regarding those around him who he had placed his greatest trust in. It was soon going to be a time of great change for Billy. Realizations about people around him and their true motivations would soon leave deep and indelible scars on his psyche, and in the process fruitful relationships that he'd established with many would go out the window. For some time to come Billy's life would be in a great upheaval, and his inner strength and resiliency would be put to its biggest test to date.

During the time he was recording *The Bridge* album Billy had received a notice from the (IRS) that he owed five and a half million dollars in back taxes and penalties for income prior to 1984. In another testament to Frank Weber's integrity, he and Billy sat down to discuss the situation in the Home Run offices one day prior to *The Bridge* tour. Frank theorized that because Billy and Elizabeth had split the proceeds from their years together right down the middle that his sister should pay fifty percent of what the IRS was after. Then, in order to insure that would be the case, Frank saw to it that Elizabeth's share of Billy's copyrights were held as a lien to satisfy his sister's share.

Subsequent to that Billy went out on tour and to Russia and pretty much forgot about the situation, being told by Frank each time the issue rose that everything was being taken care of.

Then early in 1988 Billy was asked to participate in the making of Disney's animated movie *Oliver and Company* as the voice of the canine version of the Artful Dodger. Thinking about Alexa and how much she would surely enjoy the movie, Billy accepted the role, recording his lines with her in mind and even singing the song "Why Should I Worry?" At the premier in November 1988 he and Christie sat watching the almost three-year-old Alexa's reaction. She finally made the connection after a little probing, telling her father that "he was a cute doggie." Billy the dedicated father was pleased he had taken the role.

Meanwhile Christie's influence over Billy was growing. She continued to offer her opinions of business situations and also personnel, and she made it increasingly clear to Billy that she didn't like Frank Weber, who she found to be "common' and "crass' among other things. But Billy's loyalty held on, at least for the time being, until one night when Billy was having dinner with his buddy Walter Yetnikoff, and as they were discussing Billy's money a seed that would later turn out to be fruitful was planted.

"Billy and I were having dinner at the Italian restaurant Fontana di Trevi over on 57th Street in New York City one night and he was telling me about how he was putting his Central Park West apartment up for sale to raise money to buy Christie a bigger house in East Hampton," Walter said.

This totally baffled Walter, who wondered why Billy, whose copyrights alone were worth in the millions annually, would have to sell his apartment to raise cash.

"I told him that something didn't smell right," Walter continued, "I told him that I smelled a rat, and that he should consider auditing his people. He told me to 'mind my own business,' so that night anyway I shut up and we drank more wine and ate more fettuccine Alfredo."

But Walter didn't forget, even with all the wine that night. In addition to being one of the biggest moneymakers for Columbia, Billy was and is Walter's friend and Walter had an idea.

"I called the guy that I had made Billy's lawyer, Alan Grubman, and told him that something was wrong with Billy's finances," Walter said. "I asked him to talk with Billy and asked him to hire someone to audit Frank Weber's books on Billy's behalf."

In a response that was very un-Grubmanlike, particularly when it came to his relationship with Walter, Grubman told him that he wouldn't do it because, if he did, he was afraid that Weber "would fire him as Billy's attorney." This bothered Walter to no end because he had essentially handed Billy to Grubman as a client, making Grubman's career, and besides Grubman never said no to Walter.

Subsequent to Walter's efforts Christie was also working on Billy about Weber and had gotten him to change his mind about having his books audited. Christie had no love for Grubman either, and when she and Billy got wind of the fact that he'd balked at hiring an auditor to look into Billy's money that was the beginning of the end for him. Billy sensed that something was terribly wrong now too and fired Grubman.

He immediately hooked up with John Eastman, who was Paul McCartney's brother-in-law through Paul's marriage to Linda. Eastman was also an East Hampton, New York neighbor of sorts to Billy. Billy liked Eastman because of his relationship with McCartney that Billy felt made him beyond reproach. Besides Eastman was also sort of living a dual identity that

Billy loved and found great humor in. Eastman was the consummate WASP, at least on the surface. His father was originally named Lee Epstein, hardly from a WASP lineage, who changed his surname late for business and social reasons. He also was a showbusiness lawyer, who had married Louise Linder, the heir to the Linder Department store fortune. Lee practiced law in New York City and had been introduced to Paul McCartney through his daughter Linda who Paul would soon marry. McCartney wanted Lee to represent him during those days in the late sixties when The Beatles' company Apple Corps was in financial trouble.

Early in 1969, Lee Eastman and another attorney from New York named Allen Klein were both being considered to take the reins of the Apple company. John Lennon didn't like Eastman and favored Klein, whose background was similar to his. George Harrison and Ringo Starr agreed with John and were leaning towards going with Klein. McCartney, however, was as impressed with Lee Eastman as a future son-in-law could be and was lobbying the other three to sign on with Eastman. Klein was the kind of guy who preferred to work without obstacles, which the Eastmans stood to give him. Eastman also wanted sole authority over Apple which was a big bone of contention for all The Beatles. Nevertheless, all four band members were willing to consider both sides, and see if a way could be found for Eastman and Klein to work together so a meeting with everyone was set up.

However, any hopes of a compromise was pretty much dismissed when Eastman and Klein met with The Beatles that day in Klein's London hotel suite. Lennon and his wife-to-be Yoko Ono were not impressed with the attempts of Lee's son, John Eastman to get on their good side with arty talk about the Czech writer Kafka or by the way the father and son both patronized Lennon. They saw through John Eastman's superficiality immediately. Meanwhile, Lee Eastman clearly disliked Klein, and became more and more insulting as the meeting went on. Klein kept his cool, but he and Lennon began needling Eastman by calling him "Epstein." Eastman finally lost his temper, and turned red, shouting at Klein; Lennon made his mind up then and there that neither of the Eastmans would ever represent him. Harrison and Starr followed John, and all three signed a management contract with Klein. McCartney stuck by the Eastmans, and signed with them—further dividing the already-troubled group.

Billy liked the idea of being represented by Eastman as McCartney was one of his childhood heroes and was now a friend. One of the first things that John Eastman did after becoming Billy's attorney was to hire Ernst and Young to audit the books for Billy, something that made Frank Weber visibly nervous. When they were finished, the accountants informed Billy and Eastman that indeed he was worth considerably less then he should have been, telling him that at best it was a result of sloppy management, but more realistically of criminal actions.

Billy was crushed, and rightly so. He had never wanted to spend the time with his nose in his books or financial affairs, instead allowing the huge responsibility to go to Weber, who Billy had trusted unconditionally. Weber for his part would brag to anyone that would listen that Billy didn't "even know how much money he has to send to his mother each month, he's so out of the money loop."

Weber had plundered Billy's finances, often ending up with more money from Billy's tours and recordings than Billy himself had. He also invested Billy's money in things like racehorses and oil wells which Billy had repeatably told him never to invest in. But Weber had a personal interest in both, allowing him to collect commissions on those investments as well. In one well-known case Weber had invested in a racehorse that belonged to Morris Levy and then ended up "burning it" in order to collect insurance on the animal. He also invested in a long list of risky oil and natural gas syndicates and real estate deals that left Billy liable for over a million dollars. Then in a deal that poured salt in the already gaping wounds Billy had, he found out that Weber had been overcharging Billy for the cost of music videos that were made by Rick London who was also related to Billy through his marriage to Elizabeth's sister Mary Sue. Mary Sue, however, knew nothing about what was going on.

Billy was livid and devastated by the violation of his trust. The anger he carried around reached a new level, and at Eastman's suggestion Billy hired the attorney Leonard Marks, another East Hampton summer resident who had represented Bruce Springsteen successfully in the eighties when he wanted to change managers. Marks is a skilled litigator with a strong background in the music business and would do well by Billy.

In the end Yetnikoff had indeed been right. There was something very wrong with Billy's finances as he'd suspected, and there should have been no reason for Billy to have to sell his Manhattan apartment to raise money to buy the East Hampton home. Then, in a testament to Billy's integrity, Walter received a phone call one night from Billy and Christie who at the time were riding in the back of a limousine somewhere in New York City.

"Walter, you were right," Billy said. "Christie and I want to thank you for the wake-up call, and for being such a loyal friend."

Billy really appreciated Walter's loyalty, but the audit and its results had been an eye opener for him in more ways then one. Today with his finances in the hands of Ed London (no relation to Rick), Billy is in the strongest place financially he has ever been, and equally as important, with someone he can really trust.

# Chapter 26

1988 had been a year of great upheaval and change for Billy Joel. It brought with it much sadness as he discovered how his trust had been betrayed, but also it made him determined never to allow it to happen again and never again be put in a precarious position financially. Through his anger, Billy looked at the situation with Frank Weber and Rick London as yet another one of life's lessons, and although he remained embittered by it all, he would prevail as he reached inside himself to find the strength and tenacity that had been passed down through those generations of Joels that was so much a part of him. He was determined that this latest stumbling block in his life was not going to adversely affect him or his immediate family and that he would rise above it all in a short time.

He was already in the studio finishing up his next album *Storm Front* when he fired Frank Weber and some others associated with Frank Management on August 30, 1989, just as Weber was about to obligate Billy to a six million dollar loan which would have spiraled Billy into financial ruin. Billy buried himself in what he knew best, his music, as he worked in the studio. But here too there were to be great changes in Billy's professional life as he chose Foreigner's Mick Jones, now an East Hampton neighbor, to be his producer for *Storm Front*, putting an end to his incredibly successful seven-album relationship with Phil Ramone. At the time Billy passed the change off casually in his usual manner as simply a desire on his part to go in another direction, but the reality of why Phil Ramone was out now in fact had to do directly with the Weber situation, and the bad taste that Frank had left in Billy's mouth about Phil as well as Billy's desire to essentially just sweep the slate clean of the past and move on.

Not surprisingly it appeared as if Weber had successfully poisoned Phil to Billy in his desperate attempts to cover his own tracks before the lid blew off the entire situation.

Phil was not after any more money or an increased royalty—as far as he was concerned he and Billy had the perfect working situation. But Weber was desperate at the time to cover his tracks and to take the focus off him, so for the next two albums at least Ramone would not be Billy's producer. In what would later become a reality to Billy and others about the way Weber did business, he was taking two commissions, or "double dipping" as it is known, when he'd set up album deals for Billy and Phil. One commission would come as his role as Billy's business manager and the other for setting up the deal with Phil Ramone. It isn't illegal, but is certainly unethical, yet Weber at the time was in a precarious position financially and desperately needed the money.

Exactly how Weber influenced Billy into dropping Phil Ramone is unknown, although many involved back then have their own theories. Essentially the belief is that Weber approached it from a position that he knew Billy was more susceptible to than any other—the artistic aspect. The consensus is that Weber led Billy to believe that after seven albums things might be getting stale, and that a change in the record producer would also result in a change in the music, giving it a freshness that fans and even non-fans would respond positively to. Whatever the reason, one of rock and roll's most successful partnerships, and one that certainly had benefited Billy as much as his relationship with Elizabeth had, was over, although maybe only temporarily.

But not bringing Phil Ramone in as the album's producer was not the only musical change for *Storm Front* either. In a move that Billy said was the result of money taking priority over the music, but that those affected by it vehemently denied, Billy had decided to make some personnel changes in the band as well. In typical Billy Joel fashion instead of picking up the phone and explaining his decision to those that would be affected, he simply did not invite Russell Javors or Doug Stegmeyer to the studio when they started work on the album. It understandably was a devastating blow to both musicians who felt that their loyalty and hard work over the years deserved better.

"To say that I was in it for the money is a joke," Javors said. "I can understand an artist wanting to work with other musicians. That is his right to do so . . . Just do it with some class."

While hurt, Javors was in no way down and out: He was working also with The Carpenters on an album and touring, so he had a source of income to support his wife and young son. Nevertheless, it was a wake-up call for him, and made him realize that this dream he'd had since a young boy to play in a band may have run its course. He comments: "I was lucky, because we were pretty good and Billy gave us the opportunity to live out our dream. My time with Billy was an exciting and important time in my life, but that's all it was. When it was over I moved on."

And he did. In addition to working with The Carpenters, Russell also cleaned himself up after over a decade on the road living the rock and roll lifestyle. He knew that if he were going to move forward he'd have to put all that behind him.

"I was in an alcohol and drug haze in those days—you get into the rock 'n' roll lifestyle, and there are certainly the perks too. There is a code on the road and you do not betray those trusts, those friendships. It is a surreal environment," Russell continues.

"Russell is one of the lucky ones. When his gig with The Carpenters ended he sold cars, got his license and worked as an investment banker, did development deals for TV shows and anything else he had to do to keep his family together. He certainly didn't walk away from the music with a portfolio full of money in which he could live on for the rest of his life, and, because the songs were all Billy's, there were no royalties. He, like the other members of the band was a salaried employee and when he left there were no more checks coming in, yet he couldn't help feeling that things could and should have been handled differently, particularly when he saw how others handled the dismissal of their bands.

"Springsteen got rid of the E Street Band around the same time Billy got rid of Doug and me," he said. "I was talking to one of the E Street guys after it happened, and Bruce apparently took very good care of those guys when he said goodbye. We sold more records than the E Street Band did. I couldn't believe what a different experience they had . . . I didn't even get a phone call."

But Russell also knew Billy well enough to realize that was his way, and also, as the band's leader, it was his right to make changes. He was hurt, though, that Billy seemed to want to justify his actions as a result of money issues

"It was beginning to get stale," Billy said. "I didn't want to go into the studio and talk about people's deals; I wanted to talk about music."

Not surprisingly, Russell disagrees.

"Billy can spin it any way he wants, but getting rid of me had nothing to do with money," Russell added. "I could show you my tax returns for the years I played with Billy. But I prefer to look back on my years with Billy and remember the positive things, not the negatives. I'd rather take the high road. I would hate to be perceived as being bitter or broken or living in the past, because that just isn't the case."

But Doug Stegmeyer took being let go a lot more personally and much harder then Javors did. While an incredibly talented bass player, he had let his entire life and identity get wrapped up in being a member of Billy Joel's band. Add the fact that Doug also had a fondness for alcohol and drugs that he used, some say, in an unsuccessful attempt to fight off the deep depression that plagued him, and you have a very toxic combination. His firing surprised many people at the time because he was perceived as someone who was truly loyal to Billy. But at times when alcohol and other substances got the best of him, his demeanor turned very negative and he made sure that everyone within listening range was reminded of his stature and his role in putting them in the band. Understandably this behavior created a lot of bad feelings at times and very possibly may have contributed to the undermining of the band.

Doug was also someone that Billy turned to for advice about his music, and was one of the few people allowed in the control room when they were recording. Billy had valued his musical input possibly more then any other member of the band, which again made his firing that much more senseless to many in Billy's inner circle. After being let go Doug continued to work in other bands and the music business for about six more years before his demons got the best of him. On August 24, 1995 Doug shot and killed himself in his home. It surprised everyone who knew him, because he seemed to be maintaining a busy schedule recording and producing.

"Doug gave his heart and soul to Billy," Russell Javors said. "He was devastated when he was fired. I would tell him to keep his chin up, and that he should be proud of what he accomplished and that it was time move on. He just couldn't turn the page."

Sadly, Russell's analogy of Doug's demons is accurate. Whatever the reasons for the actual firing, whether because of money and artistic matters, or because of excessive drinking and drug use, or a combination of factors, Doug and Russell were no longer part of the band that they'd started as teenagers on Long Island, long before Billy hired them as his band. But even long after Doug's death the hard feelings still seemed to prevail.

"I was the one who called Billy to tell him that Doug had killed himself," Russell said. "The first thing Billy said to me was 'You think that this is my fault.' I told him that I didn't, but that he could have been a better friend."

After Doug killed himself, Russell walked away from the music business. The nerve that had been so much a part of him was now dead. He couldn't understand how something that he loved so much and which was supposed to bring such happiness to people could turn so ugly. Adding salt to the wounds was the fact that when Russell and Doug were fired, many people who they thought had been their friends stopped calling and avoided them both, figuring that they'd better be seen as Billy loyalists to protect their own positions.

"When it was over, no one talked to us. It's one thing to lose a job, but we lost our job and most of our friends," Russell said.

Billy, from his perspective, continued to pass off the firings as the result of money issues and, at times, artistic differences. Russell and others agreed that, if in fact that were the case, Billy was certainly within his rights to have done it. It was just the way it happened and then would continue to be portrayed in subsequent interviews Billy gave left such a bad taste in their mouths, but that is and always has been Billy's way as another long-time band member would find out some years later.

★

Another big change in Billy's life and one that again was greatly influenced by his relationship was Christie was going to be where he lived. Billy had been enjoying the very comfortable life of a rock star with a spacious apartment in New York City and a waterfront home in Lloyd Harbor, New York. He'd also spent parts of the summer renting houses out on Long Island's East End. First, in the tiny hamlet of East Marion in a big old rambling Victorian house that he and Christie rented but rarely stayed in because it made both of them break out in sneezing attacks from allergies. They also visited friends on the South Fork of the East End, a place better known as The Hamptons, where the wealthy spent summers in their trophy homes, doing business among themselves and the inevitable social climbing. Granted this wasn't Billy or Christie's style really, but they did love the ocean beaches, had friends there, and also discovered Montauk and its Deep Hollow Ranch. Deep Hollow and its sister ranch Indian Field are the oldest running cattle ranches in the United States, located just over one hundred miles west of New York City. There Christie could ride her quarter horses and Billy could explore Montauk's fishing community which is made up of some very down to earth and colorful characters, exactly the type of people Billy usually gravitated toward. It was the perfect set-up for both of them and they soon were living in a rented house in Montauk and looking for a more permanent place on the ocean to buy.

In a short time they found an ocean front estate in East Hampton that had belonged to one of the area's consummate WASPs, Dickson Potter. Before his death, Potter had been a long-time member of the East Hampton's Maidstone Club and Devon Yacht Club, both East Hampton strongholds of old New York WASP society. Billy and Christie loved the house's location on over five acres of ocean front property and far enough off the road that they could be insured of their privacy. Billy also loved the idea that once again the little Jewish kid from Hicksville would be buying what had until recently been a prized trophy house of some uptight WASP. Potter in fact was so uptight that in his will he stated that his house could not be sold to someone who was in showbusiness or who was Jewish. Billy bought the place, and so loved the irony of it that on the day he closed on the property he drove over to the house and, getting out of his car, unzipped his fly as he began to urinate all over the side of the house, shouting, "What do you think now Potter? A showbusiness Jew is going to be living in your house."

With a rented house in Montauk he and Christie began a renovation of the old Potter place that when done would bear little resemblance to the original house. It was clearly a house they built only for themselves to live in with only a few bedrooms, a studio, music room/two-storey library over-looking the ocean, and a professional kitchen. Guests were banished to the very comfortable five-bedroom guesthouse in the grounds, while Billy, Christie, and Alexa stayed up in the main house.

Billy immersed himself in life on the east end and befriended many of the commercial fisherman there, people again who he respected greatly and whose struggle he could relate to. It wasn't long before Billy was becoming a vocal advocate of their plight as they were being pushed out of business by over-development, pollution, government regulations, and the sport-fishing lobby. Billy was particularly touched by how the old time "haul seiners," fisherman who for generations had used large nets to catch the valuable striped bass, had been put out of business by government pen pushers who felt that their method of catching fish was wasteful and too effective. They blamed the decline of the species stocks on them, when in reality they were only a very small part of the problem. This enraged Billy who stepped up his efforts to help them. At their request he participated in a demonstration on a beach in East Hampton where a net was set illegally and fish harvested. It was supposed to call attention to the plight of the haul seiners, but only ended up being about Billy.

On July 28, 1992 Billy was proudly arrested on the beach for what turned into a Billy Joel freak show, fueled by the media. Afterwards Billy was attacked over and over by the press sympathetic to the "sporties" side, and as a result Billy Joel albums were burnt in public protests. This took the spotlight off what was the true issue.

Although stung by the negative press and fan reaction he was getting, Billy believed in the cause, and continued to lend his name and money to helping to further it, even donating a portion of the royalties from the song "Downeaster Alexa" to the East Hampton Bayman's Association. Unfortunately, the politicians held firm and the fishery was never reinstated. Gradually Billy's interest waned too until finally he realized that the Bayman's Association secretary, a wannabe actor and one-time magazine editor with no background at all in commercial fishing, had his own personal agenda, which caused Billy to wisely back away completely. However, he remains interested in issues regarding the waters and fishing communities, as well as building boats, which would soon become evident.

With a new band and a new producer, Billy entered the studio for what would be another new recording experience. For the past seven albums with Phil Ramone, Billy often relied on the spontaneity of the studio experience to add substance, lyrics, and music to songs that were still raw and unfinished. That naturalness in such an unnatural environment was the secret to the magic between Phil, Billy, and the band which made their time together so successful. This time the studio experience would be much different and take on an atmosphere of greater structure for the first time. Mick Jones wanted

Billy and his band to show up with ten or so songs that they'd rehearsed and were ready to record—a totally new concept for Billy.

"I was horrified," he said. "What about the spontaneity?"

But Billy was enough of a professional to know that if he had enough belief in Mick Jones to choose him as his producer, he'd better follow his lead in the studio. Besides Billy had been successful and during the subsequent years of big studio budgets for albums, Billy had always rehearsed songs before coming in to record them. "So I went back to that', he said. "I started by throwing out five songs." They were songs that he felt sounded good live, but in a studio environment they just didn't make it. It was a traumatic experience for Billy initially, but it ended up making the album that much better because he had to write five even better songs that took their place. *Storm Front*, like other Billy Joel albums, had started with a musical concept in mind, but Billy discovered long before that it wasn't a good idea to limit your material to the concept you think the album will be.

"Once you get a certain distance into writing or recording an album, it begins to take on a life of its own," he said. "You become a captive of that. You are no longer the master of what the concept is."

Billy realized that once that happens and the music begins to take on its own momentum, then you have to go with it. To try to change course at that point would be a disservice to himself as a composer and musician, and that theory would certainly hold up on *Storm Front*.

The song "Leningrad" was written by Billy about a friendship he's made on the Russian tour with a clown named Victor. Victor and Billy had hit it off right away, and Billy was particularly taken by Victor when he saw how he could make his daughter Alexa laugh. When it was recorded Billy reached back into his past and called his old teacher Chuck Arnold to see if he was interested in bringing his current chorus from Hicksville High School to the studio to sing backgrounds. Chuck accepted the invitation from his former student for what would be an experience that all would go on to remember.

Arnold said: "I brought the kids in and we did the background stuff, the kids enjoyed it immensely. Billy gave me a framed record before I retired. It was a really nice gesture, you know, because he could have put a professional band in, but he wanted to use kids from his old hometown. That's what kind of a guy he is."

Almost eighteen months after Billy had begun writing material for the album, *Storm Front* was released in September 1989. It earned him four Grammy nominations but Billy wouldn't come home with any. Instead Billy saw his friend Steve Winwood win two of them that year. The album is clearly a diary of baby boomers' doubts about their generation's pointlessness and diluted values. It also contains themes of much personal uncertainty as in "I Go To Extremes," the gloomy love song "And So It Goes" and the single that preceded the album's release, "We Didn't Start the Fire," whose lyrics are a brilliant string of historical facts. The single became a huge hit, reaching number one and inspiring history students across America. It was inspired by a conversation that Billy had briefly with a twenty-something student who told Billy that he felt sorry for him because "no history" had happened during his lifetime.

"I was talking to this young guy in his early 20s," he said. "And he was talking about what a hard time this was to grow up in, with crack and AIDS. And I thought, we said that when we were that age. Jeez, there was Vietnam, the Kennedy assassinations, drugs, Nixon . . . the song is saying, 'Look, we didn't start the fire, we tried to fight it, but it was burning and it's gonna burn on after we're gone and it's gonna burn on after you're gone, too. That's the way the world is, imperfect; you have to learn to deal with it. But don't give up! Change what you can change; don't fall into cynicism and despair."

The song begins with events in 1949 the year of Billy's birth and goes to 1989, the year of the album's release, covering one hundred and twenty historical events. A stream of consciousness type of song, it conjures up memories of Bob Dylan's "Subterranean Homesick Blues" in its quick-fire half rap-style, half sung-style format, and is one of the few Billy Joel songs whose lyrics were written before the music. Billy has mixed feelings about what others including Walter Yetnikoff feel is the "work of a genius" and he hates to sing it in public because, as he puts it, "It's a nightmare to perform live, because if I miss one word, it's a train wreck." Consequently, it's not a song that is often played at a Billy Joel concert, although when it is, it receives an enthusiastic response.

*Storm Front* is an album that speaks of changes that are about to come and for Billy that would remain the way. "Something's going to happen, something's coming," he said about the album's messages. "Sometimes you have to create a crisis to get things to happen." Although he hadn't created the crisis this time, he was still in the midst of a big one and it would still be some time before the storm-warning flags were to be taken down for Billy Joel.

# Chapter 27

On May 1, 1989 the lawsuit that Jack Powers had filed against Billy for defamation was thrown out of court. Billy had called Powers a "creep" during an interview with *Playboy* magazine when he was asked about Powers' charges that Billy had taken his song and turned it into "My Life." The judge cited Billy's rights under the First Amendment and threw the frivolous suit out. Billy was understandably pleased, but still pissed off that he'd had to settle at all with the guy. Nevertheless, there were bigger fish to legally fry now in Billy's life, and he knew it made sense just to move on.

Although he'd never received his high school diploma because of his excessive absences, Billy has always been a great reader and student of history, and in fact today in his home he often has a television tuned to the History Channel, while close by at least one book having to do with a historical subject or a prominent historical figure can be found. As he has said many times, if he hadn't chosen a career in music he might just as easily have ended up a history teacher somewhere. It was with particular delight that Billy accepted an invitation to conduct a master class about his music and career at Long Island's C.W. Post college on July 31, 1989. The format was to be a very casual and informal unscripted evening of exchanging information on such subjects as his career, writing music, life as a rock star, influences, including his family and a long list of other subjects that arose in this unstructured two or so hours with a very candid Billy Joel. The classes were also going to show his fans yet another side of his complex personality—that of Billy the actor.

"The master classes are very Mark Twain-ish," Phil Ramone said. "Billy has that going for him. He's also an actor in addition to everything else."

The idea to hold the first on Billy's home turf worked wonders. His audience reacted in an enthusiastic and respectful manner and there was that immediate synergy between them and Billy so often seen at his concerts. Billy walked away that night excited about this new aspect of his career and ready to book more of the classes. The classes not only satisfied his long-time fantasy about being a teacher but more importantly gave him the opportunity to spend what were very intimate times listening to and talking with his fans, the people who he has always felt a great deal of gratitude towards and who he has always tried to insure have good experiences with him, whether in Madison Square Garden, or a fifty-seat club somewhere. He's always been a true champion of the fans and fought for their rights, including tying to eliminate ticket scalping of his shows and anything else that wrongly takes advantage of the fans.

As the press started writing about them, the classes began to take on a life of their own, and they eventually became a part of his touring life. He did them in colleges and universities all over the world, including such prestigious halls of learning as Columbia, Harvard, Princeton, and in equally prestigious venues like the Meistersingerhalle in Nuremberg, Germany, his father's and grandfather's hometown. The classes were not big money makers for Billy, in fact in most cases he got only expenses and maybe a small fee, but he did them nevertheless because he loved the intimacy of the performer/fan experience, as well as the intellectual stimulation he himself got from them.

Meanwhile, the turmoil surrounding Billy's life continued. With the skilled litigator Leonard Marks representing him, a lawsuit against Frank Weber was filed on September 25, 1989 on Billy's behalf. The lawsuit sought ninety million dollars from Weber, including sixty million in punitive damages and thirty million in compensatory compensation. Billy was livid about the violation of his trust and rightfully so. In addition to being Billy's ex-brother-in-law, Frank Weber had been one of Billy's closest confidants. He was the executor of his will and, perhaps most indicative of his stature in Billy's life, was Alexa's godfather.

"I trusted him totally," Billy said.

As the suit was being filed Billy was in a car on his way to Kennedy Airport in New York to catch a Concorde to London. He was scheduled to do a series of promotional interviews and appearances at Sony studios there for the *Storm Front* album. As the car approached the airport, a pain that he'd had in his stomach area intensified to the point where it became excruciating and he asked the driver to turn the car around and bring him to the emergency room at a New York hospital. There he was admitted for immediate surgery to remove kidney stones, a malady which had also briefly and not as severely plagued him back in Hicksville as a teenager. Needless to say the trip to London was cancelled and Billy recuperated at his East Hampton home for about six weeks before heading out in early December for the *Storm Front* tour which for the better part of thirteen months would take Billy all over the world in a tireless attempt to recoup his lost fortune.

Meanwhile, back in New York Leonard Marks was working his magic. Frank Weber and his co-defendant Rick London were trying to buy time by having court appearances postponed, but Marks held their hands to the fire.

He filed eight lawsuits against a total of 37 defendants on Billy's behalf, including one that stopped Weber and his wife from transferring money they had from the sale of their 9,000 square foot home in Lloyd Harbor, New York that Weber had built with money that Billy felt was his.

Weber, in a desperate effort to redeem himself, tried to countersue Billy in a couple of court cases that his lawyer filed in Georgia and Virginia, places they thought might be more sympathetic to his claims. He sued Billy for fifteen million dollars in commissions that he said were owed to him for deals he'd done for Billy prior to being fired. The frivolous cases were quickly thrown out and Weber filed for bankruptcy in May 1990, listing assets of just over six hundred and fifty thousand dollars with liabilities of over twenty-three million. His fall had been hard.

Rick London, who was Billy's tour manager for many years, who was married to Elizabeth's sister Mary Sue, was also a defendant in the proceedings. Mary Sue was not involved, and by all indications, knew nothing about what had been going on throughout the years. London tried to stonewall the lawsuit against him by changing lawyers, repeatedly not showing up for depositions, and once even being excused because he was in Europe on vacation. When he finally did appear in court after numerous no-shows, he answered questions put to him by Leonard Marks with vague answers such as "I don't recall" or "I believe."

Rick London had been involved in numerous Billy Joel-related companies, including Billy's pension fund. In that capacity he was accused of conservatively causing hundreds of thousands of dollars in loans to be made without Billy's knowledge to outside interests such as a three hundred thousand dollar loan to a record company executive to redecorate a New York apartment, a two hundred and fifty thousand dollar, interest-free loan to the Weber company Silver W Stables in 1987 and a four hundred and fifty thousand dollar interest free loan to Jericho Breeding Associates, another horse-breeding partnership that both Weber and London had an interest in. He was also involved in, or on the board of, a number of other companies that were supposed to be support mechanisms for Billy, such as Frank Management, Hicksville Productions, and Loco Productions. In that capacity he used his position to repeatedly funnel other monies to Weber-controlled companies or to Weber himself without ever mentioning it to Billy. In the end it was determined that London, who in addition to being Billy's friend, relative, and successor trustee of Billy's will, had made millions of dollars of loans which were either never repaid or at best paid partially.

When it was all over both Weber and London were ruined. London ended up moving to California and living with his parents where he remains today. Weber stayed on Long Island but no longer living the lifestyle that he once had. Billy with the help of Dennis Arfa, the Eastmans, and Ed London took over his own management and financial responsibilities, forming Maritime Music as the parent company. Two people from the Frank Management days that stayed with Billy were Jeff Schock, who became his de facto manager, and Jeff's wife Elaine, who was also retained to continue her role as Billy's publicist and spokesperson. In what turned out to be a total cleaning of his corporate house, this was very unusual, but Billy Schock today casually brushes off why this was the case.

"I never counted the money, I only made Billy money," he said. "I guess that counted for something."

And indeed it does with Billy Joel. In the showbusiness world that Billy is so much a part of, back stabbing and "looking out for me" is too often the norm. Billy, who has a more principled philosophy is known to often reward loyalty within his ranks. Schock was then and today remains a true Billy Joel loyalist who was determined to help his friend emerge from the ashes. Billy, who was justifiably shell shocked, paid him a flat fee as a consultant instead of a percentage as often was the way, and Jeff skillfully set out to help Billy put things back together in his personal and professional life, leaving the biggest responsibility of managing Billy Joel to Billy Joel.

"If I screw me, I'm making love with somebody I know," Billy said in typical Billy Joel manner.

It had all been a painful wake-up call for Billy, but unbelievably there were still more legal nightmares for him on the horizon, the next one having to do with conflicts of interest that had occurred and would later arise between his former lawyer and Weber.

But first and always first there was the music, and now recovered from his surgery, with Leonard Marks handling the first stages of putting his financial life back together, Billy went out on the road to recoup his losses, and to get himself back in a comfortable financial position. He did 165 shows during the *Storm Front* tour, and played to an estimated three and a half million people. He'd been told by his new business people that he was facing a "deep, deep, deep financial hole," so in his typical unyielding manner he faced the problem head on and set out on the road. He wasn't crazy about having to do it, but he realized that if he were going to insure the financial health of his family and himself, it had to happen. The one thing that bothered him more then anything else about having to spend so much time touring was having to leave Alexa, who soon would be turning four. He realized correctly that his time away from her was time he'd never get back, and so he made sure that any concert dates around her birthday were close to home, and additionally that he had a few days off to celebrate it with her.

"When I was a kid, my dad was gone a lot, and I swore that when I became a father, I was going to be home," he said.

A true survivor, he made the best of it and in addition to being a financial success the tour also had its share of milestones, including a two-night concert at Yankee Stadium in late June 1990, which was the first time that the sacred shrine of baseball had ever hosted a rock and roll concert. In years past the Pope had visited and held a mass there and boxing matches had also been held on the infield, but never had a rock and roll show unfolded there until now, and when you think about it, who could have been a better choice then Billy Joel, whose life had started just blocks away. At the time, Billy recalled that he had "gone to Shea Stadium to see the Stones," New York's other baseball mecca that had also hosted Springsteen and The Beatles.

Always aware of the historical significance of these events in his life, Billy called his former bandmate, husband-in-law, and friend Jon Small, who was now trying to carve out a living making rock videos in New York. He wanted to capture the concert event for a full-length concert video, and chose Jon out of loyalty and friendship. Jon worked his magic and within just a year, the video was certified platinum. The video also became a launch pad of sorts for Small as it was nominated for a Grammy Award for Best Music Video, Long Form. It didn't win, but by that time Jon had met Billy's friend country and western star Garth Brooks and would soon be leaving New York for Nashville where he'd make music videos for Garth and a long list of other music stars. Today Jon is one of the most successful video director/producers in the country doing television work and videos for a number of other recording artists. At the awards that February in 1992 Billy was given the Living Legend Award which had been initiated just a year before. His co-honorees that night were Johnny Cash, Aretha Franklin, and Quincy Jones, causing Billy to remark, "How does a little pup like me get in here? It's wild!"

Right after celebrating New Year 1991, Billy and his band took off for a seven-show tour of Japan to support *Storm Front*. He now had a huge following in Japan and not surprising all venues were sold out. On his way back to the states for a rest that essentially would last the rest of the year, with only a few concert dates scheduled and mostly close to home, Billy stopped in the Philippines to give two USO concerts for troops stationed there during the Gulf War.

Then in May 1991 Billy, who still had no high school diploma, received an Honorary Doctorate of Humane Letters from Connecticut's Fairfield University. It would be the first of four that he'd receive to date. Additionally the town of Huntington, New York named a waterfront park in *Cold Spring Harbor* "Billy Joel Park" on July 17, 1991 in recognition of Billy who had named his first album after the small picturesque town that he and his buddies had first discovered as greasers in Hicksville when they would drive over there to hang out in the park, throw frisbees, and try to pick up local girls. Later when he had become successful, Billy would live in Huntington when he bought the waterfront house on Lloyd Neck. In the ceremony there were the usual speeches and proclamations read by politicians before Billy and his proud mother left to have lunch with friends and town officials. Just a month later the plaque with the park's name on it disappeared, into some fan's collection of Billy Joel memorabilia no doubt.

The rest of 1991 was spent in relative quite except for two concerts down the road from his Amagansett, NY house at Indian Field Ranch in Montauk. These were a relatively new series of fund-raising concerts put on by Rusty Leaver, who was a co-owner of what is the United States' oldest cattle ranch thanks to his marriage to the owner's daughter. Rusty was now enjoying a celebrity-type lifestyle of sorts as Christie and some of her friends boarded their horses with him. He saw an opportunity to endear himself even more to the growing list of celebrities moving to the area and also to take some substantial fees for himself as a consultant, and decided to stage what became known as "Back at the Ranch" concerts to benefit local charities. Billy, who loved being part of this community, jumped on the opportunity to help without knowing that Leaver was pocketing a large amount of money for himself and on August 8 and 9 performed shows to sold-out crowds of ten thousand plus that raised money for the local chapter of the Nature Conservancy and Billy's pet organization, the Easthampton Bayman's Association. It was just one more charitable effort that Billy supported for his beloved Long Island.

When Billy had invited his old teacher Chuck Arnold and the Hicksville High School Chorus to participate on the *Storm Front* album it put Billy back in touch with officials from the school district. Aware that Billy had never graduated, they offered to give him another chance at his diploma if he'd simply complete a missing English paper, which he was happy to do. The principal at the time, Richard Hogan, told Billy that if he'd submit some of his original songwriting, then it would qualify as a substitute to the exam, so on Wednesday night June 24, 1992 Billy Joel graduated along with 305 other graduates. Dressed in a gown but no cap Billy received his diploma and then after the other valedictorians had given their speeches, Billy approached the stage podium for his.

"Well, here I am, Mom," he said. "I'm actually going to get my high school diploma, and it's only 25 years after everyone else got theirs. But Mom, don't worry. I can finally pull myself out of this dead-end job I have and start working on a career with a real future."

The kid from Hicksville who back in the sixties had dropped out of school when he was told he'd have to go to summer school now was a high school graduate. While it may have seemed insignificant to many with the huge success that Billy was enjoying in his professional life, having the diploma gave Billy more of a satisfaction then many of the awards and gold records that he'd already received because now a link that had been missing in his life was in place.

Meanwhile, things in Billy's personal life were showing signs of strain. His marriage seemed to be in trouble as rumors spread across Long Island's East End about transgressions by both partners. Billy had been on the road a lot in the past couple of years, and with Alexa now in school, many times she and Christie could not be there with him. Christie was spending much of her free time out in Montauk at the Indian Field Ranch working with her cutting horses and rumors spread about time she was spending there with Hamptons' cowboys. The marriage that people loved to live vicariously through and which had had done so much for each other's career when it came to keeping their names and faces in the news was now in trouble and they were now seen together less and less. Storm clouds were once again on the horizon for Billy Joel.

# Chapter 28

As 1992 began, lawsuits between Billy and Frank Weber, Rick London, and others associated with Frank Management and other Weber and London related companies were being filed in what at times must have seemed to be a record-setting pace. Billy's trust had been violated, he wanted blood and wasn't about to settle for anything less. Leonard Marks, who worked tirelessly on Billy's behalf, buried the defendants in not only suits but paperwork, causing Frank Weber's attorney at the time to comment that "I get five pounds of paper a week from Billy's lawyers."

The situation, as something like this often does, brought out the worst in people, many who were grasping at straws in their desperation to justify their past actions. Frank Weber filed a suit against Christie for destroying his relationship with Billy because Weber had advised Billy on what should be in his prenuptial agreement with Christie. A New York judge threw the frivolous suit out of court in March 1992, stating that all the things Weber accused Christie of were protected under state law. Then Weber filed a thirty-three million dollar countersuit against Billy for, of all things, "breach of contract." That too was thrown out of court in short order.

If it wasn't bad enough that Billy and Weber were at legal war, Elizabeth sued Billy for three million dollars, claiming that it was money Billy owed her from their divorce agreement. Billy settled with her only to see Elizabeth get sued by her brother Frank who now claimed that she owed him money from commissions that were due him for income Billy had prior to 1981. Billy again stepped in promising to cover any commission shortfalls. But after that settlement, Elizabeth turned around and sued her brother for seven million dollars, charging breach of fiduciary duty and contract. That suit would go nowhere essentially because Weber was so ruined financially and had no ability to remotely consider paying any damages. To the outside observer, it looked like a legal litigation circus between the groups that once had been family, and indeed it was.

Meanwhile life was going on for Billy, and that meant time in the studio or, more often then not lately, receiving awards for his work. On May 27, 1992

Billy was to be inducted into the Songwriters Hall of Fame. This prestigious organization was founded by Johnny Mercer and others in 1969, back when Billy was a member of The Hassles, to recognize and honor the accomplishments and lives of those men and women who create the popular songs that serve as the soundtracks of our lives. By the time Billy was inducted he joined the ranks of some of the greats of our generation including Chuck Berry, Jimmy Webb, Billy's old Brill Building friend Carole King, and Lennon and McCartney. It is an organization that truly connects the generations through music.

Now, 23 years since its founding, Billy, Elton John, and his songwriting collaborator Bernie Taupin would be inducted, along with founder Johnny Mercer and others. It was a big deal, and Billy and Christie sat in the audience as Marc Cohn performed a warm version of Billy's "She's Always a Woman." Billy's buddy from Montauk, Paul Simon, was asked to do the introduction and after the award was presented Billy spoke briefly, noting that on his 1987 Russian tour he had witnessed first hand the power of music as he noticed many Russians listening to songs like "Blowin' in the Wind," "Stormy Weather," and "Georgia on My Mind" in his travels around the streets, often on the most primitive radios or tape players he'd seen.

"The Cold War didn't turn into a hot war," he said, "not because of Nixon and Agnew, but because of Mort Shuman and Doc Pomus. They knew us through our music," Billy said.

Of course he was right. After accepting his award Billy performed "Just the Way You Are" with the help of Leslie Uggams, Ray Charles, Judy Collins, and Jimmy Webb among others.

But perhaps the most pertinent event of the night was when the organization's president Sammy Cahn related a story about the first time he had met Billy just a few years earlier. Sammy had been at a London concert and afterwards came backstage to meet Billy who was there with his father Howard. For Billy, who has strived tirelessly his entire life for some sort of acknowledgement from his father regarding his music, it must have been a great moment too, if only a short-lived one. Billy introduced Cahn to his father that night, saying, "Dad, I want you to meet a real songwriter." He relished the position of power that he had that night, being courted by a great like Sammy Cahn in the presence of his father Howard, the musician who had been denied the career in music he'd really wanted by his father. Tonight as Cahn introduced Billy to the award's audience he returned Billy's compliment, telling the audience, "I want you to meet a real songwriter." Continuing, he noted that "In fifty years of songwriting if you have five songs that are immediately identifiable, you have a medley. This man has twenty!"

★

As lawsuits of the magnitude that Billy's was often do, cans of worms are often opened that never can be shut. This was certainly the case with the Joel versus Weber suit, as in May 1992 the FBI became involved when it started investigating possible "criminal activity" by Frank Weber. They discovered numerous instances of suspicious activity as well as questionable money transactions between Weber and Billy's attorney at the time, Alan Grubman. Grubman's law firm at the time, Grubman, Indursky, Schindler, and Goldstein, was the most powerful entertainment law firm on the East Coast and certainly one of the most powerful in the country, with the possible exception of one in Los Angeles headed up by Bert Fields. Since being handed Billy by Walter Yetnikoff over a decade earlier, Grubman's firm had represented such superstars as Bruce Springsteen, Michael Jackson, Madonna and Mariah Carey. The firm also represented top-level music executives such as Al Teller, who then was the chairman of MCA Records, and Tommy Mottola, president of Sony Music, formerly Columbia and then Mariah Carey's husband.

Filed on September 23, 1992, the suit also sought a total of ninety million dollars in damages, listing a broad range of charges including fraud and breach of fiduciary responsibility. Marks charged that Grubman, who was also an attorney for CBS Records at the time he represented Billy, one of the record company's biggest artists, never told Billy about this dual relationship. This they claimed, Billy should have known about so that if there was a concern on Billy's part, a conflict-of-interest waiver could have been signed by both parties. This would turn out to be a pivotal issue in the lawsuit, and one that other attorneys with similar conflicts would watch closely. This intrinsic conflict of having an attorney represent both a record company and one of their recording artists would be the subject of much debate during the life of the lawsuit and afterwards. Donald Passman, an entertainment lawyer himself and the author of *All You Need to Know about the Music Business*, saw a real conflict with Grubman's roles.

"If you're a lawyer getting paid by a label year in and year out, how hard are you going to push somebody's contract?" he said.

But the lawsuit also alleged other issues with Grubman that weren't in Billy's best interests. It additionally charged that Grubman had "curried favor" with Frank Weber because of his eagerness to build a clientele of "A" list artists and had used kickbacks, payoffs, and other illegal forms of payment to keep Weber happy and ultimately Billy at his firm—all without Billy's knowledge about what was going on. Specifically Mark's accused Grubman of passing checks to Weber for such bogus things as a $27,000 fee, for "tax planning and consulting," and also $100,000 for other "consulting services." Subsequent to these alleged incidents, and as the FBI investigation was going on, Grubman and his partner Arthur Indursky claimed that they could not recall any tax-consulting services they might have performed for Joel. The suit also charged that Weber was the one setting the fees that would be paid to Grubman's firm, who ultimately received a minimum of $750,000 from Billy.

"I thought that having a manager, accountant, and attorney, I was protected from the wrongdoing that was detailed in these complaints," Billy said.

Unfortunately that wasn't the case. Weber had been working Grubman in other ways too for fees, the suit charged. He had gotten Grubman and Indursky to invest in a number of tax shelters that he was involved in and that Billy had no knowledge of, and then paid them "rebates" on their investments. Billy, who had repeatably told Weber that he never wanted to be involved in investing in racehorses, not surprisingly never saw any rebate money. In one bizarre instance that was cited in the suit, Tommy Mottola, who was an investor in one of Weber's racehorse tax shelters, was said to have made clear to Weber how unsatisfied with his investment he was. Weber assured Mottola that he was on top of the situation, and that "he could have a horse killed in order to collect insurance." The horse later purportedly died of "natural causes" and the tax shelter collected the insurance.

Meanwhile the media was having a field day as these two giants of the music business fought it out. Both were experts in the manipulation of the press and as the lawsuit unfolded it often was fought out more in the media then in the courtroom. So in what became a public relations war of sorts, Leonard Marks started appearing on television talk shows to give Billy's side of the story, while Grubman hired the PR crisis management firm of Dan Klores to spin his side of the story. Klores immediately used the David versus Goliath formula in his PR spin, portraying Grubman as the victim of the powerful music industry giant Billy Joel. This infuriated Leonard Marks, who was adamant about sticking to the facts as he saw them.

"I had no ax to grind," Marks said. "Many lawyers in the entertainment business have forgotten what they learned in law school—that there are substantial limitations in representing both sides of the table."

John Eastman who now represented Billy, agreed with Marks, and not wasting words said simply, "I have a number on Billy Joel's balance sheet, and if Grubman pays it, this is over."

Billy for his part was either in the recording studio that year or on the road. But in his free time he was often found dealing with the lawsuits that had been filed on his behalf, either giving depositions or answering those others had given.

In March 1993 Billy did win a judgment in New York State Supreme Court against Weber for over almost $700,000 plus interest. The money was awarded because the judge had found fault with some unnamed specific transactions Weber had made. The judge held back from deciding on all cases against Weber which forced the suit to go to trial, leaving Billy outraged as he looked at even more legal fees in the future. Fortunately he had his music to escape to and that is exactly what he did.

It had been just about four years since Billy had been in the studio recording *Storm Front*. Not that he hadn't been busy, but lawsuits and touring had gotten old real fast and Billy missed making music; besides the whole legal mess was incredibly stressful and also taking its toll on his personal life and particularly his marriage. The events of the last three years or so had forced Billy to accept that the ultimate trust he had placed in those closest to him had been violated and it hurt Billy deeply, while at the same time throwing fuel on an his smoldering anger. The whole mess was also depressing for Billy who through the years had had more than his share of dealing with depression. Nevertheless, all the drama and emotional pain that had manifested itself in Billy these past years would soon begin to emerge as something good and positive.

It really started in fragments in early 1992. Billy was in the shower in his East Hampton home when that unexplainable feeling, somewhat like the tingling anxiety your body feels just as LSD kicks in, started. In its most abstract form, the concept and some of the lyrics for a new album just started to flow out of him in a true stream of consciousness. Knowing enough about this type of phenomenon from past history, Billy realized that he just had to go with it and, if it continued, let it materialize in whatever form it took.

He got himself out of the shower and into his two-storey library/music room where he shut himself off to wait for the process to continue. Although he wasn't aware of it at the time, this time the results would be on a completely different level, and one that Billy had not ever really been in touch with. In fact it was one that he'd steered clear of in the past because he just didn't have the spiritual belief to fully comprehend it. Gradually, though, it came to him over a period of days, not as it had with *Innocent Man* or even *The Stranger*, where the music pretty much just poured out of him, but this time again in abstract fragments that he would later fine-tune, often with Danny Kortchmar in the studio.

He and Danny had started working together on the origins of the album early in the summer of 1992. Billy was recording two Elvis Presley songs for the soundtrack of Nicholas Cage's movie *Honeymoon in Vegas*. Cage is a fanatic Elvis fan, and the movie soundtrack was full of other Elvis songs performed by great musicians such as Willie Nelson, Trisha Yearwood, and Jeff Beck, but Billy had been the only other musician to be chosen to do two cuts, "All Shook Up" and "Heartbreak Hotel." Billy's version of "Heartbreak Hotel" was released also as a single where it rose to number six on the Billboard Adult Contemporary chart.

The songs were recorded in Southampton, New York in of all places a Catholic Church, where they'd set up a studio in the basement. Both Billy and Danny liked the experience so much of working together that they decided to continue the partnership. But because the church wasn't a long-term option, Billy rented what was once an old boathouse on Alfred Tuthill's property on Shelter Island, New York, and had it converted it into a recording studio. It was a perfect spot for Billy, right on the water, in an old shipyard, and he could run over from home in his boat, tie up, and go inside to work, which is exactly what he did, often with friends and family.

Billy and Kortchmar entered the studio with a long list of new musicians and singers and began to work on fine-tuning the songs that had started pouring out of him in the shower that day. Kortchmar came with a long and distinguished musical career and had produced albums and played instruments for a long list of musicians since the sixties, including such greats as James Taylor, Neil Young, Carole King, and Jackson Browne. These new songs they were working on were much more driving and harder-edged than most of Billy's earlier albums, and Billy and Danny agreed that bringing a bunch of new musicians into the studio who had experience playing rock and roll would help them reach the sound and feel they wanted to.

Drummers Zachary Alford, who had played with David Bowie and the B-52s, was invited to participate, as was Steve Jordan, who had played with The Rolling Stones, James Taylor, and Steely Dan, to mention just a few. This was the first sign to anyone that Billy's long-time relationship with Liberty DeVito was not what it once had been, and that Billy was looking for a drummer with perhaps more reach. T.M. Stevens and Lonnie Hillyer were brought in as bass players. T.M. had played bass for Joe Cocker and Tina Turner. Lonnie is a jazz drummer and had played for jazz greats like Charles Mingus and Thelonious Monk. Topping it all off was the guitar player Leslie West who Billy knew from back in the sixties when he played lead guitar for the Long Island band The Vagrants and he and Billy, who then was in The Hassles, often were found playing the same venues. West went on to play guitar for the band Mountain who back in the late sixties and early seventies was one of the first "supergroups."

Having these musicians on board was the perfect complement for the songs that would make up Billy's next album, *River of Dreams*. Billy decided to name the album after the song which for him in many ways is a first, as it allows the listener deeper inside Billy Joel then he'd ever allowed before.

"It's really a play on the phrase 'stream of consciousness,' " he said about the song and album's title. "There are biblical phrases in there, evocations of baptism and resurrection, and a great deal of symbolism in the river and seas. I am always using water as a metaphor."

From a musical perspective, both Billy and Danny had been influenced by the same kinds of music as kids in the sixties, and these influences are obvious too on the album.

"It sounds like he's playing with a rock band," Kortchmar said of the album. "It's his songs rendered with a real fire and intensity. It's not over-thought or over-produced. It's a real straight-ahead thing."

From the perspective of just music Kortchmar was right, but this album, which many believed was Billy's most significant artistic achievement yet, was also without a doubt his most personal album ever. Listeners were allowed to see a part of Billy that until then had remained unknown.

"It is the story of a person who's in crisis," Billy said of the album. "It's obvious in the first couple of songs that it's a pretty angry person."

Indeed it is, but it is also the story of a person, who after going through these series of harrowing transformations, emerges from the ashes and, wiser because of it all, reestablishes his faith.

Billy agrees, as he confirms that the rebirth is one that now will have substance and spirituality "in the things that really matter, what's really important, the things that sustain you."

While Billy has always drawn from his own life experiences as well as his cultural observation to write, this album is a lyrical stretch for Billy, whose words are clearly much more philosophic and dark than in any other album.

The album was also a turning point of sorts for Billy. "I knew I was coming to the close of some book in my life, and even the last song, 'Famous Last Words,' says, 'These are the last words I have to say.' I felt that made a quantum leap in lyrics—those lyrics were dead against any other lyrics I have ever written. It was the culmination of all the songwriting I had done."

As usual Billy was right on about his music. This time the words that would make up the album would speak of and relate to the listener what was essentially a loss of faith, and a search for, as well as an understanding of, just how to deal with that. But also on the yang side of things, an emergence from the darkness as a renewal of another sort of faith occurs. For Billy that would stretch beyond just the lawsuits that were lingering. Things in his personal life also were changing fast now and a clear indicator of this were the words to "Lullabye (Goodnight My Angel)," written by Billy for Alexa. Whenever Billy spoke about the song he'd relate the tender story about how Alexa had asked him, "What happens to people after they die?" inspiring him to write the song. But as in many of Billy's words there was another meaning too, one not so happy about what was then going on in his relationship with Christie and the events which lay ahead in their marriage. Billy, who had never had anyone to reassure him as a child after his father left, wanted Alexa to know that, no matter what, he'd be there for her, as he was, and today remains.

With no other real demands on Billy's time, Billy and Danny worked through September 1992 in the converted boathouse and when they were done had the first draft of the *River of Dreams* album which in its rawest form became known as "The Shelter Island Sessions."

Both knew that it wasn't yet a finished product and that winter and spring they booked time in recording studios in New York City and on Long Island, where ultimately the album was finished up to their liking. When it was finished Billy realized that this album was going to be totally different in so many ways from anything else he'd ever written. He knew that just to write about himself as he'd done so successfully before was not an option this time. This time he would write about the more abstract things out there that might not be so simple to explain as the "King and Queen of the Prom." Things like spirituality, again a first for Billy.

"I still feel very much like an atheist," Billy said. "But there are spiritual planes that I'm aware of that I don't know anything about and that I can't explain."

Then speaking of our culture and the revered position that musicians often are perceived as having in it, as well as an awareness that had come to him during the *River of Dreams* writing process, Billy continued:

"We're the wizards, we sort of reveal a little bit of this extra-powerful communicative force. I recently rediscovered that I was enchanted with music and the creative arts as a little child because I thought there was an element of alchemy in them."

*River of Dreams* was released in August 1993 and debuted at number one on the Billboard Albums chart, where it stayed for about three weeks. Ultimately the album was another huge success for Billy as it sold over five million copies, and led to a new tour that would last almost ten months. But Billy also found that he was still a target of some who saw him as a way to put a quick dollar in their pocket. He was sued by a Long Islander named Gary Zimmerman, who was described as a "struggling songwriter." Zimmerman claimed in his high-profile lawsuit that "River of Dreams" and "We Didn't Start the Fire" were in fact spawned from a 1986 song he wrote called "Nowhere Land" and that through a friend Billy was aware of the song. Billy wasn't going to be backed into a corner again and with Leonard Marks in his corner Zimmerman and his lawyer were no match. The case was dropped about a year after it had been filed.

During the tour there was a break for Thanksgiving in 1993 and during these days off Billy and Christie announced the end of their marriage. It'd been a long time coming, but both parents wanted to try and make it work right until the end when it became obvious that it was damaged beyond fixing. One of the great showbusiness marriages of the eighties was over.

"My divorce was a long time coming" was all Christie would say about it.

Both parents were dedicated to keeping Alexa out of their nightmare and didn't tell her about the break-up of their marriage until months after they really had split.

To say that 1993 was the year of lawyers and lawsuits in Billy's life would be a gross understatement. It seemed that every time he turned around there was some legal nightmare that was raising its head and although Billy wanted those who had screwed him to pay for it, giving depositions, meeting with attorneys, and testifying in court was getting old really fast. It was also incredibly stressful and depressing, and Billy was now self-medicating more and more.

By the early fall of 1993 Billy's lawsuit with Alan Grubman had been settled, but in a very unconventional way. Billy reportedly received three million dollars from Grubman, but not directly. In Grubman's own innovative way the money was paid to Billy by one of his major clients, Sony Music. The number that Eastman had on his balance sheet had been met, but as part of the settlement agreement both Billy and Grubman refused to discuss any of the settlement details, although things would change later on in 1995 when Grubman could no longer keep quiet.

Meanwhile Billy was still on the road with the *River of Dreams* tour and then, shortly after it ended in June 1994, would go back out on the road again in July for the first of the hugely successful Face to Face tours with Elton John.

Right after the 1994 New Year Christie left New York and took eight-year-old Alexa out to Colorado skiing. There they joined a friend of Christie's at the home of Rick Taubman, the black sheep son of A. Alfred Taubman, who is the multimillionaire owner of high end commercial real estate around the globe and the once jailed chairman of Sotheby's Auction House. Christie and the charming Taubman hit it off right away, and shortly after returning to New York City Christie and Alexa returned to Telluride to join Taubman in April for home helicopter skiing in the Rocky Mountains. This type of skiing takes the skier by helicopter to remote locations in mountain ranges, where they are dropped off to ski back down towards a pick-up location. It is often dangerous from the perspective of both the skiers who are essentially exploring uncharted areas of the mountain ranges and the helicopter pilots who often are at the mercy of volatile weather patterns. During this trip, Christie and Taubman, as well as two pilots, were attempting to locate their drop-off point when all of a sudden the helicopter was hit by severe crosswinds and crashed into the side of a mountain, rolling end over end, over two hundred feet until it came to a stop. Taubman was thrown from the copter breaking some ribs and ending up for a short time in the intensive care unit of the hospital. Christie stayed inside the helicopter and escaped with a broken left wrist. "We just dropped," she said. "All of a sudden it was like someone cut the cords to the elevator . . . I would look out the window, and see sky–mountain–snow, sky–mountain–snow." The accident devastated Billy and he cancelled a number of dates to fly to Telluride and be with Christie as she recovered and then had her flown back to New York in a private jet to recuperate.

The press was still not aware of the break-up in their marriage and when *People* magazine reported on the crash in their April 18 issue, they referred to Billy as Christie's husband. But in reality the announcement of their separation had been made just after the magazine went to press as Billy was in Nashville recording "Light as the Breeze" for a Leonard Cohen tribute album.

Soon after returning to New York City Christie returned with Alexa to Colorado to be with Taubman. Shortly afterwards she and Rick Taubman were married in a lavish mountaintop ceremony and living in the small Colorado town of Telluride. For Billy, who still was suffering through many personal issues, having Alexa in Colorado was not a situation he was pleased about. Besides he was Billy Joel, and he was used to things going his way. "I was enjoying the fact that I was getting some closure on that part of my life from age 16 to 43 or 44," he said. "It was hard work and I felt like I had bled, and really suffered during that album, and I got divorced at the end of that album, and my daughter was taken to Colorado. Ultimately, though, the divorce would improve his relationship with Alexa. The time that they did spend together now was often in between what were grueling tour schedules, and Billy, aware of their importance, made the best of them.

When you have scheduled time, you make the time," Christie said about the new arrangement. "And he dove right in and became a really good dad."

For Billy, though, it was a wake up call in not only fatherhood, but also the limitations of being a wealthy rock and roll star.

"I got a great insight into real life," he said "It does not matter how big you are, how rich you are—when you are divorced you are nothing, a second-class man, a second-class parent."

As is his usual manner, Billy made the best of it. He is a devoted parent and the relationship he shares with Alexa is the only one in his life so far based purely on unconditional love. He is a nurturing father who long ago made the vow to himself that when he had children they would not suffer the plight that he had of growing up alone.

"The love of my life was taken to Colorado . . . and I have to go visit her," Billy continued. "That's life, but when that happened a certain part of me died, you know I may be Mr. Rock 'n' Roll, but you can take my kid away from me, after all the work I have done . . . after all the success I have . . . I mean I have to charter planes to see her—what do guys who have regular jobs do?"

Then it was back to the road on tours that were too lucrative to turn down. Billy also was now trying to emerge from the ashes of his marriage to Christie, and had started seeing the artist Carolyn Beegan, a stunning red-headed amazon who lived nearby in Sag Harbor, New York.

Christie was still married to Rick Taubman and living in Colorado with him and Alexa as she pursued her successful modeling career, but their marriage which had been based on a series of lies from Taubman was quickly in deep trouble despite the fact that she was pregnant with Taubman's child. Taubman had led Christie to believe that he was the recipient of a large trust fund when in reality he had little if any money of his own. In June 1995 Christie gave birth to a son, Jack Paris Brinkley, while on an assignment and separated from Taubman in Orlando, Florida. Billy, after finding out, flew immediately to Orlando to be with her, setting off all sorts of speculation about a reconciliation that was never to happen. Despite this he made it clear to her that if she needed anything, he would be there for her. She returned to Telluride and Taubman to try and work things out, unsuccessfully as it happened.

Finally, Christie had had enough of Taubman's bullshit and she decided to pull up stakes and move back to New York City. Billy, in typical "Godfather" fashion, hired the necessary people to get her packed up and sent a jet to pick her and Alexa up for the ride back to the East Coast. Shortly after arriving in New York, Christie filed for divorce from Taubman, using the high-powered New York divorce attorney Eleanor Alter, who had handled her divorce from Billy. Taubman, meanwhile, filed his own divorce suit against Christie, seeking a multi-million dollar settlement. Desperate to put the whole nightmare behind her Christie agreed to a lump sum settlement with Taubman after he agreed not to pursue a custody battle for their son, referring to the matter as "My two million dollar nightmare" from then on.

No matter, though. As a result of her marriage to Billy, as well as her own career, Christie was a very wealthy woman. She and Billy set out to put the past behind them for Alexa's sake, which to a large degree they would end up doing. But Christie made it perfectly clear to Billy right away that, despite all he had done for her, and her gratitude as a result, things were over between the two of them. The dinner invitations and times spent together were primarily for Alexa's sake, and Christie made this perfectly clear to Billy, who may have had other ideas. Shortly after returning to New York, Christie met architect Peter Cook from Southampton, New York through her friend Jill Rappaport. Cook, who had modeled himself in his younger years, was from a local family with deep roots in Southampton. Their relationship quickly flourished as Peter offered Christie the stability she thought that she'd found with Billy years earlier. They were later married during the summer of 1995 on the beach in East Hampton, New York.

Meanwhile, Billy closed out 1993 with a concert in the Nassau Coliseum, just miles away from where he'd grown up in Hicksville. The last twenty years had been an extraordinary ride for Billy who, despite all his success, still had not found the thing that mattered the most to him a stable family life. And as the years ahead would show it would be some time before Billy would become comfortable enough in his own skin to attain all that.

# Chapter 29

Elton John and Billy had started talking about doing a tour together some years before it actually happened. "It was my idea to tour," Billy said. The two had been long-time friends and spent time together during *The Stranger* tour in 1978 when they were both staying at the same hotel in Amsterdam just prior to the plane ride that gave birth to the song "Scandinavian Skies." Billy had first raised the issue of touring together then, after a talk when both had expressed a mutual admiration for the other's work. The idea surfaced again in 1989 when the two crossed paths just prior to the *Storm Front* tour, but Elton's schedule wasn't right and the idea remained dormant for five years until 1994 when Billy raised it again to his booking agent Dennis Arfa, who then contacted Elton's people and put the first tour together.

Billy and Elton knew that pairing the two would be a huge draw at the gates and make them both extraordinary amounts of money, and they were right. The Face to Face tours that Dennis Arfa put together were record breaking in terms of profits. They also gave a wide range of fans the opportunity to see two masters of piano playing over four hours of rock and roll with their bands. Ironically, just two decades or so earlier, it had been Billy who had passed on recording with some of Elton's musicians because he didn't feel they were the right fit for his music. But now they were playing together, each band doing their sets while the other waited backstage, until the end of the show when all played a set together. The Face to Face tours gave the audience a diverse selection of songs that were not only theirs but other musicians' as well including The Beatles, Jerry Lee Lewis, and Chuck Berry, and the fans ate it up.

The pairing of these two rock and roll icons took the music world by storm. They not only sold out eighty thousand seat stadiums in hours, but they did it time after time at the same venue, including three nights in Philadelphia and six at Giants Stadium in New Jersey. Billy and Elton became the most successful duo of all time eventually grossing over forty-six million dollars in just twenty-four dates, a record that has yet to be broken.

The spectacle blew even Billy away. "When we're on stage together, part of me is wishing I could see this," he said, adding that playing with Elton was also a competitive experience of sorts: "It definitely lights a fire under you. He's knocking out hit after hit and I'm wondering how I am I ever going to follow that?"

Initially Billy and Elton went out on the road in early July 1994 and wrapped up their first tour together just six weeks later in late August. Billy returned to East Hampton for some R&R and time with Carolyn Beegan. By now their relationship had really heated up and Carolyn, a talented artist, was having a show of her work that summer which Billy had helped arrange. Billy wanted to be there to support her and in the month he had off they also spent some time on his boats traveling around to places like Martha's Vineyard and Nantucket, as well as enjoying many of the local East End restaurants and watering holes where Billy's reputation as a drinker was beginning to emerge.

After the brief rest, it was back out on the road in October for some more *River of Dreams* concerts as well as a few master classes. After a two-week break Billy left for Australia, playing the first concert there on November 13th. Australia had long been home to legions of rabid Billy Joel fans, and he'd stay there for about one month, playing thirteen concerts, including seven sold out nights in Brisbane. While he was in Australia, Billy received the Century Award from *Billboard* magazine. It was presented to him live via satellite for viewers in the United States by Tori Amos from Melbourne. Tori explained that as a young artist Billy had been a mentor to her, as she had often been asked to play his songs while she was performing. Billy accepted the award, stating in his usual modest fashion that, "Gosh, I can't believe I got this, considering the musicians this century has seen . . . Gershwin, Igor Stravinsky . . ." He also mentioned that he was happy to be there with Tori, and said how happy he was that women were finally starting to make it into the rock world, which "used to be a male-oriented domain." Ending his brief speech, he said thanks, and said that the award reaffirmed his belief that going into music as a career was the right decision.

Then it was back on the road for two more Australian shows, the last on December 10th. The plan had been for Billy then to rest up a little before doing one more show on the 17th in New Zealand before returning home to New York, but plans would change. The New Zealand concert wasn't selling tickets. In fact just 10,000 had been sold for a nearly 20,000 seat arena in Auckland so Billy pulled the plug on the show citing "personal reasons," stating that he had to fly home immediately, which he did in mid-December.

He spent that Christmas at his East Hampton home with Carolyn and friends. Carolyn was now living in a waterfront studio in Sag Harbor, New York that Billy had arranged for her through his friend Patrick Malloy, a businessman that owns almost all the waterfront property in the old whaling village. Carolyn would accompany Billy in January on the Japanese leg of the *River of Dreams* tour where both of them would live through an experience that humbled them like no other.

About one week into the Japanese tour, Billy and Carolyn were in bed at the Imperial Hotel in Osaka, Japan when about 5 a.m. on January 17th, the Kobe earthquake woke both of them from a sound sleep. The earthquake which registered a 7.2 on the Richter scale would kill over five thousand people and injure almost thirty thousand in its quick but powerful devastation. Although Billy's hotel was over twenty miles away from the earthquake's epicenter, it shook the building violently, but because of its earthquake proof design did no serious structural damage.

"I still don't know how that room held together," Billy said.

After being thrown from their bed. Billy and Carolyn dressed as quickly as they could and ran downstairs trying to get themselves out of the hotel, which they were sure was going to collapse. They met up with Billy's band and road crew as they got outside, and then soon afterwards learned the extent of devastation the earthquake had caused. The concert for that night was cancelled and rescheduled for the 19th. But after seeing and hearing about the extent of the devastation, Billy quickly made up his mind to do something to help, and decided to donate the proceeds of the two Osaka concerts to the victims of the earthquake, a move that further endeared Billy to the Japanese press and fans.

While all this was happening Leonard Marks was again working his legal magic on Billy's behalf. Back in 1993, when Billy had withdrawn his ninety million dollar lawsuit against Alan Grubman and accepted a three million dollar settlement, part of the deal was that both Billy and Grubman were to remain silent about the terms. Grubman had not lived up to his end of the deal, though, and for sometime had been bragging to anyone who would listen that he'd forced Billy to back down without any money changing hands. Marks in Billy's defense filed an affidavit on April 12, 1995 in New York Supreme Court, contending that the three million "was funneled through Sony" to Billy as the settlement for his suit against Grubman. "Sony's payments were for one purpose only," Marks said. "To get Billy Joel to settle his case against Grubman. Billy Joel had refused to stop the case against Grubman unless he received three million." Grubman, through his attorney Bert Fields, disputed Marks' statement, saying emphatically that "Grubman, did not directly or indirectly pay one dime to Mr. Joel, nor did they funnel any money through Sony."

According to Leonard Marks the settlement included a check for $2,400,000 that the Sony Corporation wrote to Billy on October 22, 1993, which coincidently was also the same day that Billy dropped the lawsuit. Also on that exact date a contract between Billy and Sony was drawn up for Billy to endorse some Sony products in Japan for the company for that exact figure. Then in another strange coincidence, on that same date Billy's business manager received an agreement that promised to pay Billy six hundred thousand dollars in additional royalty payments for record sales. It was indeed a series of coincidences that raised many questions about the validity of Alan Grubman's assertions.

After what had been five pretty intense years of performing, Billy was now comfortable enough professionally, and certainly financially, to begin taking some time off, and that is exactly what he would do for the rest of 1995, after finishing up yet another leg of a Face to Face tour with Elton John in April 1995. He immersed himself in his life on Long Island's East End, spending as much time as he could with his daughter Alexa and Carolyn Beegan. With the exception of Christie's wedding to Peter Cook that summer, Billy remained out of the public eye except to the locals.

Then in 1996 he found himself itching to perform again, but not with a band. He wanted to really explore what was going happening on college campuses with regard to music. He took his master class tour out on the road for four months on the East Coast. "I think it's a good thing for people to be able to listen to a professional when it comes to the creative aspect of this gig," Billy said about his art. "When I was starting out there was nobody to ask." Billy attacked the college tour with the same intensity that he always had playing on the road. He booked 33 dates in those four months to try and learn as much from the college students as they would from him. It wasn't a new concept, classes such as this had been done for centuries, but usually by classical musicians or actors. Billy was confident that there was enough of an interest in his type of music that the classes would be successful and he was right. He'd wanted to communicate with a core audience of students who were interested in some sort of career that had to do with music. Not necessarily just performing, but writing, producing, directing, the whole thing.

"I wanted to concentrate on students," he said.

He knew that these intimate gatherings would be mutually beneficial, while at the same time satisfying the desire he'd had since a boy in high school to teach and be part of the education process, something that he would take to a new level within a decade.

The rest of 1996 was spent pursuing his own interests, many of them outside of music. Billy has always had an innate love of the water. As a boy growing up in land-locked Hicksville, he made sure that whenever he could he was at or on the water. Whether on trips to the beaches with his mother Roz, sister Judy, and friends, or later on living in Oyster Bay, Billy always was drawn to the water, a place where he can truly unwind and be at peace with himself.

"I love the water. When I get a few miles inland I feel like Lawrence of Arabia. I get parched and panicky,' he said.

From this love of the water comes Billy's great respect for those who make their living harvesting the resources the seas produce. For a short time as a teenager Billy had worked on Oyster boats, and dug clams to survive. He also has been always fascinated with boats themselves and the people that build them. In fact Billy could often be seen after a concert back in his hotel suite, reading through books or magazines about boat design and building or sketching boats on pieces of hotel paper.

Certainly with a long list of boats that Billy had owned since buying his first row boat back in Hampton Bays, New York, even before he fled to California, Billy was knowledgeable about the vastly different types of boats and their designs. He's owned somewhere between twelve and fifteen boats until now, some that he used for fishing, and some for just cruising including the 65-foot trawler yacht *Redhead* that he'd named after Carolyn, and the 36-foot BHM swordfish boat he was often seen piloting himself throughout the northeast. So in addition to reading everything he could put his hands on about boats, Billy often would sketch hull designs in the never-ending quest for the perfect boat. It was this pastime that would evolve into a business for Billy and one that would satisfy at least part of his addiction to boats, while at the same time creating jobs for an industry that until then had all but died on his beloved Long Island.

"Over the years I've developed a pretty good idea of what a boat should look like," Billy said.

With a million dollars of his money Billy set up a boat-building partnership with a small marina on Long Island's East End. Billy owned the rights to the boat's hull which he had designed with a young yacht designer named Doug Zurn in Marblehead, Massachusetts. Billy had seen examples of Zurn's work and liked the traditional lines that his boats featured, as well as their timeless characteristics. The boat was a classic picnic boat similar to those that had been built and used in Maine for generations, and was now enjoying a resurgence in popularity at a few builders thanks to all the new yuppie Wall Street and dot com fortunes that were being made about this time in the United States. Like clockwork, every Christmas a handful of Wall Street yuppies, pockets bulging with their year-end bonuses, would place an order for this new version of what once had been a boat limited to a few of the old guard WASPs from Bar Harbor. That was fine with Billy, who never wanted to crank these boats out like cookies. His idea was to build a modern version of this old traditional design, and by doing so hopefully create new jobs for ships' carpenters, finishers, mechanics, and other people in the boat-building business. Like most of Billy's ideas, it worked.

Because Billy wanted to build a quality boat, only about fifteen or so of the boats were built each year. This way the quality craftsmanship that he strived for was maintained. They weren't cheap either, beginning at about $350,000 each, but that didn't deter his buyers who for the money got a very traditional, very fast, lobster-type yacht that they could use for overnight or day trips with families and friends.

As the owner of the hull design and mold, Billy receives a royalty for each built that is sold. "I'm not going to get wealthy from it," he said. "I wanted to help revive a traditional boat-building industry," and he did. Today, after almost a decade of building his boats, the company he started is profitable thanks to his design and his insistence that the boats roll out of the shop with only the highest of quality.

"It's a disease, I don't know how I'll kick it," Billy says of his boat business. But in reality it is unlikely he ever will.

As 1997 opened its doors Billy had a totally open slate. The intense touring was over and Billy had all but said goodbye to rock and roll, at least for now. At each opportunity he vowed never to again do any of the extended tours he had during recent years, which he said were just too demanding and time consuming, taking him away from his daughter Alexa too much. He also began to distance himself more and more from rock and roll music, instead concentrating on writing classical music instead.

Columbia Records, though, had other ideas. They wanted a Billy Joel album out there and since Billy had no new material to release they decided yet another *Greatest Hits* collection would do.

Columbia had approached Billy with the idea, telling him that there was more then enough new material since the first *Greatest Hits* collection was released in 1985. And indeed twelve years and four albums later there was. Billy choose fifteen songs that he felt would make a good album, but still it just wasn't enough for him. He felt his fans deserved more then a repackaged bunch of songs, but even if Columbia agreed to it he had no new rock and roll to offer, and they certainly weren't interested in putting any of his classical pieces on the album. So Billy did something he'd never done before: he included three cover songs that he'd done.

The first was the Leonard Cohen song "Light as the Breeze" that he recorded in Nashville just prior to Christie's helicopter accident.

The second was the song "Hey Girl" written by Carole King and Gerry Goffin in the Brill Building days, and recorded by Freddie Scott in 1963. Billy had performed the song back in the mid-fifties with his first band, The Lost Souls, and loved the idea of putting his version on the album. He'd recorded it right after he and Christie had split, thinking of Alexa as he sang it that day, because he had just discovered that Christie was taking her out to live in Colorado with Rick Taubman.

The third cover song was the previously unreleased Bob Dylan song "To Make You Feel My Love," which Billy had heard after Jeff Rosen, Dylan's publishing representative, personally brought it out to his East Hampton house for Billy to listen to. "Dylan's people wouldn't send the tape by mail," he said. "I guess he's paranoid about tapes getting out." Billy listened to the tape and knew immediately that he wanted to record the song. "I almost stopped breathing when I listened to the song," Billy continued. "I knew right away that I was going to do it." Billy's version was released as a single to call attention to the entire album and it worked, riding up to number fifty on Billboard's Hot 100 that year after the album's release. The album itself was sort of a disappointment for Columbia, reaching only number nine on the Billboard 200 albums chart, although it did sell over one million copies.

But most significant, the release of *Greatest Hits 3* signified a long end to Billy's involvement in pop music. "I think it's interesting to note that the last pop song I wrote was "Famous Last Words," Billy said. It certainly would turn out to be an epilogue of sorts for Billy's career. It was obvious that he was burnt out from thirty plus years of what was often a grueling schedule both in and out of the studio, as well as in his private life.

With no concerts of any significance except some private corporate events that year, and an appearance at buddy Garth Brooks' Central Park Concert in August, 1997 was pretty devoid of music for Billy Joel. Yet that would change shortly as the promise of more quick money and life on the road would pull Billy out in early 1998 for the Billy Joel 1998/1999 world tour, some of which he'd do with his band and for part of which he'd be joined by with Elton John and his band to set more attendance and money records that would amaze the powers that be in the record business. That tour would begin in January 1998 with Billy and his band. They'd then meet up with Elton and his band in Australia in early March for about a month together in Australia and Japan, before splitting up and returning again to the United States in late April 1998 for a month of shows, and then to join Elton again for three shows in Ireland and Scotland, before taking off the summer and some of the fall. Then, on November 1st Billy was back on the road with a vengeance as he kicked off six more months of shows with his band before quitting in April for a seven-month rest to count his money. Billy may have been amassing one of the great fortunes of rock and roll, but he also was not taking particularly good care of himself and many in his inner circle were beginning to be concerned about what they regarded as increasingly odd behavior and events that were potentially embarrassing to Billy. Most were attributed to Billy's increasing appetite for alcohol, something that Billy had always had a fondness for, certainly more than the stereotypical rock and roller who favored drugs over booze. But still Billy was surrounded by a lot of "yes" people and although many were not inhibited at all about discussing this outside the bubble Billy lived in, no one wanted to be the one to say anything to Billy about his drinking for fear of losing their jobs or access to him. It was the quintessential story that had happened so many times in rock and roll music, and those who truly cared about Billy hoped that it wouldn't end in the tragedy that it often did.

# Chapter 30

By 1998 Billy had also won a large and diverse number of awards for his music that included honorary doctorates, humanitarian awards for charitable work, inclusion in the Songwriters Hall of Fame, *Billboard* magazine awards, and a long list of others. In addition he had to date seventeen Grammy nominations and had won six Grammys including the prestigious 1990 Legend award. His career had certainly been recognized by the powers that be in the industry as one of the great ones of our time, and it seemed that few if any awards had escaped Billy.

Then as 1998 drew to a close it was announced that Billy would be inducted into the Rock and Roll Hall of Fame alongside many of the greats that had influenced his career and music, as well as his contemporaries. It was, even at this point in his career, the culmination of what had started thirty-plus years earlier in his first garage band back on Long Island, an amazing series of events for someone whose talent no longer could be questioned. Billy Joel, like his music or not, was indeed one of the great icons of our generation, and on the stage that night in Cleveland, Ohio on March 15, 1999 Billy was inducted into the Rock 'n' Roll Hall of Fame by his friend and collaborator Ray Charles. It was one of the proudest moments of his life, causing Billy to remark in his typical understated fashion that "I've had the most amazing life, and it's mostly because of rock and roll music."

While his professional life was unquestionably a success, his personal life was not. Billy had been living alone in his ocean-front estate now for almost six years since he and Christie had split up, and he was thinking about a change. Sure he loved the east end of Long Island, its natural beauty, and interesting people, particularly the locals, but in the last decade or so it had become sort of a Hollywood east as more movie stars, recording artists, and captains of industry had bought or built trophy homes there. The once sleepy little town of East Hampton was now during the summer months and year round on weekends, in addition to being home to people like Steven Spielberg, Sting or Revlon's Ron Perlmen, also an extension of Manhattan's East Side with throngs of New Yorkers and their crazy energy all jockeying for some imagined sort of social position. With that came the hoardes of tourists, many of whom believed that if they drove out to East Hampton they'd be sure to see people like Billy or Alec Baldwin standing in their yards watering their lawns. Of course it was a ridiculous idea, made even more surreal by changing attitudes brought out to the country by these city people who quickly were changing the face of what East Hampton had been for centuries into their own sterile version of life in the country.

Another consequence of being discovered for East Hampton and the entire surrounding area was that the value of real estate, once cheap enough to attract great talent like Jackson Pollack and William DeKooning from the city, had skyrocketed to absurd levels. It seemed that just about every Wall Street executive who got a bonus would run out east to buy land or a home just to be able to be part of this very superficial scene. Billy had paid just over a million dollars for his home and property from Dickson Potter, and then renovated it to the tune of three or so more million as he and Christie turned it into their home. As part of his divorce settlement, he paid Christie five million dollars for her fifty percent of the home, so all together he had close to ten million invested in his palatial estate on the six-plus ocean-front acres. It was yet another example of the incredible good fortune that Billy would have over the years with real estate investments. Still it was an awfully big bachelor pad, that came with a lot of ghosts from Billy's past and besides Billy had never been one to put down deep roots in a home. In fact besides his mother's house in Hicksville, Billy had lived in this East Hampton house longer then any other he'd ever owned.

Then in August of 1999 Billy was having lunch with Jerry Seinfeld, a Manhattan resident who now like many showbusiness celebrities also just had to have a home in the Hamptons. He had been to Billy's ocean-front house before and loved the location, and that day, as they sat in an East Hampton restaurant owned by advertising executive Jerry Della Famina, the subject of Billy's home came up. Jerry eventually asked Billy if he'd be interested in selling it, and Billy, thinking it over, grabbed a napkin and wrote a figure on it, folding it in half and in typical Godfather fashion, pushing it across the table for Seinfeld to read. Jerry opened it and looking at the figure looked up at Billy, who was sure that he was going to laugh at him. Instead Seinfeld told him OK, and in doing so helped Billy to set a record for a real estate sale that would last for five years on the Hamptons.

The price for the entire six acres and two homes was thirty-four million dollars, a lot more than what the five million Billy paid Christie represented for fifty percent of the home. Billy told Jerry Seinfeld that before he could give him the final OK, he had to check with Alexa who later told him "Yes" because "Daddy, change is good." That was enough convincing for Billy who surely thought he'd better lock this deal up before Seinfeld woke up and changed his mind. Seinfeld, who loved the seclusion of the house's location, and the privacy the property offered, never did wake up and the deal went through. But money was no object to Seinfeld either. He'd just been paid over one hundred million for the syndication rights to his television show, from which he'd already make a sizable fortune, so what was thirty-four million dollars when you're dealing in Monopoly money?

Billy would remain in the home until the next spring as he sorted through the almost fifteen years of his life that he'd spent there. He also had a mini-tour set up for that December which would take him to ten cities in a month, including winding up in New York City for his second New Year's Eve concert there. The first one in 1982, where tickets were priced at an average of fifteen dollars, was a huge success. For the 1999 show tickets would sell for ten times that amount, and concert goers got to listen to an almost four-hour show that included thirty-five songs done in two sets. In addition to featuring a long list of Billy's material, Billy also did songs by such greats as Jimi Hendrix, Sly and the Family Stone, and even Elvis. The concert was yet another milestone in Billy's career and was recorded that night to be released in May 2000 as a two-disc set.

Although he was beginning to show signs of burning out, Billy couldn't seem to turn his back on the many millions that were his if he toured. *Fortune* magazine had recently done an article in which they estimated that Billy made over thirty million dollars from one year of touring, and with that kind of money around Billy would find the energy to go on the road no matter what. Besides he wasn't writing any rock and roll music these days, saying that "I feel no desire to" when asked about it.

It seemed that Billy truly was at the end of a road in his life. The passion, compulsion, and desire which had burned so intensely in him for over thirty years had been doused and he was totally burned out on this guy Billy Joel the rock star.

"I'm really tired of him," Billy said. "He only has a certain range and vocal timbre. He only has a particular range and vision as a performing artist, and I'd like to write for some other people."

Which is exactly what he would do. He wanted to return to his roots. Billy had really wanted to be a songwriter thirty years or so earlier when he was with Irwin Mazur, but had gotten sidetracked into being a rock star. Not that he was complaining, which of course he wasn't.

"I've caught a couple of good waves," Billy said about his career.

It was becoming increasingly clear that Billy wanted a change in his music. He wanted to return to his roots and focus on his first love, classical music. It wasn't a new concept for a rock star. Peter Townsend had been the first to combine classical music with rock in 1969 when he wrote the rock opera *Tommy*, as had others such as Frank Zappa and Billy's friend Paul McCartney. Billy wasn't sure what form his work would take, but he had been listening almost exclusively lately to classical music, and knew enough about himself to realize that it meant something.

Classical music, as well as music by such great composers as George Gershwin, have, next to rock and roll, always been Billy's great loves. After all, it was the music that he had been trained in beginning as a four-year-old child, and even before that the music that he had listened to at his father's knee. Not surprisingly the influence of classical music is also obvious in many of Billy's songs.

"I started out writing classical music before I ever wrote a pop song," Billy said. "I played Mozart before I played Lennon and McCartney. I played Beethoven before I played Billy Joel."

While it wasn't clear to anyone, including Billy, if he was indeed closing a book for good in his life, it was clear for now anyway that rock and roll was over and classical music was again his focus. Yet this time it wouldn't be the impromptu pieces he wrote to bullshit his mother about his music lessons. Billy was really serious about this new direction in his music and, like everything else he did career wise, he would approach it with the greatest degree of integrity.

But some in Billy's inner circle questioned why he had this new interest in classical music. Was it because he was burnt out on rock and roll and felt a need to return to his roots, or did it have something to do with his relationship, or non-relationship with his father Howard? Billy has always been deeply affected by Howard's abandonment, as any young child is, and although Howard certainly could not deny the great success that Billy had achieved, he was still a musical snob and looked down his nose at rock and roll, believing it to be a sub-form of music. Consequently Billy had always felt a deep-seated need to prove to Howard that he was wrong, that he was a true musician, worthy of all the praise and awards he'd received.

Those who have been closest to Billy believe that this is one of Billy's biggest demons. That despite everything he has achieved, he has never achieved what is truly most important to him, the acknowledgment from Howard that it's all been worth it. In fact the song "Vienna" is probably Billy's first attempt at reaching out to try to meet Howard on some sort of middle ground. When asked, Billy will say it was inspired by a trip to the city that is Howard's home where he saw an elderly woman sweeping a street with great pride. The scene made Billy realize that in life everything doesn't have to be done at breakneck speed, that there is time in life to accomplish our goals.

A reason which is closer to the truth is that Vienna is a place where a musicians have always gone to be truly tested. It also wasn't a coincidence that about this same time Billy's half-brother Alexander, who lived in Vienna with Howard, was beginning to emerge as a successful conductor in Europe.

He had taken Billy's advice and done one year of law school to pacify Howard before dropping out and dedicating himself to music. Billy was certainly proud of Alexander but he also knew that Howard looked at Alexander's career as one that was worthy of great respect. He'd show Howard, he'd write a classical piece that once and for all would undeniably prove his worth as a musician.

Some of the music Billy already had been working on. Some of the "sketches," as he often refers to them, had been lying around or in his head for some time. The fifth piece "Soliloquy (On a Separation)" was inspired by a visit Billy had with Alexa years earlier just before she left for Colorado to live. That goodbye had been really difficult for Billy and he later sat and put the notes to paper, deciding that the sad and dark piece spoke for itself and needed no words.

"If you put your own words in and you make up your own story . . . you can imagine, what was the composer thinking?" he said about the piece.

Whatever the interpretation, the album was well received by his fans and critics. It was released in September 2001 rising to #1 on Billboards Classical chart where it stayed for eighteen weeks. Although not a multi-million selling album it was received by the classical music community as a worthwhile work. Like Billy's rock and roll songs its influences are firmly rooted in Romanticism and cover a wide range of moods.

"Sometimes I'm writing to a particular person and I want to convey an emotion. And usually it's a woman. All my life I've been writing for women. But they seem to like that. Girls like that. They like it when you write stuff for them," Billy said in typical fashion.

Musically there are hints of Chopin and Schumann in the solo piano pieces. Wisely Billy decided not to record the album himself, aware that he is not a talented enough classical piano player to pull it off. Instead he chose Richard Joo, a highly regarded British-Korean piano player, for that role. Not surprisingly the album was recorded in part in Vienna where Howard was able to attend. Did it finally put to rest the demons of Billy and Howard's past? Unlikely, as Howard, who suffers today from debilitating Parkinson's disease, is too dark and too cold emotionally to be in touch with those feelings, many believe.

On Tuesday September 11, 2001 events unfolded in New York City that would forever rob Americans of their innocence. Two commercial jets crashed into the twin towers of the World Trade Center about eighteen minutes apart killing about three thousand innocent people, many of them New York City policemen, firemen, and office workers. Two other hijacked planes also crashed, one into its target at the Pentagon and one into a farm field in Pennsylvania, thanks to the brave passengers who took back control of the jet and forced it down, saving what now was thought to be either the White House or the Capitol as its target. The profound psychological, political, and economic effects that followed in the United States would change Americans forever. Throwing the country into a war like never fought before, but also causing Americans to bond together in ways that had not happened since World War II. Billy was certainly no exception. The terrorists had attacked his beloved New York City, the town whose blood ran through Billy's veins, the place that had inspired so much of his work over the years and that was his true home.

Within days the rock and roll community led by Billy's friend Sir Paul McCartney had scheduled "The Concert for New York City" to be held at Madison Square Garden on October 20. Many top name bands and musicians including The Who, U2, Eric Clapton, Elton John, and Billy signed on to raise money for the victims of 9/11 in this once in a lifetime, six-hour event. The audience that night was filled with police, firefighters, 9/11 survivors, and families of victims in what became for everyone an unforgettable burst of pure emotion.

Billy, looking particularly sad, took the stage that night and donned a police hat that had been left near his piano, causing the packed Garden to roar with approval. He then performed a somber and touching version of "New York State of Mind" before ripping the place apart with his eerily apocalyptic "Miami 2017" a combination of songs that couldn't have been more appropriate.

The concert raised over thirty-five million dollars for the victims and their families, and was recorded and released as a five-hour two CD set and a DVD. The concert could never undo the pain of 9/11, but it did for that brief six hours bring people together as only music can.

Billy's drinking had now become local news on Long Island's East End and in Manhattan. He was regularly seen in restaurants or bars drinking excessively and often being loud enough to attract the sort of attention he didn't want. Some attributed it to his January 2000 break-up with artist Carolyn Beegan, but the reality is that even before that Billy was seen at times in New York City and Long Island's East End drinking excessively, either with friends or alone. It seemed that the disease that had often plagued his mother was also leaving its mark on Billy, and stories about him having to be helped into elevators or polishing off a bottle of brandy alone at a New York sidewalk café table were happening too often for them unfortunately not to have some degree of truth to them.

Then almost three months to the day after the melt down at Madison Square Garden, Billy totaled his car one night while returning home alone. It was about two weeks after former girlfriend Trish Bergin had married a lawyer that she'd been dating.

"I took this very hard," Billy said of the break–up. "I then began what was a prolonged period of overindulgence."

That night Billy was returning to his rented house in East Hampton's Northwest Woods after a night out eating and socializing when he lost control of his 1999 Mercedes Benz and totaled it. As he came to an intersection he realized that he wasn't going to be able to make the left turn but tried anyway, skidding and losing control of the car, as it plowed into a group of three fire–well stanchions demolishing them.

Billy suffered some head wounds and subsequent bleeding but refused medical attention. Although no tickets were issued and Billy was not given a sobriety test, the police report did state that he was traveling at a high rate of speed as judged by the severity of damage to his car. He had to cancel an appearance he was supposed to make the next night at the Songwriters Hall of Fame dinner because of blackened eyes and a puffy face. But then, to the delight of many, he checked himself into Silver Hill Hospital in New Canaan, Connecticut for ten days to deal with what was described by his publicist as "a specific personal problem."

Silver Hill is a well–known one thousand dollar per day country club type rehab and psychiatric facility that has hosted such well knowns as Marilyn Monroe, Mariah Carey, and Liza Minnelli on its beautifully landscaped sixty acres.

"I told my daughter that I recognized I was having a problem. And my gift to her for Father's Day was going to be cleaning up my act," Billy said.

But like many people with addiction issues Billy didn't "get it" the first time. Denial is a strong force and Billy still thought that he could end his excessive drinking on his terms. Besides no one in his inner circle was telling him any different, although many were quietly talking to members of the press and others about what they considered a rapidly growing and very serious personal problem. The depression and subsequent self-medicating that Billy was caught up in had him in a vicious cycle and one that was gradually worsening. It was a serious situation, but Billy, who for decades had done things his way, was determined that he could overcome any issues himself. He participated in the programs at Silver Hill, but in reality only half-heartedly.

"I felt like I was disrupting their program, so I had to get out of there," Billy said of his stay at Silver Hill. "I felt like an amateur. I had been on a bender but at Silver Hill I was listening to 18-year-old heroin junkies and guys who had been drinking a couple of bottles of vodka a day for 20 years, I was just drinking too much wine . . . I said I could pull myself out of this, I said to my self just don't drink, prove to your self that you can go a whole summer without drink, and I did . . ."

Billy left Silver Hill after his ten–day stay and for a while was on his best behavior, really trying to put his drinking behind him. For the rest of the summer he immersed himself in meetings about a Broadway project that he'd been working on with chorographer Twyla Tharp while staying in a suite at Manhattan's St. Regis Hotel where he could be found at times drinking champagne and wine, as well as giving guests impromptu mini concerts in the dining area. Always the dedicated father he could also be found spending time with Alexa both in New York and out east on Long Island.

Then in September he joined Elton on a mini Face to Face tour that lasted about one month. They did eleven shows including eight in the New York/New Jersey area and one in Boston where he met a twenty-eight-year-old beautiful blonde who worked at the local Ritz-Carleton Hotel named Ann Maxwell. It seemed that the darkness of the past couple of years was behind Billy as friends immediately noticed a dramatic change in him for the better.

Billy bombarded Ann with flowers, notes, and phone calls and Ann, who was originally from the New York area, invited Billy to have Thanksgiving dinner with her family just two months after they met. Billy, who was nervous about the dinner, pulled it off and was invited back for Christmas with the Maxwells. The speculation about a wedding as soon as the spring of 2003 was rampant, but it wasn't to be. Billy was soon seen again with Carolyn Beegan on his arm, and no one was talking about what happened with Ann.

The break-up with Ann also took its toll on Billy who was scheduled to go out on tour with Elton John again in February 2003. On Saturday January 25, 2003 Billy was having dinner at Sag Harbor's American Hotel, a favorite of Billy's when he was in the Hamptons. With him was Carolyn Beegan, Arma Andon, and Biana Stepanian, a real estate agent that Billy often used when buying, selling or renting property on the east end. They had dinner and ordered at least one bottle of wine and champagne before leaving around ten o'clock. Billy had now replaced his 1999 Mercedes with a 2002 S600 and about ten thirty, after dropping Carolyn off, was headed back towards East Hampton from Sag Harbor when he lost control of the car, causing it to hit a tree on the passenger side and bounce back into the middle of the road.

He was "lucky to be alive" according to Sag Harbor fire Chief Matthew McAree, who added, "If it was head on it would have been a different accident altogether."

The $125,000 car was totaled and when police and firefighters arrived, they found Billy conscious, but trapped behind the wheel of the Mercedes. Using a special saw, they cut Billy free of the car and treated him for head wounds before airlifting him to Stony Brook Hospital where he was treated overnight and released the next morning.

It was Billy's second serious car accident in seven months, but again he was not given a sobriety test in what many saw as a double standard for famous people in the Hamptons. Billy admitted to having "a glass of champagne" with his dinner, a statement which was later retracted by his publicist who stated that Billy had "abstained" from drinking that night. Police justified their not performing the sobriety test by saying that there was no smell of alcohol on Billy's breath or in the car. Billy, who had recently bought a twenty-two million dollar home on Long Island's North Shore, was also renting a house in the Hamptons to be near Alexa.

The next day the media had a field day when Christie, who lived nearby, arrived at the firehouse to take photographs of the demolished Mercedes.

"The seat Alexa was sitting in only hours before the latest crash was completely decimated," Christie said, adding: "I'm worried about Billy but, like any mother would be, I'm alarmed and concerned about my child's safety by this frightening pattern of events."

In his defense, Billy told police and the media that he had recently had minor surgery on his nose and face which had caused a great deal of swelling, adding that since the operation he had also been on pain medication and that the combination of medication and swelling had impaired his sight that night, causing him to strike the tree.

Then, despite a witness who stated that Billy's car had "gone by him at a high rate of speed and the struck the tree," police refused to charge Billy with anything or ticket him. The situation set off a tirade of rumors and speculation about Billy, who is a hero of sorts on Long Island and particularly the Hamptons, receiving preferential treatment. Whatever the reality, Billy could not seem to emerge from an ever-deepening hole that he was digging for himself.

# Chapter 31

Billy has always had a great love of the theater and particularly its music. As a young boy show tunes would often fill the small Joel house as Roz played records and often sang along with them. "There was always music," Billy said of those days. Additionally some of Billy's greatest heroes are songwriters like George M. Cohen and Cole Porter.

For many years Billy had entertained the idea of writing the music for a Broadway play but his schedule and private life always kept it from happening. The cross-over from rock and roll to Broadway was nothing new. *Grease, Jesus Christ Superstar,* and *Hair* were early Broadway shows and more recently *Aida,* a show written by Tim Rice, a former partner of the wildly successful Andrew Lloyd Webber, with music by Elton John, the seemingly tireless rock star, was enjoying a successful Broadway run. Also the original sixties rock opera *Tommy,* written by Peter Townsend, was brought to Broadway in a new incarnation by Townsend. Interestingly it was Townsend who in 1986 ran into Billy at the opening of the Rock and Roll Hall of Fame in Cleveland, Ohio who had first sparked a serious interest in the idea with Billy. He told Billy that he thought he was the musician best suited to write a Broadway musical because of what Townsend believed was Billy's ability to bring "pop and rock music sensibility into musical theater." Billy had also been approached by others prior to 1986, but because of the great respect that Billy had for The Who's brilliant songwriter and guitarist, this was the first time that the idea really took hold.

The idea lay pretty much dormant until March 1994 when Billy was giving one of his master classes at Princeton University. Asked by a student if he had any aspirations for Broadway, Billy downplayed the idea, citing a long list of areas he saw as problems, such as the great commitment of time and money, the number of songs he'd need to write, and other issues such as with production people and actors. Billy had clearly been caught at a bad time.

So it was with great interest that he met with Twyla Tharp to discuss her idea of a Broadway production based solely on his music. Ms. Tharp is a highly regarded professional with a forty-plus year distinguished history.

She'd already worked on five movies, one Broadway show and choreographed over 125 dances since graduating from college and striking out on her own. In addition she was a two-time Emmy winner and had worked with such prestigious dance companies as the Paris Opera Ballet, the Royal Ballet, and the New York Ballet. So when she called Billy to pitch her new idea of a Broadway show based on Billy's songs, she got his attention.

The suggestion for the play actually came from her son, Jesse Alexander Huot, who one day said to her, "You love Billy Joel. Why not dance to Joel music?" The seed was planted.

Twyla loved the idea but like everything else there was a hitch, even if a minor one. She didn't know Billy, nor did she know how to contact him.

"But these things can be done," she said. "You always know somebody who knows somebody."

In this case she did, and soon after she was calling Billy's agent to introduce herself and get his number. She called Billy and, briefly explaining her idea, invited him to her apartment to discuss it in more detail. Billy, who knew Twyla by reputation, was intrigued and accepted the invitation. Before the meeting, Twyla made a twenty-minute video choreographing several of Billy's songs with six dancers who later would be part of the actual cast.

"He liked it," Twyla said of the meeting and video.

"I never imagined that my music could look like this," Billy said.

"I think that basically he had seen dancing on his videos, but that was pop dancing, which is fine," Twyla added. "But Billy's a serious composer and he has a sense of a bigger framework than the pop culture. And I think the fact that his music sustained that kind of serious approach had been gratifying to him."

Indeed it had. Billy gave her the OK before leaving the apartment, and promised that the next day, Twyla would have all his CDs and sheet music to study.

"It was risky, it was kind of crazy," he said. "There was so much potential for it to be a nightmare. I loved it."

But ultimately he had faith in Twyla, or he never would have let it get that far. Twyla spent that weekend listening to the CDs in chronological order, and when it was all over she was both inspired and drained, calling Billy to tell him, "OK, I have it."

That was when she asked him about what happened to his characters Brenda, Eddie, and Anthony. He had never thought about it, he said.

"Well, that's the point," she answered. "I want to do a show using your songs to tell a story. I don't know what it is yet."

Twyla's idea was to do a narrative based on Brenda and Eddie, but in doing so the story would also be much more. It's ultimately a story about war, and the generation of American men who went to Vietnam. The end result is a musical that tells the story of five friends during the 1960s, their loves, their lives, the Vietnam War, and its aftermath, in a way that is very close to the life that Billy led in Hicksville.

Using Billy's songs, Twyla was able to draw the community that would represent the Eddies, the Jameses, and the Brendas, and construct it from those points in his narrative. "All I did was take a whole selection of short stories and make a novel," she said.

The musical novel uses only Billy's music, and is played onstage by a rock and roll band similar to Billy's with a piano player playing a Steinway grand piano. There are no speaking roles yet it works in such a way that the end result is a moving and poignant tale.

In fact as *Movin' Out* was taking shape Billy came one day to watch a rehearsal. He had purposely been absent during the musical's development.

"We agreed from the beginning that his job was done when I started," Tharp said, adding: "It's collaboration with his music. That's different then a collaboration with him."

"I kept myself away," Billy said. "I wanted to walk in dumb."

"It was so exciting," recalled Holly Cruikshank of Billy's appearance at the rehearsal. Holly was in the original cast and plays Brenda in the road show.

He saw the rehearsal, Holly said, and "he started crying."

"It's really hard to see your songs go," said Tharp about Billy's reaction. "Like he said, they are his children and he was letting them out. It's not easy to disengage. Billy's songs are very personal to him and he's performed them a lot. And to suddenly see them in another context is not easy. But also to see that others are moved by them, it's not easy. It was a new experience for him."

The first preview was on June 25, 2002 at Chicago's Shubert Theatre. Billy was there and liked what he saw, although like the doting father he is, he made a few notes of suggestions that he gave to Twyla the next day over lunch. Twyla was receptive and made the changes which involved making Brenda more sympathetic and the Vietnam battle scene less confusing. The real issue was going to be the scathing reviews that the play received, and after looking seriously at the points raised, Twyla ended up revamping part of the production. It was clear to her after watching the audience that there was a certain level of confusion, and that changes were in order.

"From watching the audience you gain a real awareness of where it is playing and where it is not," Twyla said.

On September 30, 2002 the show previewed in Manhattan at the Richard Rodgers Theater. This time with the changes in place the reviews were different. "It was such a relief," recalled Cruikshank of that night. "We found out at the opening night party that it got good reviews, and it was a relief to everyone." The show ran on Broadway for over 1300 performances, finally closing on December 11, 2005, to begin an international tour. In 2003 *Movin' Out* was nominated for eight prestigious Tony awards, winning two for Best Orchestrations and Best Choreography. It also received a number of other prestigious awards, but perhaps the one that Twyla Tharp is most proud of is the Vietnam Veterans of America's President's Award, presented to her for outstanding artistic accomplishments, including *Movin' Out.*

"The time had come and the wound was healing and we could give honor to these guys without it being controversial," Tharp said of the Vietnam vets. "That's why I made it."

She went to Nashville, Tennessee to accept the award and found the experience particularly profound.

"They are so moving and so brave," she said of the Vietnam vets. "They have been so ingenious and so courageous with what they've had to go through to return to this culture. It was a very moving experience to be able to say, 'Hey, here's a tiny, tiny little gift of thanks.' Which is what I always intended *Movin' Out* to be. That they received it as such, I feel very privileged."

Billy had achieved yet another incredible milestone in his career with the success of *Movin' Out*, and although this time it was a collaborative effort, there was no denying that without Billy's timeless music this great story and its testament to the lost heroes of Vietnam may never have been told, certainly not in such a profound way. At the same time that *Movin' Out* was receiving awards there was also an indication, that maybe, just maybe, things were happening in his personal life which were indicative of a change for the better, but before that could happen completely Billy still had to experience that great darkness which always occurs just before the dawn.

# Chapter 32

When the three month Face to Face tour with Elton ended in May of 2003, Billy returned to Sag Harbor to live in his recently renovated new home. He had bought the beautiful old whaling captain's house during one of his real estate buying sprees where he also purchased an eight million dollar estate down the road from Jimmy Buffet's summer place outside Sag Harbor, and a five million dollar waterfront home on Shelter Island, New York that he ended up buying because he fell in love with its huge dock where he envisioned keeping his boats. The captain's house sits on a quaint one-lane street on Sag Harbor's historic waterfront and has a seven-slip marina on the property where Billy could dock his growing personal navy, second only in the area to Jimmy Buffet's.

That summer Billy was also busy renovating the Centre Island home that he'd recently bought for about twenty-two million dollars while he lived in Sag Harbor. The Centre Island home would eventually be his year-round home, and sat on fifteen waterfront acres of some of New York's most expensive real estate. It had previously been the home of another consummate WASP, or "Mr. Golf" as Billy often referred to him, because the house was decorated in a style which reminded Billy of a clubhouse at some country club. The house itself is a beautiful old twenty-plus room, brick and stone Georgian mansion with sweeping views of the water, and set far enough off the road that it insured Billy the privacy he wanted. On the surface it seemed that Billy had the world by the balls, and in some ways he certainly did. The one thing that continued to escape him, though, was the relationship he wanted so desperately, and which he sought out so aggressively. In the past couple of years Billy had been linked with a number of beautiful women, and had two well-publicized relationships, both of which were wildly speculated to end in marriage, but which melted down before that ever happened. Billy was determined, though, that he'd have this, and like must things that he's wanted throughout his tumultuous life, he'd get it.

'The happiest times in my life were when my relationships were going well —when I was in love with someone, and someone was loving me," Billy said, adding: "Being in love has always been the most important thing in my life."

Each spring in the Hamptons a rising of the population occurs as second-home owners descend on their houses, and with them hordes of seasonal laborers, made up largely of college students who work in countless positions that insure that these city dwellers will have the most comfortable and smooth-running summer season of their lives. Then with the advent of September and Labor Day, these hordes leave, causing the populations to drastically fall as the streets, beaches, and other spots are returned to the year-round residents to enjoy. It has been this way now for decades, and each year a few that made their way to the Hamptons will end up staying and joining the year-rounders, many times the result of a summer romance that has continued.

This was the case in 2003 when Katie Lee, a recent graduate of Ohio's Miami University, arrived in Sag Harbor looking for a summer job as a waitress in one of the seemingly endless number of restaurants that are packed to the rafters with second-home owners and tourists. She found a job in the newly opened seafood restaurant, Jeff and Eddy's. Aside from having degrees in both English and Journalism, Katie's real love is food, which she developed as a child while cooking with her grandmother home in West Virginia. She had also taken numerous culinary classes over the years and studied cooking in Florence, Italy while there one semester. Katie had heard about the Hamptons, the beautiful beaches, wonderful natural beauty, and great summer scene, and wanted to have some fun that summer before deciding whether to continue her education or enter the workforce. She was interested in continuing to learn about cooking wholesome foods and the job in this new Sag Harbor restaurant that also featured a fresh fish market seemed perfect.

Jeff and Eddy's had opened on Sag Harbor's Main Street that April. Its owners are Ed Burke Jr., a young, aggressive prominent defense attorney, and with a better then average winning record, and Jeff Resnick, a successful local restaurant owner already. They envisioned a New England-type seafood restaurant, with a fresh local fish store alongside the bar. The place was an instant success, and mobbed each night. On one of his nights out for dinner Billy stopped in the new restaurant and ran into its newest employee, twenty-two-year-old Katie Lee. Billy was immediately attracted to Katie and vice versa and they soon were inseparable. Katie was soon living with Billy in the old house, and once again a noticeable change in Billy for the better was obvious to all that knew him. That's not to say that his drinking was letting up any because it wasn't, and in reality if anything, it occasionally reached the critical point according to those around him. But there was no denying that this latest woman in his life was making him happier in many ways and, for the time being at least, taming some of those personal demons which Billy often wrestled with.

Quickly, rumors were flying that Katie was the one and that a marriage was imminent, but having heard this in the recent past many were skeptical. Nevertheless Billy and Katie were soon seen together out of the Hamptons as their relationship became more serious. She accompanied him to the Tony Awards early in June where they were photographed with Alexa and Billy's mother Rosalind, and she was also accompanying Billy on his trips to the Centre Island house to meet with architects and designers where her input was soon as important as Billy's.

Then, in early October, bad luck that many attributed to a night of too much wine once again plagued Billy. In his Sag Harbor home with Kate he got out of bed to go downstairs, and fumbling around for the light switch, fell down the stairway breaking his right wrist. Although Billy tried to make light of the accident, which resulted in some minor surgery as bones were set, again it was clear that too much alcohol had played a role once more.

Soon after the accident Billy and Katie moved into the Centre Island home permanently and set up house. Right after the Christmas and New Year's holidays of 2004 they boarded a jet to escape the New York winter for a while down on St. Bart's. Here, over a romantic dinner, Billy asked Kate formally to marry him and presented her with a five-carat diamond ring, which she accepted. Both were very happy on their return to New York about a week later, as plans for the October wedding at their Centre Island home began immediately. It would be the third marriage for the now fifty-four-year-old Billy, but it didn't matter to him, he was convinced he'd found his soulmate this time, and nothing was going to stop the wedding from happening.

"One of the reasons the relationship works is because she's much more mature than me in many ways," Billy said.

But, unfortunately, despite his newfound happiness, troubles still lay ahead for Billy. On April 25, 2004 Billy was driving from his Centre Island estate into neighboring Bayville town to pick up some pizzas that he'd ordered. It was about 4 p.m. and Billy had jumped into a 1967 Citroen that he kept in the garage with his collection of motorcycles and other vehicles. About a mile from the entrance to his home, Billy skidded on the wet pavement and lost control of the small car as it skidded up onto the lawn of a house owned by 94-year-old Maria Dono and smashed into the house's side, damaging a small wall and the home's siding.

"I can't believe I got in another accident," Billy moaned as he exited the car, clearly embarrassed.

Billy, who was alone in the car, suffered a minor cut to his left ring finger, and refused any medical attention. In his defense it had been raining pretty much all day, and the roads were slippery, but it didn't matter, the media had a field day with news of Billy's third accident in less then two years. Police didn't ticket Billy or test him for alcohol because, according to a statement they released, "there was no evidence alcohol or drugs played a role in the crash."

It was a situation that Billy would not live down for some time, if ever. A local radio station disc jockey quickly came by the crash site upon hearing of the accident to find the car towed away. He did find some front-end parts which the next day were auctioned off on the radio station to raise money for a local charity. But, like any mention of the accident, it only threw fuel on an already more then smoldering fire. Billy for his part denied that alcohol played a role in that accident or any of the others, but many believed by that time that three accidents couldn't be written off solely to bad luck. Something was going on in Billy's life that needed professional attention. It was clear that drinking or no drinking, Billy had problems that even he could not overcome alone.

Meanwhile, plans for the wedding went on, and Billy could often now be found at the Centre Island home that summer, reluctant to go out for fear that yet another incident may happen. He and Katie remained so busy planning the wedding and shopping for an apartment in New York City that they never even went to the Sag Harbor house that summer. In fact Billy often talked about putting it up for sale, which he did for a time, before removing it from the market.

In September of 2004 Billy and Katie found the apartment they were looking for in a recently renovated TriBeCa building. The nearly three thousand square foot loft-style apartment was purchased for close to four million dollars by Billy as a gift of sorts for Katie, who now was pursuing a career as the host for a television cooking program. The apartment's kitchen was one of the things that closed the deal for Billy and Katie and they often were found there as they were on Centre Island in the kitchen with Katie preparing healthy meals for a noticeably slimmer Billy, as Billy followed her around the kitchen cleaning up. Again the perfect balance.

The weather threatened to rain on Saturday, October 2, 2004 pretty much all morning and early afternoon. But at about four o'clock, as close to 250 guests, including Billy's father, mother, and sister, Howard Stern, Don Henley, old friend Jon Small and Christie Brinkley watched, Billy stood on the brick platform in the home's formal gardens wearing a tuxedo as Katie's father Steve escorted his daughter up to Billy before placing her hand in his. As the sun broke through the gray clouds, Katie Lee, recently of Huntington, West Virginia, stood next to Billy dressed in an Oscar de la Renta white gown, wearing a fifty carat diamond necklace and carrying a bouquet of flowers. Billy stood with his half-brother and best man Alexander, who had come from Austria, as Billy's daughter Alexa stood with Katie, acting as her maid of honor. The couple read wedding vows that they had written together and exchanged wedding bands, before turning to greet the cheers of the crowd.

Afterwards everyone feasted on Italian food and chocolate cake, with Billy sitting down at the piano to give his guests a mini concert. It was a new beginning for Billy and all his friends in the closely knit inner circle were hopeful that Katie could continue to help Billy emerge from the ashes.

They spent their honeymoon in Europe where Billy decided that it might be time to go back on the road and test the waters. He was tired of being referred to as the "Greta Garbo of rock," as he spent more and more time on Centre Island. He called Dennis Arfa to discuss it, and Dennis booked two dates for him in Phoenix, Arizona and Las Vegas, Nevada. Those were in addition to a private show he was doing for Anheuser Bush Brewery at one of their corporate retreats, for which he was being paid over a million and a half dollars. With these three concerts booked far enough apart Billy knew that he could gradually ease himself back into performing while not putting too much strain on his fifty-five-year-old vocal chords.

He returned from his honeymoon to begin putting together a band for the concerts with one notable change. His long-time drummer Liberty DeVito would not be going on the road with Billy, something that startled many. While Billy had often made band changes, Liberty was the one member of the band that many believed was irreplaceable. He had been with Billy since the days back in Ultrasonic Studios when Topper became the Billy Joel Band, and was Billy's highest paid band member, a testament to Billy's loyalty to him. But Liberty had broken the cardinal rule when it came to Billy Joel: he'd talked behind his back, and word of it had gotten back to Billy. That was it. Billy who had used other drummers on the *River of Dreams* album, but who from loyalty had taken Liberty on the road with him to promote the album, had been looking for a new drummer for sometime, and upon hearing that Liberty was letting out secrets about Billy's private life, the ax had fallen for him as far as he and Billy were concerned.

"Liberty and I are not talking," Billy said. "We have had a falling out and there was something that happened with Liberty that he denied being the source of, and I found out that it was Liberty and it hurt my family situation."

The rumors about exactly what had happened between the two were rampant. Some said Liberty had talked to people outside Billy's inner circle about his drinking, while others said it had to do with something that Liberty and his second wife Mary, who was close friends with Christie Brinkley, had said to Christie about Billy's relationship with Carolyn Beegan—how it had actually started long before they had split while on a concert tour that Carolyn had been secretly flown back and forth on. If that were the case then Liberty had broken a cardinal rule of life on the road that "what happens on the road, stays on the road." Whatever the reason, things were over between Billy and Liberty and it looked like it was for good.

On February 7, 2005 Billy was at home with Katie when suddenly he was bent over in pain. An ambulance was called and Billy was taken to a nearby hospital where doctors examined him and determined that the pain was a result of acute pancreatitus, brought on by years of alcohol abuse. Billy was checked into a private room for further tests and treatments, and it looked as though the years of alcohol abuse had finally and undeniably taken their toll on Billy. Quickly his public relations team went to work downplaying his hospitalization and asking that everyone respect Billy and Katie's privacy as he began the healing process. Behind the scenes, though, it was an entirely different story, as in addition to Billy's medical care many who cared for Billy, including Katie, urged him to check himself into a rehab facility once again. This time it wouldn't be for what essentially had amounted to a ten-day vacation in 2002 at Silver Hill. Billy was too sick to ignore what his body was telling him, and he had to quit drinking or the next time he might not be so lucky.

Finally, the denial Billy carried about his problem was a thing of the past and arrangements were made to have him check into the Betty Ford Clinic in California for a full one-month stay. The location was kept an incredibly well-guarded secret, even with the huge amount of media scrutiny. Finally, in early March, when Billy was well enough to travel, he and Katie boarded a private jet for the trip to the West Coast to check Billy in. After the news was announced, the more cynical speculated about whether or not Billy would actually complete his stay and if his five-month long marriage could survive the recent series of events. But this time Billy was determined not only to get better, but also to make his marriage work. Although he still wasn't ready to completely admit the extent of his problems with alcohol, he'd get there and in the not too distant future. In mid–April 2005 Billy and Katie were spotted in a coffee shop nearby the clinic on the day Billy checked out, just before they boarded their jet to return home. Billy had turned yet another page in his incredible life, and the tough little kid from Hicksville was determined to put his life back on track. He attended a few AA meetings, but stopped going, having trouble digesting all the "higher power" rhetoric, as many do. He gradually came around to the reality and extent of his drinking problem, and in typical Billy Joel fashion, as he began to be more comfortable about it, even started to allude to it with his own distinctive humour:

"How many people in the entertainment have gone into rehab? Just about everybody. Name me the people who haven't? It was my time to go. Everybody goes. It's like getting your teeth cleaned. You've got to go eventually. It's like 'mental' floss."

He stayed off the wine and booze that summer and fall as he immersed himself in a musical project for Columbia Records that would end up being a retrospective of his musical life from 1964 to the present time. *My Lives* featured some previously unreleased songs that he'd done with The Lost Souls, The Hassles, and Attila the Hun dug out of the Billy Joel archives by old friends Billy Zampino and Jim Bosse. Additionally some versions of Billy's newer music that had never been heard before were included on the multi-CD set, as was a DVD of a concert he performed years earlier in Frankfurt, Germany.

With Billy involved in a musical project, even if quietly, rumors began to surface about a possible upcoming tour. Then in late November 2005 the rumors became reality when full-page ads began appearing in newspapers such as the *New York Times, Boston Herald,* and others. Billy, who hadn't toured alone in six years, or with Elton John in three years, and who hadn't released a rock album since 1993, was headed back out on the road. The more skeptical down played the planned tour, saying things like Billy was washed up, that his voice couldn't stand up to a tour after all the alcohol abuse, and that he'd lost his fan base. Yet Dennis Arfa and to a lesser degree Billy knew better. Dennis never doubted that the tour would be a success, yet initially it was planned as a mini-tour of sorts covering ten cities and thirty shows, but when ticket sales started it was clear that idea was going to be revised quickly. Shows sold out in hours, and new ones were added, also selling out right away. Billy and Dennis were careful to space the shows far enough apart so that Billy's vocal chords would get sufficiently rested, but it was clear that the legions of Billy's fans around the country had not forgotten him and had been dying to see him in concert again for years. Eventually the total number of shows at Madison Square Garden reached twelve, a record at that venue, each one selling out quickly.

"What about a thirteenth?" Billy was asked by Ralph Turchiano his old buddy from Hicksville.

"Bad luck," was the answer he got from Billy.

But it wouldn't matter. This rock and roll icon, who had never been a darling of the press, particularly the music press, was kicking ass once again, and as usual doing it on his terms. Despite his detractors he was right back on top, possibly more so than he'd ever been, and the disastrous concert he had done with Elton John at Madison Square Garden on that ill-fated night of March 15, 2002 seemed a distant memory. Not only were his old fans at the shows, but many younger fans who had never been to a Billy Joel concert, whose parents first listened to Billy, were there in the audiences too. 2005 and 2006 were shaping up to be years in which Billy would have no regrets. He had faced his demons and beaten his alcohol problems. As he started the tour he looked and sounded like the Billy Joel of years past, slimmed down and kicking ass on stage.

In his personal life he and Katie had gone through a lot in a very short time, yet both of them were determined to make their marriage work, and Billy found the strength not only in himself, but in Katie too, to keep things on track. His marriage to Katie Lee today is stronger then ever, and it's a good bet that Billy will be a father once more before too long.

For Billy Joel, the little kid from Hicksville, New York with music pouring out of his veins, it hasn't always been an easy road. In most cases he's to blame for it too, yet throughout his forty-plus year career he has experienced incredible highs and incredible lows, both personally and professionally. Despite this, he has always stayed remarkably true to his most inner self, sometimes while in great denial, and sometimes not telling one hundred per cent of a story. But never has he displayed the slightest hypocrisy over the years regarding himself, and in doing so has stayed true to one of his most sacred beliefs. One that he often expresses at the end of his concerts for the countless millions that have seen him . . . "Don't take any shit from anyone."

# DISCOGRAPHY

**ALBUMS**

THE COMMANDOS (AKA THE LOST SOULS)
"Journey's End"/"What Did I Ever Do To You?"/"Time And Time Again"/"Just Another Lie" (Mercury demos), circa 1965

THE HASSLES
*The Hassles* (United Artists), 1967
*Hour of the Wolf* (United Artists), 1969

ATTILA THE HUN
*Attila* (Epic), 1970

SOLO
*Cold Spring Harbor* (Family/Paramount), 1971
*Piano Man* (Columbia), 1973
*Streetlife Serenade* (Columbia), 1974
*Turnstiles* (Columbia), 1976
*The Stranger* (Columbia), 1977
*52nd. Street* (Columbia), 1978
*Glass Houses* (Columbia), 1980
*Songs in the Attic* (Columbia), 1981
*The Nylon Curtain* (Columbia), 1982
*An Innocent Man* (Columbia), 1983
*Greatest Hits*, Volume I & Volume II (Columbia), 1985
*The Bridge* (Columbia), 1986
*Kohuept* (Columbia), 1987
*Storm Front* (Columbia), 1989
*Live at Yankee Stadium* (Columbia), EP, 1990
*River of Dreams* (Columbia), 1993
*12 Gardens Live* (Sony), 2006

WITH VARIOUS ARTISTS
In Harmony 2, "Nobody Knows Me" (Columbia), 1981
USA for Africa: We Are the World, "We Are the World" (Columbia), 1985
Ruthless People, "Modern Woman" (Epic), 1986
Simply Mad About the Mouse, "When You Wish Upon a Star" (Columbia), 1991
Honeymoon in Vegas, "All Shook Up," "Heartbreak Hotel" (Epic Soundtrax), 1992

**SOLO SINGLES**
"She's Got a Way"/"Everybody Loves You Now" (Family/Paramount), 1973
"Tomorrow Is Today"/"Everybody Loves You Now" (Family/Paramount), 1973
"Piano Man"/"You're My Home" (Columbia), 1973
"Worse Comes To Worst"/"Somewhere Along The Line" (Columbia), 1974
"Travellin' Prayer"/"Worst Comes to Worst" (Columbia), 1974
"The Entertainer"/"The Mexican Connection" (Columbia), 1974
"Summer, Highland Falls"/"James" (Columbia) 1976
"Movin' Out" (Anthony's Song)/"Everybody Has a Dream" (Columbia), 1977
"Just the Way You Are"/"Get It Right the First Time" (Columbia), 1977
"Only the Good Die Young"/"Get It Right The First Time" (Columbia), 1978
"Shes Always A Woman"/"Vienna" (Columbia), 1978
"My Life"/"52nd. Street" (Columbia), 1978
"Big Shot"/"Root Beer Rag" (Columbia), 1979
"Honesty"/"The Mexican Connection" (Columbia), 1979
"It's Still Rock and Roll to Me"/"Through the Long Night" (Columbia), 1980
"Don't Ask Me Why"/"C'Etait Toi" (You Were The One) (Columbia), 1980
"Sometimes a Fantasy"/"All for Leyna" (Columbia), 1980
"Down in the Boondocks"/"21st Century Man" (D.L. Byron) (Columbia), 1980
"She's Got a Way" (live)/"The Ballad Of Billy The Kid" (live) (Columbia), 1981
"Pressure"/"Laura" (Columbia), 1982
"Allentown"/"Elvis Presley Blvd." (Columbia), 1982
"Goodnight Saigon"/"A Room of Our Own" (Columbia), 1983
"Tell Her About It"/"Easy Money"/"You Got Me Hummin'" (Columbia), 1983

"Uptown Girl"/"Careless Talk" (Columbia), 1983[HS]
"An Innocent Man"/"I'll Cry Instead" (Columbia), 1983
"The Longest Time"/"Christie Lee" (Columbia), 1984
"Leave a Tender Moment Alone"/"This Night" (Columbia), 1984
"Keeping the Faith"/"She's Right on Time" (Columbia), 1985
"You're Only Human" (Second Wind)/"Surprises" (Columbia), 1985
"The Night Is Still Young"/"Summer, Highland Falls" (Columbia), 1985
"A Matter of Trust"/"Getting Closer" (Columbia), 1986
"This Is the Time"/"Code of Silence" (with Cyndi Lauper) (Columbia), 1986
"Baby Grand" (with Ray Charles)/"Big Man on Mulberry Street" (Columbia), 1987
"Back in the U.S.S.R." (live)/"Big Shot" (live) (Columbia), 1987
"The Times they Are a-Changin'" (live)/"Back in the U.S.S.R." (live), (Columbia), 1987
"We Didn't Start the Fire"/"House of Blue Light" (Columbia), 1989
"I Go to Extremes"/"When in Rome" (Columbia), 1990
"The Downeaster 'Alexa'"/"And So It Goes" (Columbia), 1990
"That's Not Her Style"/"And So It Goes" (Columbia), 1990
"Shameless"/"Storm Front" (live) (Columbia), 1991
"All Shook Up"/"Wear My Ring Around Your Neck" (Ricky Van Shelton), (Epic), 1992
"The River of Dreams/"No Man's Land" (Columbia), 1993
"All About Soul" (with Color Me Badd)/"You Picked a Real Bad Time", (Columbia), 1993
"Lullabye (Goodnight), My Angel)"/"2000 Years" (Columbia), 1994

## UNRELEASED SONGS

Although Billy always says that he has no backlog of unreleased music, the truth is that indeed he does. The following list is from the Library of Congress for songs copyrighted under Billy's name.

"Alexa's Theme" (1988)
"Attitude Road" (1992)
"Bye Bye" (*Cold Spring Harbor/Piano Man* days)
"December Song" (*Cold Spring Harbor/Piano Man* days)
"Every Time (Falling in Love)" (1982)
"Great Ships, Great Oceans" (*Cold Spring Harbor/Piano Man* days)
"Handball" (1979) (though he performed it in concert as early as 1977)
"Indian Love Ball" (1981)
"It's All Right" (1982)

"It's Not Easy" (written for *Cold Spring Harbor*)
"Josephine" (written between *Cold Spring Harbor* and *Piano Man*)
"Long, Long Time" (written between *Cold Spring Harbor* and *Piano Man*)
"Money or Love" (1989)
"My Journey's End" (1964)
"New Thing in C" (1989)
"Numbers" (1982)
"Only a Man" (*Cold Spring Harbor/Piano Man* days)
"Oyster Bay" (*Cold Spring Harbor/Piano Man* days)
"Prime of Your Life" (1981)
"Rosalinda" (written between *Cold Spring Harbor* and *Piano Man*)
"Song for Alexa" (1989—possibly became "Lullabye"?)
"Tell Them You're in Love" (1985)
"The Moment at Hand" (1988)
"The Purple Heart" (1982—possibly became "Goodnight Saigon"?)
"Until You Come to Me" (written for *Cold Spring Harbor*)
"We All Have Our Cross to Bear" (written for *Piano Man*)
"Wide Awake" (1982)
"Where is My Lady?" (written for *Cold Spring Harbor*)
"Where's the Revolution?" (written for *Piano Man*)
"You Got Your Reasons" (1989)